TWILIGHT OF THE ASSHOLES

It's Not About

November 24th 2004

Twilight of the Assholes

Somebody Stop the Spike Machine

VOLUME II OF
THE CHRONICLES OF THE ERA OF DARKNESS
2004-2009

by Tim Kreider

FANTAGRAPHICS BOOKS
7563 Lake City Way NE
Seattle, Washington 98115

Edited by **Gary Groth**
Designed by **Alexa Koenings**
Associate Publisher: **Eric Reynolds**
Publishers: **Gary Groth** and **Kim Thompson**

Distributed in the U.S. by W.W. Norton and Company, Inc.
(800-233-4830)

Distributed in Canada by the Canadian Manda Group
(800-452-6642 x862)

Distributed in the United Kingdom by Turnaround
Distribution (44 (0)20 8829-3002)

Distributed to the comics specialty market by Diamond
Distributors (800-452-6642 x215)

ISBN: 978-1-60699-398-9

First Fantagraphics printing: January, 2011

Printed in China

For George

"Looks like we're all goin' to Spooky Island, dudes!"

-Shaggy

Tim Kreider is a brilliant artist and has a rare talent for capturing the disgusting essence of a person in a few pen strokes—

Here I have to digress for a minute on the topic of those disgusting essences; in this book you will find literally dozens of people, from oxygen-sucking William Rehnquist (seated next to curiously absent Supreme Court nominee Jesus Christ) to Dick Cheney (face contorting with wicked opportunity when he learns he has a potentially fatal heart disease; now he can hurry up and bomb the fuck out of someone before he dies) to the sneering pantsuit-clad old lady in the "Americans vs. 'Muricans" cartoon, whose faces all look equally like engorged, wrench-tightened anuses, which I guess gives extra meaning to the *Twilight of the Assholes* title. And what's amazing is that Tim Kreider is a person who can bring out the subtle character differences from one wrench-tightened anus-face to the next. You have to have a deep and passionate sensitivity to all the different shades and gradations of human assholedom to produce such loving and varied portraits of such faces.

Kreider definitely has that passion, in industrial warehouse-sized excess, which is probably a real bummer for him (i.e., in the attempting-to-lead-a-happy-untroubled-existence department) but is a real plus for us, because when wedded to his obvious talent for drawing and caricature it made him the perfect person to chronicle the astonishing rogues' gallery of truly repulsive and cowardly people who made up much of our cultural and political elite during the time period covered in this book.

Moreover what makes Kreider really interesting as a political satirist is that he's the polar opposite of most of our pundits these days. Whether it's cable TV hosts or radio blowhards or columnists like me or cartoonists, most of the people who trade in political commentary for a living in this country adhere to a simple and reliable commercial formula: you side with the "left" or the "right," and then you stick with your team no matter what, always rooting for your party to win and never crossing the line to criticize your own.

This isn't who Kreider is; in *Twilight of the Assholes* he even admits later on in the book that he was never a true politics junkie, and once you go through all of his work you can easily see that his views on politics are drawn not from some corporate team-building instinct but from a general sort of hatred for liars and cowards of any kind, which makes him an iconoclast in the purest sense of the word. There is venom in this book for Bush and Cheney of course, because they *were* liars and cowards both, but also equally for sexual prudes, angry Muslim chanters, Jesus (well, his particular dislike is for "Jeezus" – the gun-toting, blond-headed, ass-kicking jock/book-dumping high school sadist that Americans have made the icon of their particular brand of Christianity), Santa Claus, and liberal protesters (his "Liberals vs. the Empire" cartoon depicting sixties wannabes "fighting back" against the approaching Death Star by holding up a big Darth Vader puppet at a march unfortunately sums up the left's accomplishments during the Bush years perfectly).

The cartoons in this book stop shortly after the election of Barack Obama, which means that the author thankfully missed a great many of the disappointments of this particular administration, but even so Kreider's pre-election cartoons are infected with a profound fear that Obama might turn out to be a fraud and a fake just like the others. His hilarious strip about his angst-ridden love affair with candidate Obama ("Obama and Me, a Love Story"), which shows cartoon Kreider having a cartoon-relationship-fight with cartoon-Obama over his stance on the FISA bill, perfectly sums up the terror a lot of us felt when we were invited to have hope that Obama really represented a new day.

And again, Kreider is such a pure iconoclast that the

slightest suggestions of campaign-trail fakery in Obama leaped out at him as monstrous and terrible disappointments. He made a great strip out of the notorious "Ok, now I'll eat anything" quote issued by Obama, after Hillary won Pennsylvania by quaffing beers and whiskies with the same "regular people" she and her husband spent their entire careers trying to get away from. Unlike the reporters who cover this stuff every day for a living, Kreider caught the larger symbolic significance of candidate Obama's pronouncement – the raw desperation of even America's best and most intelligent leaders to do *anything* to get elected – and drew Obama stuffing his face with a procession of noxious things to impress idiot voters, from spotted owls to Palestinian babies to, finally, his own words (this last panel would have been considerably broader and more elaborate had Kreider had the last year or two of broken campaign promises to work with). Obama is one of the heroes of the book, and like me Kreider was moved by America's willingness in electing him to rise above not only its racial prejudices but above its hatred for nuance and intellectualism; but an honest thinker sees flaws even in one's heroes, and Kreider proves his intellectual honesty when he takes aim at candidate Obama's occasional cravenness.

I bring that up only to point out that *Twilight of the Assholes* isn't a partisan rip-job. Kreider strikes me as the kind of guy who started off hating everyday outrages like pop culture gossip (I love the cartoon of him not giving a fuck if Letterman and Oprah made up) and the Christmas season (I nearly fell over laughing at his "War on Christmas" cartoon: I once had the exact same fantasy about debearding mall Santas and screaming "Your parents are Santa!" to all the kids) and had to work his way up to having opinions on free trade, Iraq, etc. Kreider's satirical anger is less about the policy decisions of the politicians he writes about

than it is about their characters, what sort of people they are: their meanness, their smallness, their cowardice, the grotesque sexual insecurities and fears that they always feel it necessary to project onto us somehow.

The time period of "The Twilight of the Assholes" happens to cover a period in our history when all of those qualities were in supreme abundance in our population. This was a time when Americans went from being merely incredibly lazy to being actually atrophied intellectually, and allowed themselves to become so desensitized by crap entertainments and mechanized propaganda that they were literally *glad* to follow drooling illiterate leaders whose entire political platforms were centered around bombing faraway peoples to a crisp to make ourselves feel better about shit (and who cared if they were the wrong people). Kreider captures the horror and stupidity of this period with his pitch-perfect drawings (the ass-faced old bag worrying about the missing girl in Florida in the "Silver Linings of the Holocaust" strip reminded me of every "Dernit, I'm entitled to my stupidity" voter I've ever interviewed on the campaign trail) and dares throughout the drawings and the texts to hope that this Bush-Cheney era was just temporary, some kind of psychotic episode that will pass with time. Hence the "Twilight" of the title, hoping that the curtain is really closing on this shameful period of ours, or perhaps already has.

I personally have my doubts. But it's exactly this doomed and very genuine optimism of Kreider's that makes the art in this book so painful and excellent. This isn't just about choosing sides with him, these issues aren't a football game. It's life or death and his whole happiness and sanity is at stake in every drawing. It makes these cartoons beautiful stuff, and some of the few good things to come from a time period most of us would rather forget.

I've had it with the Christians. You know the ones I'm talking about. Not the Good Christians who believe in, like, helping people—feeding the hungry, aiding the sick, housing the homeless, fighting injustice—but the ones in the news and in power these days, who are so keen to judge and punish and so suspiciously obsessed with sex. The ones scheming to overturn Roe v. Wade. The ones downplaying the effectiveness of condoms to teenagers. The ones preaching abstinence in Africa. The ones who believe in Creationism and want prayer back in the schools and think George W. Bush is "a godly man." The born-again, Bible-believing, face-of-Christ-in-a-pancacke-seeing Evil Christians.

All quotations from scripture are bona fide, although I mixed up the language from the King James and New International versions a little. I will admit to quoting scripture somewhat selectively—I am not the first to do so—to highlight the contradictions and hypocrisy of the Christian right. It would be anachronistic to try to define Jesus in terms of contemporary political philosophies, but I think it would be fair to say that he was what we would call, by today's standards, something of a hardass. He said that if you divorced your wife for any cause other than infidelity you were making an adulteress of her. He also said that anyone who even looks at a woman lustfully had already committed adultery in his heart, meaning (as I choose to interpret it) that we're all fucked anyway so why even bother trying. And there's no getting around it, the Old Testament explicitly condemns homosexuality as an abomination, and Jesus did say that not one letter of the law would be deleted or changed before Judgment Day. But he also told us to love our enemies, and warned, "Judge not, that ye be not judged."

But then he also seems to have believed that the apocalypse would come during the lifetimes of many of the people listening to him in the first century. I myself don't believe anything it says in the Bible so I can do whatever I want until I die and am cast into the lake of fire. People who call themselves Fundamentalists, however, don't get to choose which Biblical dictates to follow and which they're free to ignore. So when do they start selling off all their possessions and giving the money to the poor?

Jeezus is the embodiment of the Christianity I despise: sanitized, kitschy and sentimental, racist and jingoistic—a big cheerful Midwestern football star with twinkling blue eyes and feathered blond hair. I grew up in an Anabaptist sect that was persecuted early on for its insistence on the separation of church and state, so the sight of an American flag in church would have been tacky and offensive when I was a kid, like selling ad space on the altar. We were also one of the historic pacifist churches, so the image of the Prince of Peace wielding an M-16 is, to me, sort of obscene. But people actually talk as though they imagine that God manages their acting careers, or roots for one football team over another, so why not believe that he's on our nation's side against all the others? Pretty much everyone in every other nation-state in human history has believed the same thing. (The ancient Greeks' vision of the Gods choosing up sides in mortals' wars, sitting on the sidelines to watch the slaughter like a cockfight, sneakily intervening on behalf of their favorites and capriciously fucking with their enemies, better reflects the vagaries of warfare in real life.)

Drawing the "real" Jesus is, of course, an exercise in naked projection. I regret that mine came out looking like Gandalf.

At heart, I'm a fundamentalist myself; I'm just one who doesn't believe. I was disillusioned with Christianity because it turned out not to be literally true. I've always loved what Flannery O'Connor said about the Eucharist: "If it's a symbol, to hell with it." In the unlikely event that I ever do convert, I won't be some pot-smoking Unitarian who says he kinda believes in a mystical something; I will be a sandwich-board street prophet telling passersby to repent of their sins now or burn in hellfire everlasting. If I ever give my heart to Jesus it'll be to Jesus, not that feel-good impostor. If that happens, just watch out, is all.

JESUS VS. Jeezus

	JESUS	Jeezus
ON SEXUAL IMMORALITY:	"IF ANY ONE OF YOU IS WITHOUT SIN, LET HIM CAST THE FIRST STONE." (JOHN 8:7)	I hate fags!
ON ALCOHOL AND DRUGS:	"WHAT GOES INTO A MAN'S MOUTH DOES NOT DEFILE HIM, BUT WHAT COMES OUT OF HIS MOUTH, THAT DEFILES HIM." (MATTHEW 15:11)	But only say 'Nay'! Get ye high on Me!
ON ABORTION:	——	Bring the little fetuses unto me, for they are precious to Me. On this issue shalt thou vote, and this alone.
ON WAR:	"ALL WHO DRAW THE SWORD WILL DIE BY THE SWORD." (MATTHEW 26:52)	Slay ye every one of them, and I shall sort them out!
ON SEPARATION OF CHURCH AND STATE:	"RENDER UNTO CÆSAR WHAT IS CÆSAR'S, AND RENDER UNTO GOD WHAT IS GOD'S." (MATTHEW 22:21)	I am the state!
ON MONEY:	"IT IS EASIER FOR A CAMEL TO GO THROUGH THE EYE OF A NEEDLE THAN FOR A RICH MAN TO ENTER THE KINGDOM OF HEAVEN." (MATTHEW 19:23)	Make thy pledge now, at Our toll-free number.

Republicans hate sex: they oppose premarital sex, oral sex, anal sex, homosexual sex, pornography, breasts (especially black ones)[1], Bill Clinton, abortion, and contraception, even if it means solemnly tsk-tsking while every man, woman and child in Africa dies of AIDS. They also famously hate sex's two traditional accompaniments, drugs and rock n' roll.

So how can these people be the ruling party in the United States of America, famously the most sex-crazed nation in the history of the world since the decline of the Roman Empire? (Possible exception: the Japanese, notoriously obsessed with visions of multitentacled aliens raping schoolgirls). Every male in this country, from N.A.M.B.L.A. members to Promise-Keepers, now has high-speed access to fantasies more depraved than Caligula's, and I fear that behind closed doors they are all jacking off like chimps to images of their daughters' friends with Malamutes. All those guys with "W" decals and "Support Our Troops" ribbons on the backs of their trucks who voted on "moral values" are also posting photos of their passed-out wives' asses on voyeur sites, arranging full swaps in Vegas over swingers' chatrooms, meeting other guys in local parks or bus station bathrooms for furtive blowjobs, going to ERs in the middle of the night with implausible stories to explain the light bulbs jammed up their rectums.

I guess the simplest and most obvious explanation is hypocrisy. They're not so different from those arty hipster types who claim that their favorite film is *Salo: or, 120 Days of Sodom* when secretly it's *Krull*. It's always gratifying when we learn that Jimmy Swaggart gets handjobs in cheap motels or that Bill O'Reilly's as crude and bullying to his employees as he is with his guests, or that Rush Limbaugh's loading up on Viagra for paid sex tours, because it exposes the pompous lie of Republican virtue that they all espouse in public. I sometimes like to imagine that if everyone were somehow to be simultaneously exposed, if we learned exactly how weird everyone else really is—if, as an old cartoon of mine has it, we had X-ray vision—we might finally agree to let drop quite a lot of the posturing nonsense that passes for public discourse in this country.

The truly creepy ones are those few who aren't faking it, who really do wait until marriage and then only ever do it in the missionary position in the dark for the divinely-sanctioned purpose of procreation—that fringe culture of incorrigibly depraved fetishists we might call the Normal.

---

[1] A reference to the accidental exposure of Janet Jackson's nipple during the Superbowl halftime show, an outrage that commanded the moral attention of the nation in a month that saw 23 coalition deaths and an estimated 604 civilian deaths in Iraq.

IT IS NOW OBVIOUS TO ALL BUT THE DEMOCRATS THAT THE DEMOCRATIC PARTY IS MORIBUND. THE TIME HAS COME FOR THEM TO REINVENT THEMSELVES —— AS

The Sex Party

MOTTO: "ARE YOU GETTING ENOUGH?"

THE SEX PARTY PLATFORM:

ON ABORTION, GAY MARRIAGE, SEX & AIDS EDUCATION: 👍!

ON GOVERNMENT: *BIGGER IS BETTER!*

ON CHURCH & STATE: THE CHURCH HATES SEX. FUCK 'EM.

ON FOREIGN POLICY: *MONG WHORES, NOT WAR.*

ON DRUG POLICY: *WHAT GOES TOGETHER BETTER THAN SEX & DRUGS?*

ON CIVIL LIBERTIES: *WHAT HAPPENS IN AMERICA, STAYS IN AMERICA.*

SYMBOL OF THE REPUBLICAN PARTY:

THE ELEPHANT

SYMBOL OF THE SEX PARTY:

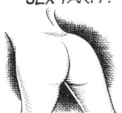

THE *ASS*

SEX PARTY PARAPHENALIA

* "EAT ME" FOR LADIES

CONFRONTED WITH CHARGES OF SEXUAL IMPROPRIETY, THE SEX PARTY CANDIDATE RESPONDS:

YES. I FUCKED THAT WOMAN FROM HELL TO BREAKFAST. I FUCKED HER LIKE I WAS PAUL BUNYAN AND SHE WAS A FLAPJACK THE SIZE OF LAKE TAHOE. I INTEND TO FUCK HER AGAIN IMMEDIATELY AFTER THIS PRESS CONFERENCE.

NEXT QUESTION —?

THE REPUBLICAN PARTY FUCKS THE POOR.

THE SEX PARTY FUCKS THE POOR!

"The Conservative Christian's Guide to Compassion," March 30th 2005

My colleagues Tom Hart and Jen Sorensen and I have been on tour this week, driving up and down the East Coast from New York to Providence to Boston to New Haven and back, talking politics all the way. On the radio the lurid, pitiful Terri Schiavo case grinds on and on, serving as a diversion while the Republicans sneak through legislation on bankruptcy and class action lawsuits, quietly removing legal tools for individuals to protect themselves against corporate power. None of us can quite reconcile conservatives' deep concern for the embryonic and the comatose with their apparent indifference to the poor and the foreign. Why these maudlin protests over the brain-dead but no word about the thousands of civilian casualties in Iraq?

I'm affecting a rhetorical naïveté here; I think I understand the dissonance very well. Fetuses and the brain-dead are abstract—blank, passive objects on which the empathetically impaired can project their vague sentimental notions of innocence and upon which they can lavish their misplaced, tacky, simple-minded love, not unlike the pets the childless anthropomorphize and creepily dote upon. Grown-up, conscious human beings are by contrast annoyingly flawed and contrary, full of wrong opinions and apt to behave badly. A lot Fundamentalist Christians don't seem to be up to the daunting charge to love thy neighbor. Witness the scary, weepy love they profess for their invisible friend Jesus, a guy they never met who died two thousand years ago, versus their rabid loathing for abortionists, homosexuals, secular humanists, Muslims, Jews, Papists, Wiccans, pornographers (and pornographees!), rock musicians, college professors, children's authors, and closet Marxists and yippies like David Souter and John McCain.

I have a relative respect for the doctrine of the Catholic Church, which is uncompromisingly pro-life across the board: anti-contraception, anti-abortion and anti-euthanasia, but also anti-death penalty. They are, at least, consistent, insisting that all life is sacred, not just cute life. Even the lives of the Bad. I can't help but admire moral hardassery. Though it's the same sort of highly qualified admiration I feel for hardline libertarianism, in that it's consistent to the point of insanity: *an AIDS epidemic is no excuse for using condoms; sure, I guess ten-year-olds should be able to carry concealed firearms.*

As I've written before, the apparent contradictions of Christian conservatism are incidental, all on the surface. The real impulse behind it is the will to judge, to mete out reward and punishment, to be God's little suck-up teacher's pet, His safety patrol, the instrument of His will, which, luckily, happens to coincide exactly with your own.

The Conservative Christian's Guide to Compassion

THE UNBORN

O WEEP FOR THE INNOCENT BABIES
MURDERED IN THEIR SLEEP!

THE BORN

OUR HARD-EARNED TAX DOLLARS ARE
SUPPOSED TO GO TO THESE PEOPLE WHO
KEEP HAVING CHILDREN THEY CAN'T AFFORD?

THE BRAIN-DEAD

PRAY FOR THE SOULS OF THOSE
HELPLESS UNFORTUNATES
CONDEMNED TO EXECUTION BY
OUR ATHEISTIC CULTURE OF DEATH.

THE RETARDED

I GUESS THEY WERE INTELLIGENT
ENOUGH TO COMMIT THEIR CRIMES.

BUNNIES

O BOO BOO BOO!

FOREIGNERS

WELL I'M SURE GOD WILL
SORT OUT THE RIGHTEOUS.
YOU CAN'T MAKE AN OMELETTE
WITHOUT BREAKING SOME EGGS!

Another idea we came up with on the "Laugh While You Can" tour. I imagined America, after the end of its global dominance, as the bitter, broken-down drunk at the end of the bar, boring everyone by going on and on about his glory days. I personally look forward to the inevitable day when our hubristic ambitions fall apart on us and we lose our empire. After that, hopefully, we can concentrate on becoming the greatest country on Earth instead of just the strongest. Former empires are generally civilized places to live, with fine cuisine and world-class museums stocked with plunder. (It's easy to forget that Belgium committed such ghastly atrocities in the Congo now that they make such tasty ale and chocolates.) It was Tom Hart's suggestion that it should be England who would take America under its wing; that's John Bull gamely trying to teach Uncle Sam how to take

post-imperial life easy and age gracefully, kick back, have an ale and not fret so much about water under the bridge. The French embodiment of Liberty, rather loosely adapted from Delacroix, is looking a little frowsy but still holding herself together with a Gallic hauteur. Our bartender stands in for all the people of the third world who've always been oppressed imperial subjects and never had a shot at the top. And that's the poor Russian bear up on the wall. If I'd had enough space, or better compositional acumen, I would've found some way to include Germania as an aged and bloated Valkyrie, quaffing pilsner from a stein in a desperate effort to forget, forget, forget.

Chinese translation: "Eat shit, foreign devils."

It will perhaps come as no surprise to my readers to reveal that Thompson was a formative influence on my own work. His wild and perfect swoops between high literary diction and poetic Kentucky profanity made him the best American political polemicist since Mencken. Would that he had influenced no more than my prose. My copy of *Fear and Loathing in Las Vegas* was inscribed with the words, "This book twisted and ruined Tim Kreider's life." I had to be very careful about taking it off the shelf, since each re-reading could trigger a dangerous bender that could last for weeks. Luckily I loaned it out years ago and never got it back.

I met the man once, at the book release party for *Kingdom of Fear* thrown by *The Paris Review* in George Plimpton's apartment, to which I'd gotten myself invited along by a friend of a friend. Thompson showed up several hours late, very unsteady on his feet, and held court in the living room, drinking a glass of whiskey and flirting with pretty young girls. Late in the evening we all crammed ourselves into the TV room to watch Thompson's interview on Charlie Rose, which had been taped earlier in the afternoon. The whole room laughed sycophantically every time he burbled incoherently in response to a question. The whole scene was distasteful and sad, seeing a man passed out on his laurels.

Recognition and praise matter more than most artists like to admit, but they're a poor substitute for productivity—like trying to live off of whiskey instead of food. Thompson was as serious about his craft as any writer, and his literary ambitions were the highest; apocryphally, he used to transcribe passages from *The Great Gatsby* verbatim on his typewriter just to know in his own nerve endings how it felt to write prose that fine. But his work in the last couple decades was an empty aping of his own old style. He had become a professional Hunter Thompson impersonator. I remember that in the introduction to the *Great Shark Hunt* he contemplated diving out his hotel window twenty-eight stories down into the Plaza Fountain. Looking back, he must've felt he'd missed his moment. I went home that night without speaking to him.

Or at least that's what I thought until a week or so later, when my friend Myla told me, "So I heard you talked to Hunter Thompson!" "Who did?" I asked. "Me?" As it emerged, in fact I had. What happened, I learned, was that I had smoked pot, something I almost never do any more. Now that I heard this, I did seem to remember accepting a small pipe and saying, "I don't usually do this..."

Apparently the esteemed Doctor and I talked at some length, in a language that no one else present could understand. And yes, now that I thought about it, I did have a memory—or was it my imagination?—of his personal assistant, a petite, self-possessed woman he would later marry, telling me very clearly and patiently, as if for the hundredth time, "Yes, Hunter has your comics and he will read them." After the party, I was told, I had loitered pathetically around on the street as if hoping to be invited into the limo when they left, but needless to say this is not what happened. I have no real memory of any of this. Which seems appropriate, in a way, but it's also disappointing now that I know that it was my only chance.

When I heard the news of his suicide I headed to the nearest bar, ordered a shot of Chivas Regal, and toasted his memory. *Requiescat in Pace*. I sat there until closing time with my pens and folder of papers in front of me, trying to come up with an appropriate cartoon I could email in by press time. But nothing came to me. I blew it. I never found the image to express this feeling that all hope was now gone. (I didn't draw this cartoon until a week later, too late for print.) Thompson once wrote, in a moment of similar bleakness, that the assassination of John F. Kennedy "broke the back of the American dream." I'm sure his reasons for suicide were personal, not political, but it's hard not to impute some causality to the correlation: George Bush gets re-elected; Hunter Thompson blows his brains out. If he gave up, what are the rest of us waiting around for? It seems to augur badly for us all, like the mass dieoffs among the frogs, those most sensitive and thin-skinned of creatures.

This idea recalls a notion my old friend Michael thought up back in middle school, of the the afterlife as a game show wherein the host would spin the big wheel like on *The Price is Right*, or turn to the big board as on *Family Feud*, to reveal: "The *right* religion was... HINDU!" And all the Hindus would pump their fists in triumph and hiss "Yess!" while all the Christians and Muslims and Buddhists and Jews and Taoists and Shintoists and Animists clutched their heads and moaned, "Ohhhhh!' The humiliating bloopy you-lose bassoon music would play as they were escorted offstage to give it another try next go-round. They'd get cases of Turtle Wax to take with them as consolation prizes.

I have no special respect for the Pope, but I didn't intend any particular disrespect to him with this cartoon, either—it was just an irresistible premise.[1] I'm sure the Pope is a very nice old man, though it's occurred to me that if he were my next-door neighbor instead of the leader of a major world religion, just some average guy who happened to believe that all forms of artificial contraception are a sin and that he himself was God's personal spokesperson on Earth, and had only admitted that Galileo was right in the Nineties, he would seem like an amiable crackpot and I would probably avoid getting into any long conversations with him.

Thanks to some guy at the Polish Club in Fell's Point, Baltimore, who gave me the Polish translation for "crap" as well as five different kinds of sausage and spherical donuts with powdered sugar and raisins.

---

[1] This was one of countless occasions when obscurity spared me from scandal. Matt Taibbi, the funniest political writer of our time, and his editor both lost their jobs at the *New York Press* after he tossed off a silly piece titled "The 52 Funniest Things About the Upcoming Death of the Pope." (Taibbi recalled maybe being under the influence of Vicodin while writing the piece.) Senator Hilary Clinton, New York City Mayor Michael Bloomberg, and Congressman Anthony Weiner— faithful *NY Press* readers all—were among those so morally troubled by this article that they felt compelled to put aside considerations of freedom of speech and the separation of church and state and made it an urgent priority to denounce it.

Lately I've been trying to think of ways for the Left to reclaim this country as our own. As "The Sex Party" suggested, I propose that if the Republicans are going to wrap themselves in the self-righteous vestment of Moral Values—by which they seem to mean prudery and intolerance—the left should just go ahead and admit to being unabashed libertines. The Democrats should be the Sex Party, the Drug Party, the Rock 'n' Roll Party. These are American values as well. Who's more obsessed with sex than any nation on earth? Americans. Who's sucking up all the drugs in the Western Hemisphere and half of Asia? Americans. Who invented Rock 'n' Roll? Africans. I mean Americans! African-Americans, anyway.

I'm tired of "the real America" being defined by obese, pious teetotalling virgins out in cow country who believe in angels and think France is our sworn enemy, while the rest of us have to feel like the faggy eggheaded cousin who ran off to The City. All my hard-drinking, drug-abusing, fornicating atheist friends are Americans. Megan and I always used to take a big American flag along with us to protest marches and rallies, and endured the occasional remark from some sneering hippie or Wiccan. During the "Laugh While You Can Tour" in '02 I wore an American flag pin in my lapel, and I found, to my dismay, that I felt self-conscious and uncomfortable wearing it—as though people seeing it must think of me what I always think of people I see wearing one: *asswipe*. I do not like letting these ignorant fatheads with flag decals and yellow ribbon magnets on their SUVs appropriate all the iconography of partiotism for themselves. Backing whatever the government does and Supporting Our Troops isn't especially American—it's what everybody does everywhere, in every country on Earth, most enthusiastically in despotic little shitholes like North Korea. Dumb assent and docile compliance are anti-American; it's criticism and dissent that are quintessentally American. This is a nation of subversives, rabble-rousers, and wrongos who got driven out of every other nation on earth because they wouldn't keep their mouths shut about their unpatriotic notions.

That's me and Boyd and Jenny Boylan standing in for all the disenfranchised losers of the left, a microcosm of the Other America: Jenny representing the transsexual soccer moms, Boyd the crazy half-breeds, and me the drunken geeks. On the right, what Harry Dean Stanton's character in *Repo Man* calls "ordinary people—I fuckin' hate 'em." This is not just George Bush's and Billy Graham's and Rush Limbaugh's country. It's Hunter Thompson's country. It's Jimi Hendrix's country. It's our country. It's America, goddamnit. It's time we took it back.

Americans VS. 'MURICANS

	Americans	'MURICANS
KNOWLEDGE OF BILL OF RIGHTS	• 1ST AMENDMENT: ALLOWS PROTESTS, PORNOGRAPHY, FLAG-BURNING, AND YOU DON'T HAVE TO GO TO CHURCH. • 4TH: THE COPS NEED A WARRANT TO SEARCH YOUR PLACE. • 5TH: IF THE COPS DO GET YOU, YOU DON'T HAVE TO SAY SHIT. • 21ST: PROHIBITION REPEALED!	• 2ND AMENDMENT: THE STATES SHALL TAKE AWAY THE PEOPLE'S GUNS WHEN THEY PRY THEM FROM THEIR COLD, DEAD FINGERS. • 1ST: THE PEOPLE SHALL NOT MAKE GRAVEN IMAGES. • 6TH: THE PEOPLE SHALT NOT COVET. • 7TH (?): FINDERS KEEPERS • 27TH: MARRIAGE SHALL BE BETWEEN A MAN AND A WOMAN.
CIVIC PARTICIPATION	• WRITING LETTERS · TO · THE · EDITOR, ELECTED REPRESENTATIVES • ATTENDING PROTEST MARCHES AND RALLIES	• LISTENING TO TALK RADIO • BUYING FLAG DECALS, BUMPER STICKERS
MORAL VALUES	"FREEDOM." E.G., UNCENSORED EXPRESSION, DISSENT, SECULAR PLURALISM	"FREEDOM." E.G., UNCONDITIONAL SUPPORT OF GOVERNMENT, SURRENDER OF PERSONAL LIBERTIES, RESTRICTED CIVIL RIGHTS FOR MINORITIES, STATE-SANCTIONED RELIGION
NATIONAL CULTURAL TOUCHSTONES	• ADVENTURES OF HUCK FINN • THE GREAT GATSBY • ON THE ROAD • RAPSHODY IN BLUE • "SOMEWHERE OVER THE RAINBOW" • JIMI HENDRIX'S STAR-SPANGLED BANNER • "BORN TO RUN."	• "HAVE YOU FORGOTTEN?" • FORD ADS

"Liberals vs. The Empire," May 25th 2005

A bracing antidote to last week's uncharacteristically affirmative fighting spirit. My friend Carolyn wrote me about last week's cartoon and the accompanying artist's statement:

> I have just recently starting thinking it's time to give up. We are the minority and they have the country. I am in lying-low mode. Hey did you notice that your examples of negative American role-models are alive but the positive ones are dead? Lying low.

This cartoon illustrates my greatest complaint about the Left in this country: we're useless. We've been playing drums and building giant puppets and "adbusting" while the Right has taken control of all three branches of the government and the media. I went to mass protests before the war in Iraq, both in New York and in Washington, D.C. History has shown that they accomplished jack shit. Protests are an obsolete tactic, routine and impotent now, and the media renders them invisible by pretending they never happened. Letters to our elected representatives have the same effect on public policy as prayers to Jesus do on cancer.

The Right no longer gives a shit about the rules as long as they win; the current fight over filibusters is only the latest blatant example of this contempt for the impediments of democracy. Like any playground bully, they change the game at their convenience to expedite whatever it is they happen to want to do—in this case, pack the Federal Courts with far-right crackpots who'd uphold the Dred Scott decision.

Some people argue that the Democrats have to move farther to the right—the Clinton Doctrine—which will ensure that they become even more namby-pamby, irrelevant, and scorned. Some argue that they need to return to their populist roots and appeal to the middle class's enlightened self-interest, which might work if the American people had taken civics class or heard about anything that wasn't on TV this season.

What I think the Democrats need to do is out-Tory the Tories: fight dirty, conduct smear campaigns and character assassinations, saturate the media with outright, shameless lies, go for the jugular, take no prisoners, kill the women and children, and seed the ground with salt. Why must we be always so timid and polite? It's like trying to reason with your torturers. Even far-right hard-liners would respect the Democrats more if they openly declared war than they do their feeble and unconvincing efforts to ingratiate themselves with the Republicans' core constituency of the ineducable and the insane. Why not just give up on those cretinous Jesus freaks and just come out and say all the obvious truths: George Bush is a liar, Jesus isn't real, Iraq's a disaster, guns are for cowards, abstinence is for the ugly, and screw the unborn.

I realize that this is an illustration of Gresham's law, which states that all political parties sink to the level of the worst player, and that by so doing we would become the very thing we affect to despise. I would rebut: what*ever*. This is a war for the soul of our nation, a war between, on the one side, a coalition of fanatical Fundamentalists and cynical Fascists, and, on the other, those dwindling few of us who are still in favor of a pluralistic, secular, free society. Our enemies do not want a dialogue; they just want us to shut up.

Me, I want our side to win. I want those fuckers beaten, humiliated, disgraced. I want to see them as furious and defeated as I feel every day. I want the Ten Commandments out of the courthouses and back in the children's books where they belong. I want to see Republican ladies in red dresses and pearls weeping on TV. I want to see gay men getting married on Martha Stewart. I want to see the local rednecks slumped over their beers as if gut-shot, angrily wondering what the hell ever happened to this country. The Death Star is within firing range. We have thirty snub fighters armed with proton torpedoes and a two-meter wide target. Who's with me?

For several weeks now we've been in a weird summer lull in which there's been no real news. *The New York Times* has been running borderline-tabloid stories about the trivial and the bizarre: a feature on "Meth Mouth," an unphotogenic syndrome afflicting habitual users of crystal methamphetamine; a human interest piece about an aspiring actress playing Curious George at a book fair whose head deflated; an article about a bag of garbage on the Upper East Side that smelled really bad. The revelation about Deep Throat was the first item of news that's really cheered me since Reagan died. It reminded me a little of the day they found what might've been a fossil in that Martian meteorite; everyone seemed giddy and elated over a breaking news story that didn't involve anyone getting hurt.

But then on Wednesday night I was listening to the radio and noticed an extraordinary thing: all the news was unexpectedly cheering. In addition to the stories listed in the cartoon, I learned that George Bush's poll numbers were falling; a majority of Americans felt the war in Iraq wasn't worth it; the Downing Street memo was belatedly getting mentioned in the U.S. press; Philip Cooney, the White House official who edited those government reports on climate change to downplay the potential effects of global warming, had resigned and gone to work for the oil industry in a more formal capacity; and even *USA Today*, the *Regis & Kathy Lee Show* of newspapers, announced that the debate on global warming was officially over.

Is it possible that things are finally turning to shit for the Bush administration? My friend Megan believes that "things will just gradually sorta fizzle for them" until they waddle limping off into irrelevance, but I am still hoping for a Nixonian day of reckoning, public humiliation and disgrace, anagnorisis, George drunk and weeping on TV, Mr. Cheney dragged away in chains. But I am an irrepressible optimist.

This week's cartoon features several unfamiliar characters I should identify for future historians:

Panel 1 is an unkind caricature of Senator Mel Martinez, the first Republican to point out that Guantanamo Bay was providing fodder for anti-American propaganda abroad. To be fair, all the images I found of him made him look goofy and good-natured, and I do respect his standing up to the Bush administration, but it's worth noting that his main objection was that Guantanamo was making us look bad, not that it *was* bad. He may not be bad for a Republican, but he's still a Republican, and here at *The Pain* our official policy regarding Republicans is: no prisoners.

Panel 2 shows Edgar Ray Killen, former Klansman, currently on trial for the murder of three civil rights workers, about which he's been more or less openly gloating for forty years. His is one of those faces, like George Bush's, Dick Cheney's or John Ashcroft's, which no caricature I could draw, however grotesque, could possibly capture, let alone exaggerate. The features etched by eighty years of caustic evil have made him into a withered, senile reptile, some vicious, toothless old thing best dragged out back and crushed with a brick. Killen really did protest that he had a lot of black friends. No doubt he is beloved in his local African-American community. I'm sure many of them will come forward as character witnesses.

I very much enjoyed drawing the plump head, tiny face, shifty eyes and sweating lip of White House Press Secretary Scott McClellan, who may be the least convincing liar I have ever seen on TV—whether he's assuring us that the abrupt departure of Philip Cooney from the Council on Environmental Quality had nothing to do with the revelation, a week earlier, that he had censored scientific information in government documents, or dismissing the Downing Street memo as just another re-hash of a debate already settled.

Yes those are neat little swastika pins McClellan and Martinez are wearing. Join the party, wear the pin.

TWILIGHT OF THE ASSHOLES

HEY IS IT JUST ME, OR HAS THERE BEEN SOME

Cheering News

LATELY?

EVEN SOME REPUBLICANS ACKNOWLEDGING OUR CONCENTRATION CAMP IS BAD P.R.

LOOK, I'M NOT SAYING IT'S WRONG— IT JUST DOESN'T *LOOK* GOOD!

FOLKS COULD GET THE WRONG IDEA.

EVEN SOUTHERNERS ADMIT LYNCHING BLACKS, MURDERING CIVIL RIGHTS WORKERS WAS TECHNICALLY ILLEGAL

GODDAMMIT SOME A MAH BES' FRIENS IS NIGGERS.

WHY, AH'M PRACTICKLY WHUTCH'Y' MIGHT CALL A NIGGER *LOVER*!

EVEN THE WASHINGTON PRESS CORPS STARTING TO ASK WHETHER THE INVASION OF IRAQ WAS A CROCK

SECRETARY McCLELLAN, CAN *YOU* COMMENT ON THE ACCURACY OF THE SO-CALLED 'DOWNING STREET MEMO'?

THIS IS JUST A RE-HASHING OF A DEBATE THAT WAS ALREADY SETTLED.

WHEN WAS THIS DEBATE, EXACTLY?

...BEFORE.

EVEN THE U.S. CONGRESS REALIZING THE PATRIOT ACT IS UNCONSTITUTIONAL

ON APRIL 15TH OF 2003 YOU CHECKED OUT THE *AUDIOBOOK* OF THE *NOVELIZATION* OF 'KINGDOM COME'.

I REFUSE TO DISCUSS THAT WITHOUT A LAWYER PRESENT.

...AND I SEE THAT WAS EIGHT DAYS OVERDUE.

Lately I've been thinking I could really use the talents of a good P.R. flack—someone who'd cover up, make excuses, dismiss, dissemble (or "disassemble," as the President has it), prevaricate, stall, stonewall, and flat-out baldfaced lie through his teeth for me as shamelessly as that stolid toady Scott McClellean does for the Bush administration. Because, like the Bush administration, I have on occasion made decisions that were not strictly reality-based and which proved to have unforeseen consequences, and, also like them, I am loath to own up to it and would rather just see if I can't weasel out of everything.

I seem to have tapped into a deep vein of visceral loathing for Scott McClellan with last week's cartoon; a number of readers wrote in just to vent about him. "He is not at all an accomplished liar, and I am pretty sure he doesn't care," wrote my lone fan in Kansas. "It seems rather galling that he lies, and we all know he is lying, but it just doesn't seem to matter. No outcry of 'Liar!'" Some got almost Lovecraftian in their prose: "The tiny face that appears to be sliding off of a thick, neckless tube, and his teensy weensy mousy hands." My colleague Emily Flake was damningly concise: "What a waxy little stooge."

There's a way in which this rancor toward McClellan is misplaced. He is, after all, just the guy who gets paid to stand there and lie about the administration's crimes; he doesn't actually commit them. It is the cruel genius of all corporate bodies whose business involves unconscionably screwing over their customers to ensure that the only corporeal representative of that company directly accessible to the public is some underpaid innocent—a desk clerk, secretary, receptionist, or phone-bank caller—who is in no way personally responsible for the institutional screwing-over and whose only real job is to be screamed at. So you either vent your impotent rage upon them and later feel stupid and ashamed of yourself, or else realize that it's not this poor schlub's fault that your rental truck is not there when it was "reserved," or that your hard drive crashed after less than two years, so you go out of your way to be nice and polite to them, even apologetic, and later you feel stupid and ashamed of yourself.

In other words McClellan's only real job is to be the object of all this displaced aggression. The appropriate response ought to be to pay no more attention to him that to a podium or curtain and direct our rage over his head at his employers. But then, it's also not as if his only other option was to bus tables at Pizza Hut. He knew who he was going to work for, and what kind of work their firm did. And there's a certain insulting arrogance evident in the fact that they didn't even bother to hire a *competent* liar; they just needed someone to stand there and formally deny everything while they went about their filthy business.

I particularly love—"love" in the sense of hate—his signature line, "The President has moved on," which he deploys any time he's asked about some error, dereliction, crime or atrocity the President may have committed or authorized even a few days earlier. "The President is not dwelling on the past. The President is looking to the future." (I have to remember this line if the cops ever dig up the bodies in my crawl space. "Are you guys still hung up on *that* whole thing? Because I've totally moved on.") The President is serenely above this petty partisan squabbling, preoccupied with important matters of state, not these irrelevant and sensational incriminating documents or civilian casualties you all are so fixated on. The President is all, like: "That is so last week."

It is a heartening fact, as pointed out in Lewis Thomas's essay on lie detectors, that lying is inherently stressful to the human body. One can only hope that McClellan secretly suffers from ulcers or piles or psoriasis as psychosomatic retribution for his daily diet of mendacity. I like to imagine that after White House Press Secretaries resign they have to spend time in some sort of rehab facility, The Ron Ziegler Clinic, behind whose doors they can finally break down and confess their years-long litany of lies and be flagellated by interns in an attempt to expiate their venal sins. Maybe as part of their recovery they have to do some sort of rigorous, penitential truth-telling, like breaking bad news to the relatives of accident victims, or writing copy for pamphlets about VD.

My Press Secretary

"The Next Supreme Court Nominee," July 6ᵗʰ 2005

On Friday morning I was struggling with the week's cartoon, among other issues, when I learned that Sandra Day O'Connor, historic first female right-wing hack appointed to the Supreme Court, had announced her resignation. This news came around noon, and my five o'clock deadline was absolutely inflexible this week. So my premise was cut out for me; all that remained to do was fill in the humorous candidates. Jesus and the fetus were the obvious choices. The disabled lesbian Latina is only an exaggeration of the minorities who support intolerant and regressive policies that the Republicans always seem able to dredge up from the ranks of mediocrity—e.g., Clarence "Long Dong" Thomas and Alberto "The Torturer" Gonzales.

The last panel remained blank until alarmingly late in the afternoon, when I finally sent out a desperate Emergency Humor Consultation to my inner circle of advisers. From webmaster Dave came the suggestion, "The Thing." Now The Thing is a flawed man in some ways, but I think I would endorse more of his court decisions than not. Dr. Doom, on the other hand, seemed more like the sort of candidate the Republicans would put forward—tough, hard-headed, unsentimental, likely to have a lenient attitude toward questions of extraordinary rendition, indefinite detainment, and enhanced interrogation techniques. It's yet another debate-framing coup for the Right that conservatives get to label liberal judicial nominees "activist judges," suggesting they're taking wild liberties with the Framer's intentions, like grad students in Comp Lit arguing that *Pride and Prejudice* is a seminal text of Queer Theory, while conservative judges who rule to deny civil rights to homosexuals, block scientific and medical procedures undreamt of in the eighteenth century, and defend the sale of semiautomatic weapons, the electrocution of the retarded, and the imprisonment of American citizens without due process are considered rigorously literal interpreters of the Constitution's original meaning. It's also extremely fun to emulate the sort of florid rhetoric spouted by the Lord of Latveria.

WHO WILL BE THE NEXT Supreme Court Nominee?

THE FIRST UNBORN-AMERICAN JUSTICE

THE LORD JESUS CHRIST

SOME REPUBLICAN DISABLED LESBIAN LATINA WHO ADVOCATES EUGENICS

(THE HON.) VICTOR VON DOOM

A new design for the Freedom Tower was unveiled last week, redesigned with concessions to security concerns. It really does have a Brutalist concrete base, like a colossal bunker in the financial district, and its bland faceted shaft is even less inspiring than the original lopsided postmodern mediocrity proposed.[1] As a childhood aficionado of extremely tall buildings I have a purist's contempt for this stubby seventy-story pretender that tries to steal the title of World's Tallest with a hollow, uninhabited superstructure and a spire. Like the Bush administration itself, it's both craven and arrogant, its head scrunched down between its shoulders while it waves a flag at the top of a very long pole. It's a building that is, in effect, cringing. If that's the best we can do, we deserve to lose out to Malaysia.

It's embarrassing even to have to call this building "The Freedom Tower." Who thought up this name—some ten-year-old boy in camouflage pants? I can only hope that, as with the corporate brands slapped on venerable old stadiums, no one will use it and some spontaneous popular nickname will stick instead. Something like Ground Zero One, George's Folly—or, perhaps to honor the former Vice President, simply Big Dick.

The Fear Tower seems to me a sadly perfect symbol for what America has become in the last four years: the most frightened nation on Earth. I was impressed by the way Londoners behaved in the wake of the last round of terrorist attacks; they just got back on their buses and subways and went to work the next day. They did not shut down the city for weeks or close their borders or round up a bunch of Arabs at random and indefinitely "detain" them without charges. New Yorkers were just as matter-of-factly courageous after 9/11; it was the rest of the country, the mean-drunk soccer moms and blubbering NASCAR dads back in suburbia, who saw it all happen on T.V., imagining the barbarian hordes storming their gated communities, who begged their big powerful daddy in Washington to please take away our civil liberties and clamored for him to kill somebody in the Middle East, anybody. So more Homeland Security funding per capita goes to the trembling yokels of Wyoming, a state no terrorist could find in a road atlas, than to the residents of New York City.

9/11 was the single best thing that ever happened to George W. Bush, next to having been born into the right family. He should be thanking Jesus for it every night and beseeching Him to please send more terrorists to kill more New Yorkers. Fear is absolutely the only thing George has going for him. Without it, even the American people might eventually notice that he's sold their country out from under them. The people who voted Bush back into office voted for him because they were afraid. I voted against him because I'm not.

---

1   In retrospect I came to appreciate Daniel Liebeskind's design—the final design made it look visionary by contrast, sort of the same way that George Bush made Nixon look statesmanlike.

George's Vacation

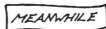

Don't Worry, George —
We All Have Our Cindy Sheehans

*Do not ask.

August 24th, 2005

I know we Liberals have a reputation among real Americans for elitism and arrogance—believing that just because we left home and went to college and live in the city now, because we read books and use fancy words and don't even have a TV and no longer give a shit who won the big game, that this somehow makes us smarter than ordinary folks, like we know what's best for everyone. So it does seem fair to ask whether this cartoon is making some clichéd and insulting generalization, insinuating none too subtly that conservatives are simply stupider than liberals.

I can assure my readers that it insinuates no such thing; it comes right out and says so. This cartoon is a big fat unapologetic "I Told You So" from me on behalf of my hundreds of thousands of compatriots who filled the streets shouting that this war was trumped up on lies and would turn into a quagmire to all the patriotic shitheads who swallowed every lie the Bush administration fed them, no matter how big it was or how bad it smelled, rallied around the flag and supported the troops and yelled "U.!S.!A.!" and called us traitors and hippies and faggots and are only now starting to wonder whether it was really such a good idea after all—and not because it was a violation of international law or morally wrong, but just because we're not winning.

I almost have to respect those delusional few—now almost exclusively limited to members of the Bush administration—who still adamantly support the war more than the millions of fair-weather fascists who were enthusiastic about it until our guys started getting killed and it turned into a big downer. Almost, but not quite. At least the latter group is able to accept reality—albeit belatedly, about four years after it was obvious to their historically literate compatriots, the same way they're finally coming around to accept the reality of global warming about twenty years after the scientifically literate community.

I don't want anyone to imagine that I take any satisfaction in the deaths of American servicemen and -women. It wasn't their bright idea to go into Iraq. I am pleased to see the political weenies who thought up this invasion, policy-paper Napoleons like Cheney and Rumsfeld and Wolfowitz, exposed as frauds and incompetents who had no idea what they were doing. But most of my vindictive rancor is aimed at my fellow Americans who enabled this atrocity with their fatassed bovine complicity.

Come on, my fellow dissenters—this is no time for liberal civility. Quiet vindication doesn't offer anything like the satisfactions of loud, obnoxious, sneering vindication. You think conservatives wouldn't be gloating and hooting and demanding we renounce our citizenship and go back to Franceland if their fantasies had all somehow come true and our troops had been greeted with dancing and flowers and democracy had flourished in Iraq? So why not be poor sports and rub their faces in it a little? Let's all say it together, just this once:

WE TOLD YOU SO, YOU DUMB GULLIBLE FUCKWITS, YOU IGNORANT GUNG-HO CANNON FODDER, YOU SUBMISSIVE BETA APES. WE TOLD YOU SO. WE TOLD YOU SO. WE TOLD YOU SO.

That was technically more than once but it does feel good, even if it's in a way one might prefer not to own up to.

The Difference

LIBERALS

JULY 2002

CONSERVATIVES

**AUGUST 2005
1,800 DEATHS**

The abuse and degradation of the word *freedom* has been the most offensive of all the Bush administration's Orwellian perversions of the language. Just as they've done to the American flag, George and his supporters have thoroughly soaked it in Republican piss to mark it as their own, made it the sole property of jingoistic, warmongering shitheads. I have to wonder whether the patriots who parrot slogans about "freedom" as a defense for the war in Iraq have any idea what they even mean by the word. When was the last time most Americans used any of their constitutionally guaranteed freedoms, anyway? Downloading porn? Shooting at deer? Telling the state trooper who's pulled them over for DUI that they got rights while trying to remember legal lingo from *Cops*?

The word *freedom* has been rendered worse than meaningless; in fact it's become less a word than an incantation, used to magically justify anything the administration wants to do—like seizing oil reserves that are inconveniently located underneath what is technically some other nation's territory. Now whenever I hear anyone use the word *freedom* I mentally substitute the word *oil* and suddenly the sentence is translated into perfect, lucid sense: "Americans love oil." "All the world's people, regardless of race, religion, or nationality, thirst for oil." "The terrorists hate our oil." "Oil is on the march." "Our heroic troops have paid the ultimate price for oil." And, most tellingly: "Oil isn't free."

What Is FREEDOM?

FREEDOM IS THE MOST PRECIOUS SUBSTANCE KNOWN TO AMERICANS. IT IS *VITAL* TO OUR CHERISHED AMERICAN WAY OF LIFE.

ALL PEOPLES THE WORLD OVER, REGARDLESS OF RACE OR NATIONALITY, THIRST FOR FREEDOM. BUT AN EMBITTERED MINORITY *HATE* OUR FREEDOM, AND WILL STOP AT NOTHING TO TAKE IT FROM US!

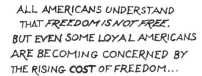

NATURALLY, AMERICA'S CLOSEST ALLIES ARE THOSE NATIONS THAT PRIZE FREEDOM AS HIGHLY AS WE.

ALL AMERICANS UNDERSTAND THAT *FREEDOM IS NOT FREE.* BUT EVEN SOME LOYAL AMERICANS ARE BECOMING CONCERNED BY THE RISING *COST* OF FREEDOM...

The Katrina disaster has been one of those rare occasions, like the first Presidential debate against Kerry, when, miraculously, the normally oblivious rest of the world suddenly seems to have noticed that George Bush is an incompetent, churlish fool. Once again his non-reality-based approach to governance has run up against its one flaw: reality. Appointing cronies to prestigious positions based on partisan loyalty turns out to be a problem when, sooner or later, those positions call for some competence or expertise. Trying to deny actual events and put a positive spin on failure doesn't work as well when those events are occurring not on the other side of the planet, where reporters can be "embedded" and effectively controlled, but in America, where we're seeing thousands of our fellow citizens looking like third-world refugees. It's an Iraq happening right here at home, where the footage can't be censored.

George, who brags about not reading newspapers, seems to have been the very last person in the world to hear about the destruction of New Orleans. He's still congratulating his appointees on "a heckuva job" while the rest of the nation is watching in horror as corpses bloat in the streets. His administration is only capable of seeing this as an urgent political problem—as a *P.R.* disaster. Their solutions are to make more trips to the Gulf, stage more photo ops, write more speeches, impress upon the American people that they are aware of the situation. "We're thinking about this every hour," they stress. Wow! That must be hard work, George, all that hourly thinking. You know, I think about sex every hour but that alone doesn't get me any closer to having any.

George and his few remaining supporters are trying to blame the locals for any little snafus in the relief effort. My friend Louise, a novelist and bartender in Austin, Texas, e-mailed me: "The other night I had a whole slew of overweight soccer moms from Houston in my bar. They really were soccer moms, here for a tournament. Boy, were they pounding the frozen margaritas and white wine! They all went on and on about how thankful they were that we have such a strong, forceful and dynamic leader in the White House, how lucky we are, bless his heart, and if it weren't for the incompetent state governments of Louisiana and Mississippi none of these problems would be happening. They were terrible tippers, too."

It should be clear by now even to shitfaced soccer moms in Texas that George Bush could not find his own ass with both hands and the entire U.S. intelligence apparatus. He has shown the world that the United States is no longer a power to be reckoned with but a pathetic, lumbering laughingstock: not only can't we win a war any more, we can't carry out the most basic functions of a government, like evacuating our own citizens in a natural disaster. The only thing he's accomplished in four years is to pass those massive tax cuts for his wealthy owners and run the country into a crippling deficit. He was getting ready to push for a repeal of the estate tax, which would only benefit societal parasites like me who've never had to do an honest day's work in their lives, before this dang hurricane thing made even Republicans realize it might look impolitic.

Bush, like his father, behaves as though he were the colonial governor of some third-world shithole, which is what large areas of the United States have come to resemble on his watch. It's never occurred to him that government was supposed to do anything but fill up the bank accounts and investment portfolios of his campaign donors. He's cost hundreds, if not thousands, of citizens their lives and humiliated us in front of the entire international community. "The king of vacations at his ranch only said, 'You must flee,'" mocked Venezuelan President Hugo Chavez. "He did not say how." (Chavez is not a very likeable character in himself, but as a comic foil and a gall for George he's as indispensable as Tweety is to Sylvester.) It'd be hard not to nod solemnly at the poetic justice if some thirst-crazed fourteen-year-old black girl put a cap in his ass from a rooftop as he toured the sodden ruins of New Orleans.

"The Pain Predicts," October 12ᵗʰ 2005

I currently have a number of bets going with my friend Myla. Myla is strongly opinionated and pretends to be utterly sure of herself at all times, so she is fun to bet against. She called me one day during the Roberts hearing to say that he seemed reasonable and moderate—she thought he might turn out to be okay. Oh, Myla, I said. Notice how everyone somehow got that same impression even though, throughout the week of his confirmation hearing, he studiously avoided saying one concrete thing about his judicial beliefs or how he would vote on any issue that he might be called to rule on? My gut feeling is that anything George W. Bush wants is bad; therefore Roberts will, once on the bench, unmask himself as a heartless authoritarian bastard of the far right in the mold of Rhenquist and Scalia, dedicated to protecting the rights of the wealthy and privileged against oppression by the poor and powerless. Myla and I are going to select one clear-cut case of good vs. evil that comes before the Supreme Court and see which way Roberts votes. (Already the court's ruled against librarians who were challenging the provision of the P.A.T.R.I.O.T. act that allows the Feds to read your library records, which does not bode well for Myla.) The loser must wear a Robert Bork T-shirt in public.[1]

Harriet Miers has no experience as a judge, no written record of any legal opinions at all, nothing but the full confidence of her dear personal friend George Bush. Conservatives are concerned because she hasn't gone on the record as saying she will save the unborn, but it's clear she is an evangelical Christian dingbat. Look at her makeup.

Myla believes that Bush, who is famously incurious, just nominated someone he personally knew rather than look around and do research to find a qualified candidate. It's as if I were unexpectedly called upon to nominate a Supreme Court justice—I'd probably just nominate my friend John, because he used to be a lawyer. (I'd also look forward to reading his legal opinions. He once advised Jim and me, around 3 A.M. the night before we were to appear for a summons, to "blow off this court thing.")

This theory does make some sense, I have to admit. You figure the deal must have been that Dick Cheney got to pick the first Supreme Court nominee and agreed to let George pick the second, betting that there weren't going to be two vacancies in their term. It's easy to picture the scene when, against the odds, George gets his chance and Mr. Cheney asks him: "Well, George, have you thought about who you'd like to nominate?" George says, uncertainly: "I pick Harriet." There's a pause. Then, incredulous, Mr. Cheney says: "*Harriet?*" He's not sure they can be talking about the same person. "Your *lawyer?*" "I think she's real smart," says George, with quiet defiance.

I read an article pointing out that Miers' main qualification as a Supreme Court nominee was the same as it's been for all Bush appointees: personal loyalty to the president. This criteria makes a Machiavellian sort of sense when applied to cronies you're going to make cabinet secretaries or bureau chiefs, but I couldn't figure out why you'd require personal loyalty from someone you were selecting for a lifetime appointment... *unless*, it occurred to me, you *also* intended to be in office for life. That's when I understood: they have no intention of leaving office. No way are they taking any chance of losing power over something as chancy and uncontrolled as an election. They are entrenched in the White House for good.

Just as I was convinced that the Bush administration made provisions to rig the 2004 elections, I believe that they will contrive to stay in office beyond their two constitutionally allotted terms. They'll repeal the twenty-second amendment, or declare martial law and "postpone" elections after another terrorist attack, or,

---

[1] I totally won this one. Myla has yet to wear the Bork shirt.

The Pain Predicts...

NEW SUPREME COURT JUSTICES WILL INDEED PROVE TO BE RIGHT-WING WACKJOBS.

BUSH ADMINISTRATION WILL CONTRIVE TO REMAIN IN POWER PAST SECOND TERM *

*O YES. MARK MY WORDS.

THOSE GAS PRICES? — NOT COMING BACK DOWN.

EVER.

DEMOCRACY IN IRAQ!

HA, HA! JUST KIDDING.

if they fail in that, the next anointed Republican candidate will also select Dick Cheney, the actual President for these last five years, as his or her running mate, thereby maintaining what John Ralston Saul calls "persistent continuity at the heart of power."

Myla calls this "a sucker's bet." She feels guilty taking advantage of me. "No way is Bush doing that," she said. "Myla, Myla, Myla," I chided her. "These people don't care about the Constitution or the democratic process. They only care about staying in power." Perhaps Myla is right; maybe I am being paranoid. Maybe in 2008 we'll throw these traitorous scum out and the entire eight grim years—the Bush Administration, the P.A.T.R.I.O.T. Act, the War on Terror—will all seem like a bad dream. But after the 2000 election I am capable of believing anything—the National Guard barricading the White House, the Commander-in-Chief given emergency dictatorial powers, George declared a god like Augustus Cæsar. Who'd stop it? The Congress is dominated by Republicans who follow the Executive Branch's orders in obedient lockstep, the Supreme Court is packed with the same partisan stooges who thrust Bush into office in the first place, the Fourth Estate accepts any *fait accompli*

it's presented with, and The freaking People are more interested in Tom Cruise and Katie Holmes' pregnancy. The stakes, besides democracy in America, are a dozen oysters, to be eaten at the venue of the victor's choosing.[2]

---

2   Any time you purport to make confident assertions about the future, you end up looking stupid. In retrospect it looks as if I might've succumbed to a strain of the same paranoia now gripping my counterparts on the other end of the ideological spectrum. They're currently buying up ammo and bracing themselves for the first wave of Obama's Socialist/Islamofascist/Negro shock troops rather than, as we were, just bitching articulately over beers about the bloodless fascist coup, but they're essentially indulging the same grandiose fantasies of the government's omnipotence and one's own special persecution. This is what being kept powerless and ignorant does to people.

In my defense, I will say that given what the Bush administration had already gotten away with—and, what was even more appalling, what we let them get away with—worst-case scenarios and dystopian fantasies had come to seem not just plausible but inevitable. (Sort of the same way that, after one authentic creep on Craigslist answered a perfectly straightforward ad I'd posted seeking a ride from New York to Maryland by casually asking for some "road head" on the Jersey Turnpike, I became easily gullible by follow-up hoaxes sent by friends.) The fact that Bush/Cheney did not attempt to remain in power beyond their Constitutionally limited two terms, or to attack Iran, I would still attribute to practical limitations rather than a lack of will.

After All the Oil Runs Out

SHORT-RANGE, SURFACE-TO-SURFACE RAPTURING

ANIMAL POWER

SLAVERY

A RETURN TO LIGHTER-THAN-AIR TRAVEL!

A court battle over evolution is currently being fought in my neighboring state of Pennsyltucky. The local school board wants to slap disclaimer stickers on their high school biology textbooks cautioning that evolution is "only a theory" and advocating "intelligent design" as an alternative. I am not going to waste any space rebutting the "theory" of intelligent design, which is taken seriously only by cowtown school boards and slave-state politicians, not in any reputable scientific circles. Recently even the normally staid *Scientific American* and *National Geographic* have spoken up, sounding more than a little exasperated, in unequivocal support of evolution. *Scientific American*'s editorial on the subject is a masterpiece of sarcastic rhetoric that makes you want to stand up and cheer. *National Geographic*, for its part, ran a cover feature called "Was Darwin Wrong?", which turned out not to be an open rhetorical question; the answer, spelled out in 168-point type on the inside, was: "NO."

Intelligent design isn't even deserving of rebuttal; in fact, like most religions, it's constructed to avoid any possibility of disproof, which makes it the opposite of a theory. The only "evidence" cited for it consists in finding gaps or inconsistencies in the edifice of evolutionary theory, most of which are based on misunderstandings or fallacious premises. But the only competing explanation creationists can offer is, "Pretty spooky, huh? Must be God." It's a theory in the same sense as is my theory that there are sea monsters because the ocean is very big and deep and there's probably a lot going on down there that we don't even *know* about, man.

But let us indulge intelligent design for a moment and try to infer what we can about the elusive Creator from what we can observe of his/her/its divine creation. Inexplicably, Jews, Christians, and Muslims have always denigrated the natural world as being in opposition to God's nature; as a fractured, distorted reflection of His will instead of mirroring it perfectly. The world, they teach, is corrupt, changeable, and ephemeral, while God is perfect, unchanging, and eternal. But suppose, as makes more sense, that the universe is the way it is because it reflects God's own nature. What we would have to infer about God from His creation is this: He loves violence, the victory of the vicious over the weak; He invented sex, in all its fleshy, squelching, pornographic glory; He has zero interest in morality or justice; He's a whiz at math; and He adores fecundity, excess, and, above all else, beauty.

I'll give the last word on this debate to my ex-girlfriend Sandi, now a science reporter. She was a grudging agnostic when I dated her and is now the sort of atheist who actually participates in atheist marches on Washington (carrying, one can only assume, signs with nothing on them). Back when I was dating her, she described her position on God, creation, and cosmology through this analogy: she had a fish who lived in a little fishbowl on her windowsill. The fish could see vague, refracted shapes sliding about outside the bowl. Once a day, fish food would rain down from the surface like manna from Heaven. These were pretty much the sum total of facts Sandi's fish could observe about the universe. She figured her fish had about as much chance of deducing that it was being kept as a pet in an apartment in Baltimore, Maryland, in the United States of America on the planet Earth, and of gaining insight into Sandi's life and personality, as we do of ever understanding our true place in the universe or the mind of God.

Arguments for Intelligent Design

WAS IT A COSMIC "ACCIDENT" THAT SLEW 85% OF ALL SPECIES ON EARTH IN THE CRETACEOUS EXTINCTION TO MAKE WAY FOR MANKIND?

ONLY HE WHO CREATED MAN IN HIS OWN IMAGE COULD ALSO HAVE DESIGNED ORGANISMS AS EXQUISITELY ADAPTED TO THE HUMAN DEFENSES AS INFLUENZA, EBOLA, AND THE FLESH-EATING VIRUS.

WHAT SUBTLE WISDOM IT WAS THAT HARDWIRED FEMALES TO SEEK LOYAL, PROSPEROUS MATES, BUT WIRED MALES FOR PROMISCUITY.

AND WHO BUT A DIVINE CREATOR WOULD HAVE DECREED THAT WE SHOULD LIVE BY KILLING AND REPRODUCE THROUGH FORNICATION?

Another sympathy-for-George cartoon. I don't know why my loathing for this man has to be twisted into perverse pity in order to be funny. In real life I am reveling in the unraveling of the Bush administration. By the time you read this Karl Rove, that useful sociopath who is by all accounts the only reason George Bush ever got elected to anything, may have been indicted by special prosecutor Patrick Fitzgerald. Democrats are staring to worry that Harriet Miers is a dangerous Fundamentalist dingbat; "intellectual conservatives" (I assume this is a relative term, like "moderate Shiites") are disgusted because she's a dumb, inexperienced Fundamentalist dingbat; social conservatives are concerned because she isn't out of the closet as a proud and vocal Fundamentalist dingbat. I'm actually considering hauling my old TV/VCR out of the closet and hooking it up to watch the U.S. Senate make cruel sport of Harriet Miers, and to scrutinize her makeup. What is it with the evangelical Christian ladies and the eyeliner?

And just a few days ago former State Department Chief of Staff Larry Wilkerson gave a speech charging that Dick Cheney and Donald Rumsfeld form a cabal that makes all foreign policy decisions in secrecy and without input from other agencies. When the disgruntled ex-aides start talking, you know it's all over but the sentencing. This most notoriously secretive administration in U.S. history is springing leaks. Now the rats begin their exodus. The Bush regime will never recover from their failure to notice hurricane Katrina. Presidential approval ratings are at Nixonian lows. A few weeks ago *The National Enquirer* ran an article about George falling off the wagon. One must be cautious about accepting uncritically any news items breaking in a publication that also monitors news of the Yeti, but the fact that a story in a tabloid, whose politics tend to be reactionary, could safely take as its premise that George is desperate, beleaguered, and out of his depth is a telling sign of the times. Such a story would never have appeared in 2002. There's blood in the water.

And I for one am a very hungry shark. I love reading reports that the West Wing is "tense" and "anxious" these days, and that George Bush is even more thin-skinned and nasty than usual. Aides are allegedly afraid to bring him bad news, and these days there just isn't any other kind. I read that story twice—the first time for information, the second just for pleasure. It was as sweet to me as Mozart's quintet for clarinet and strings in A. I love to imagine everyone who works in the White House as frightened and angry and frustrated, their agenda forgotten (remember social security privatization, and the repeal of the estate tax?), scrambling now just to salvage their careers and stay out of jail. They all deserve it, from the chief of staff to the littlest intern. I hope they lie awake at night with migraines and ulcers and nightmares. I hope George is drinking again, and cursing Jesus bitterly in his heart.

Me & George, We Got Problems

Me

ADMINISTRATION

I'VE BOUGHT AND RETURNED THREE (3) COMPUTERS IN THE LAST TWO (2) MONTHS. I WEEP WITH RAGE DAILY.

DOMESTIC

MY POWER STEERING WENT OUT, SO I GOT THE FLUID PUMP REPLACED. BUT THEY BROKE A VACUUM TUBE, SO I GOT *THAT* REPLACED.

. NOW THE STEERING'S OUT AGAIN.

FOREIGN

CAT NOW DOING THIS THING WHERE SHE WIPES HER LITTLE CAT ASS BY DRAGGING IT ACROSS THE RUG. *

*MY FRIENDS TELL ME THIS MEANS: WORMS.

GEORGE

ADMINISTRATION

KARL AND MR. CHENEY SAID THIS C.I.A. THING WAS GONNA BE NO BIG DEAL* BUT NOW KARL SAYS HE MIGHT HAVETA "GO AWAY" FOR A LITTLE WHILE (?!) AND WITHOUT KARL AROUND I AM SO FUKED!

*THIS WAS A PROMISE

DOMESTIC

MR. CHENEY GOT TO PICK A NOMNEE AND HE SAID I COULD PICK THE NEXT ONE AND EVERBODY LOVED HIS BUT THEY HAT MINE!!

IRACK

My Secret Fantasies

LIBBY, ROVE, AND CHENEY DECIDE TO SAVE THEIR OWN ASSES BY MAKING GEORGE THE PATSY.

GEORGE NOMINATES SOMEONE EVEN DUMBER AND LESS QUALIFIED THAN HARRIET MIERS.

TO SAVE FACE, LIBBY AND ROVE COMMIT SUICIDE.

I GET JENNA BUSH WASTED AND HAVE BILL CLINTON'S FACE TATTOOED ON HER ASS!

November 2nd, 2005

Things I'm Supposed to Care About

THE ISRAELI/PALESTINEAN CONFLICT

POP CULTURE

WHO WON THE FUCKING FOOTBALL GAME

RETIREMENT

Ponder, if you will, the troubling implications of this passage from Bob Woodward's *Plan of Attack,* an account of a briefing on Iraq in "the Tank," the secure meeting room for the Joint Chiefs of Staff at the Pentagon, which took place on January 10th, 2001, ten days before Bush's first inauguration:

> The JCS had placed a peppermint at each place. Bush unwrapped his and popped it into his mouth. Later he eyed [outgoing Secretary of Defense William S.] Cohen's mint and flashed a pantomime query, Do you want that? Cohen signaled no, so Bush reached over and took it. Near the end of the hour-and-a-quarter briefing, the chairman of the Joint Chiefs, Army General Henry 'Hugh' Shelton, noticed Bush eyeing his mint, so he passed it over.

I just finished reading Woodward's inside account of the buildup to the war in Iraq. It's hard to know how accurate his account is, since the Bush administration is not known for its openness and it's not as if they weren't aware that Bob Woodward is a journalist. But it sounds as though the administration didn't so much purposely lie about Saddam Hussein's having weapons of mass destruction as they simply never questioned the premise that he had them. They declared as certainties what were unfounded assumptions, and only collected evidence to back them up as an afterthought.

However, the book does confirm a number of my other suspicions. Foremost among them is that, contrary to conventional wisdom on both the right and left, George Bush really is as stupid as he looks. Bush and Karl Rove joked about the paranoid news stories on the left suggesting that Dick Cheney was really in charge of the country, but in the end George always made important decisions—such as the one to go to war in Iraq—after meeting alone with Cheney. And Dick Cheney is described by everyone who knows him as having been obsessed with the overthrow of Saddam Hussein for years—again and again his fixation is described as "like a fever."

Even more disturbingly, George has never second-guessed or doubted his decision to go to war. This might be called conviction or strength of character if it had been a good decision. But it's starting to look very much to everyone except George as if it might instead have been a bad one. Saddam Hussein did not have weapons of mass destruction. The war has not made Americans safer. It's validated the most paranoid conspiracy theories of the most rabid anti-American Arabs throughout the Middle East and turned Iraq into a rallying point for terrorists. And it hasn't made life better for the average Iraqi, not even the ones left alive; it's made it more violent and impoverished, and the future more uncertain. So George's placid certitude starts to look more like what we might call denial. Although even most late-stage alcoholics will break down and admit they have a problem after they run someone down while drunk at the wheel. I don't know if there's a word for the kind of denial that's stubbornly maintained after causing tens or hundreds of thousands of deaths.

Intelligence ought to make someone more persuadable, less entrenched in one's opinions—the hallmarks of intellectual integrity are open-mindedness, a capacity for ambivalence and self-doubt, not absolute certainty, or what the President's PR men like to call "moral clarity." (As my old dance instructor used to tell us, "Not the courage of one's convictions, but the courage for an *attack* on one's convictions!") There's a passage in *Plan of Attack* in which Colin Powell, seeming genuinely disturbed, wonders to himself exactly when, if ever, George entertains doubts. Powell does it all the time. Maybe late at night, he speculates. What Powell seems not to have understood is that George is not a person remotely like himself—his psychology is either too primitive to experience self-doubt or too pathologically insecure to tolerate it. He enjoys the same absolute certainty enjoyed by all divine appointees to sacred missions, from Urban II to Jim Jones.[1] I have no doubt he sleeps the untroubled sleep of the innocent, soothed by dreams of bottomless supplies of peppermints.

---

[1] My rhetoric here turns out not to have been as hyperbolic as one might've hoped. In 2009 Former French President Jacques Chirac revealed that when Bush called to try to persuade him to send French troops to join the invasion of Iraq, he appealed to their "common faith," saying: "Gog and Magog are at work in the Middle East.... The biblical prophecies are being fulfilled.... This confrontation is willed by God, who wants to use this conflict to erase his people's enemies before a New Age begins." Chirac confirmed this story in an interview recounted in Jean-Claude Maurice's book, *Si Vous le Répétez, Je Démentirai* (If You Repeat it, I Will Deny). It would certainly make a great deal of retroactive sense of the whole Iraq war if it turned out that George Bush was simply insane.

3 A.M.
FOR THE BUSH ADMINISTRATION

Not sure if Tim saw this… seems like there should be a cartoon in it.

George met with the president of the European Commission, Jose Manuel Barroso. Jose commented on how nice George's suit was, and George responded, "God told me to wear it." A moment later he added, "That's a joke."

Ann,

A rare instance when I deign to take over electronic correspondence from Ms. C.-H., because this suit joke is by far the funniest thing I have ever heard the President say. It genuinely delights me. Also it indicates a greater degree of self-awareness than I'd thought he possessed. Of course the joke is only ostensibly at his own expense; really it's mocking those Godless Europeans' perception of Bush as a Jesus-freak yahoo. Still, it's been cracking me up all day. If George hadn't had such powerful connections and had instead been a floor salesman at Joseph A. Bank or a Datsun lot, he might even have turned out to be an okay person. Sigh. I wish he was still drinking.

Inspired by this joke I have written a letter to the President, offering to draw any cartoon idea he sends me. We will see where this gets me.

Regards,
Tim Kreider

President Bush,

I am a political cartoonist for a number of alternative weekly papers, including the Baltimore City Paper and the Philadelphia Weekly. Since I know you to be a man of direct and simple words, I'll say plainly that I hate everything you've done to my country. Nevertheless, when I read about your straight-faced reply to the President of the E.U. today after he complimented your suit ("God told me to wear it"), I had to admit that it was hilarious. My compliments. Sounds like you really had him going for a second there. It would've had me going, too.

I have a proposal for you, one that I make without any irony or hidden agenda, and I hope you will give it due consideration: I will draw any cartoon idea you come up with. It seems only fair to give you this opportunity, having viciously mocked and pilloried not only your policies but you personally, as well as your advisors, friends, and family, for the last five years. The cartoon need not be about politics; it can be about anything you wish. If you've had a good cartoon idea in the back of your head for years, now is the time to use it. It can be either a single-panel gag, like New Yorker cartoons, or a multi-panel strip, like newspaper comics. You can just give me the general idea and I'll elaborate on it, or go ahead and write dialogue or captions, and I'll faithfully illustrate them. I will not only draw this cartoon and publish it in all the left-leaning newspapers in which I appear (giving you authorial credit, of course), but will gladly present you with the original artwork, framed, as a gift.

I realize you're a busy man, but, should you accept this offer, I look forward to our collaboration.

Sincerely,
Tim Kreider

THE WHITE HOUSE

Thank you for your generous offer. We sometimes pass around your City Paper *cartoons at Cabinet Meetings and get a chuckle out of them. We disagree on many things, Tim, but funny is funny (Show yer tits—ha ha). So here is my cartoon idea. I am talking to VP Cheney: "Well, Dick (ha ha—don't put the "ha ha" in), I guess you won't be getting to ride your scooter at Christmas this year." That's it. I guess it might be funny if Dick said something back, like "oh you got me" or something, but I'm not sure. I leave that up to your humor expertice [sic].*

Thanks,
Your President[1]

---

1 Sadly this proved to be an ingenious hoax by my friend Aaron. George never responded to my offer

"I Love Saddam," December 14th 2005

As soon as I drew the title I knew this cartoon was destined for some sort of greatness. "I [HEART] SADDAM" is one of those phrases, like my friend Mike's immortal "Babies Are Assholes," that's exhilarating just to write or say out loud, because it voices a sentiment so unacceptable it's not even forbidden; it's so outside acceptable discourse that most people would never even think it, much less print it in the newspaper.[1] Everyone in this country, from bleeding-heart left to bloodthirstiest right, before proceeding to expound his or her position on the war, must first genuflect to the conventional wisdom that Saddam was "a brutal dictator," and "a bad guy," and, whatever else we may say about how the war was implemented, we all have to admit that Iraq is better off now that he's out of power. There's some incorrigibly perverse part of me that takes a dumb childish glee in standing up and saying, "Aw, I dunno—I kinda like his beard!"

This is essentially the same puerile impulse I used to have to suppress in church all the time that made me wonder what would happen if I just suddenly stood up during the sermon and screamed. But saying such things is also part of my job as one of society's jesters, because anything that absolutely everyone across the political spectrum from NPR to Fox News agrees on, any axiom that nobody doubts or challenges not so much because

they don't dare to as because it doesn't occur to them—"America is the greatest country on Earth," "Americans love freedom," "our troops are heroes"—is a lie. It's mythology, propaganda, call it what you want—one of those unexamined assumptions that a culture finds indispensable. But it's definitely not a fact.

Which is not to say that Saddam *wasn't* a brutal dictator. More like to say, *So what?* We've sent money and weapons to plenty of brutal dictators over the years. Saddam was our brutal dictator for decades—Donald Rumsfeld was shaking hands with him back in '83. And it's certainly not inarguable that the Iraqis are better off without him. Are the ones we killed better off now? Are their families? Every day more Iraqis are killed by Americans or by suicide bombers. Now the prisoners in Abu Ghraib are being tortured by Americans instead of by Saddam. I guess that's progress. I know, I know, we did build them that soccer stadium. I'm sure it's very nice.

There is something pathetic and silly about the powerless Saddam. Now that he can't have anybody's entire family tortured and executed he's become a harmless, blustering buffoon. Hitler, who was considered clownish in the '30's, may have successfully immortalized his image as some sort of superhuman villain by committing suicide. If he'd been brought to trial at Nuremberg he might have been seen for what he was—just another greasy demagogue ranting about blood and destiny, spraying spittle and making no sense at all, his brain half-eaten by syphilis. We do these thugs too much honor by regarding them as monsters. The Devil is well known to fear mockery more than anything else.

---

1 Soon after this cartoon appeared my friend Carolyn sent me a bumper sticker that said: "I [Heart] SADDAM." It was not only a gift but a dare. Alas, I was far too cowardly to affix it to the car I have to drive around C____ County, Maryland, where even a bumper sticker for a Democratic candidate is semiotically tantamount to a rainbow flag or hammer-and-sickle or pentagram decal. Carolyn had called my bluff. I've often wondered how far I would've made it down Route 40.

I ♥ Saddam!

IT STARTED WHEN I REALIZED HOW MUCH NICER HE LOOKED WITH A BEARD.

BEFORE:
THUGGISH AND SCARY.

AFTER:
FRIENDLY AND DISTINGUISHED!

YOU HAVE TO WONDER WHETHER, IF WE'D BEEN ABLE TO BRING HITLER TO TRIAL, HE'D'VE SEEMED LIKE JUST A BUFFOON.

...AND YOU HAVE TO ADMIT HE'S BEEN CONSISTENTLY ENTERTAINING IN COURT. HE'S SUCH A CHARACTER!

*ALL ACTUAL QUOTES!

HOW ABOUT IF, INSTEAD OF MARTYRING THE GUY BY EXECUTING HIM, WE HUMILIATE HIM BY PUTTING HIM ON AN AMERICAN REALITY T.V. SHOW?

My loathing of Christmas is well known to long-time readers of *The Pain*, and I was a little worried that I might have used up all my best ideas on this theme. But driving around running Christmas errands on Saturday I heard a segment on "On the Media" about fundamentalist Christians' latest persecution fantasy: "the war on Christmas." I smiled to myself. *The War on Christmas*. My cartoon was all but finished.

Christians, who comprise 83% of Americans and have dominated Western culture and discourse for the last eighteen hundred years, seem to have a pathological need to see themselves as the same persecuted minority they were in first century Rome. I suppose this ought not to be surprising, since they worship a figure whose most fetishistically celebrated achievement was getting beaten, flogged, and executed; there's a sense in which Christianity *is* a martyr complex. Now that there is some belated and grudging official acknowledgement that ours is technically a pluralist society and there are people of other faiths (and even some Godless atheists) in this country as well, fundamentalist Christians are rallying believers to defend the baby Jesus against the infidels' "war on Christmas." It's the same tired rhetorical tactic as white mediocrities' decrying "reverse racism" when affirmative action promotes black mediocrities above them, or Republican politicians' bleating "class warfare" whenever anyone complains about another enormous tax cut for their billionaire campaign donors.

It's not like the Christians even invented Christmas. There's been a festival holiday around the winter solstice for as long as there's been human civilization, often having to do with the death and rebirth of a demigod: the Egyptian entombment of Osiris, the Greek Lenæa (depicted here), the Roman Saturnalia. Christians just appropriated it for their own purposes in the fourth century A.D. Christmas is as much an artificial holiday as Valentine's Day. Five hundred years from now someone will be lamenting the war on Kwanza.

Obviously this cartoon is a mockery of right-wing Christians' whiny martyrish paranoia, but it is also an enthusiastic embrace of their caricatured demonization of us secular humanists, as well as, yes, an unironic call to arms for a concerted, all-out War on Christmas. Down with Christmas! Death to the Baby Jesus! Christmas is a holiday that exists solely for the benefit of children and retailers. Everybody else hates it. It's a holiday that literally *drives people to suicide* every year. I don't have any kids and I can't stand shopping, and yet Christmas is still inflicted on me for over a month out of each year. You'd think that now that I'm a grownup, I could give this Christmas bullshit a rest already. It's like still being forced to go to gym class or take recorder lessons. If it can't be abolished altogether, couldn't we at least compromise on a policy of containment—maybe restrict it to a quadrennial nuisance like those other interminable, meaningless rituals that nobody cares about anymore, the Olympics and elections?

NOW THAT THE ACCURSED CHRISTIANS HAVE UNMASKED OUR PLAN, THERE IS NO LONGER ANY NEED TO CONCEAL OUR TRUE PURPOSE. THE TIME HAS COME TO DECLARE AN ALL-OUT

WAR ON Christmas

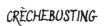

PASSIVE RESISTANCE

CRÈCHEBUSTING

REVIVAL OF PAGAN WINTER SOLSTICE TRADITIONS

DEPICTED: LENÆA, FESTIVAL OF THE WILD WOMEN, IN WHICH A MAN IN THE GUISE OF DIONYSUS IS TORN APART BY DRUNKEN GIRLS.

SHOPPING MALL DISEMBEARDINGS

Since I have been mocking the dingbat beliefs of creationists lately I thought it only fair to expose some of my own dodgier convictions. I've also been angling for a way to get my Dick Cheney theory into print for months now. I genuinely believe in each of these crackpot theories. Permit me, like a man sitting next to you on the bus, to discourse upon each of them in turn, and at length:

CRACKPOT THEORY #1: George Bush's story about giving up drinking is too neat and implausible. Supposedly, he quit on his 40th birthday when he found Jesus. This is not how these things typically happen; more often people quit drinking only after waking up in a car parked around a tree. More importantly, just quitting without getting into some sort of recovery program is not really sobriety—the President is what in AA they call "white-knuckling it" (not a reassuring image of the fingers on The Button). More likely, I think, is that he solved his drinking problem the same way he solves all other problems—he lied about it. Think about it: choked on a pretzel? This is such an embarrassing story that you'd invent another story to cover it up unless the real story was even *more* embarrassing, so embarrassing and potentially damaging that you'd have to invent a cover story embarrassing enough that no one would ever suspect it of being a cover story.

A disclaimer: it was not George Bush who was injured in drunken lightsaber horseplay. That was me.

C.T. #2: Mark Crispin Miller's book *Fooled Again* is a full examination of the evidence that the 2004 election was rigged. I remember raising this question on the road with my colleagues on the Laugh While You Can tour back in April; did *they* think the Republicans had rigged the election? They were both hesitant, hedging their answers for fear of seeming like paranoid left-wing conspiracy nuts, but finally they sheepishly confessed that, although there was no hard evidence, yeah, they kind of believed so.

My own reasons for believing so are based less on any evidence than on my sense of the Bush administration's

mentality; secretive, hostile to democracy, contemptuous of the electorate, concerned above all else with holding, consolidating, and expanding their power. No fucking way were they going to take even the smallest, most marginal statistical risk of losing the election. Everyone knew it was going to be close. You think they would leave it up to the American people, for whom they have never shown the slightest trust or respect, whose opinions or interests they have never permitted to interfere with their policies? The company that manufactured the voting machines, Diebold, is owned by a Republican campaign donor who publicly promised to do everything in his power to deliver the election to Bush. There were no paper ballots, no way of monitoring or double-checking the accuracy of the results. Exit polls all showed that Kerry would win. You figure it out. We are living in a dystopian parallel universe, the one where everyone wears daggers and Mr. Spock has a goatee. In the real America the government responded swiftly and efficiently to Katrina, no one is debating whether torture is wrong, and George and Mr. Cheney are co-hosting a cooking show.

C.T. #3: The invasion of Iraq is all about Dick Cheney's heart condition. Hear me out here. It is well documented that people who have had heart attacks and/or open-heart surgery very often subsequently suffer episodes of clinical depression. The reasons are obvious; it's a confrontation with one's own mortality, an existential shock that often precipitates major personality changes. A sane, decent person (fig.1, my friend Jim, who did not require bypass surgery but did have a heart attack last April and these days is a new man) might resolve to worry less about trivial things like work and money and devote more time and attention to the people he loves. Because Dick Cheney is neither sane nor decent, he decided that his great achievement, his gift to humanity, his lasting monument in human history, would be the invasion of Iraq. Cheney suffered his first heart attack in 1978, when he was 37, and underwent quadruple bypass surgery in 1988. Friends and confidantes of Dick Cheney have repeatedly described his monomaniacal obsession with Iraq as being "like a

My CRACKPOT Theories

ALL GEORGE'S WEIRD INJURIES: DRINKING MISHAPS.

THE 2004 ELECTION WAS RIGGED.

THE REAL REASON FOR INVADING IRAQ: DICK CHENEY'S HEART CONDITION

SANE, DECENT PERSON   ME   MR. CHENEY

fever." His old friend and colleague Brent Scowcroft said of him, "I don't know him anymore." And by all accounts it was Cheney who pushed insistently and unrelentingly for the necessity of war throughout the deliberations and buildup to the invasion. It was, essentially, a one-man war. I'm sure there is a delicate protocol in the Bush White House whereby the idiot boy king is carefully allowed to believe he is making all the decisions himself, but I'm also sure that, like a rube being taken in by a card trick, he is presented with a narrow, pre-selected range of options and subtly directed toward the one he's supposed to pick. It's been documented that he makes his final decisions—including the decision to invade Iraq—only after meeting with Cheney alone.

I'm convinced that 2000 Americans and, by the President's own conservative estimate, 30,000 Iraqis—ten times the number of Americans killed on 9/11—have died for no reason other than that a sick old man who was too cowardly to go to war himself when he was called years ago is afraid of being remembered as nothing but the inept, forgettable technocrat he's always been. He is suffering from delusions of grandeur, dreams of being the architect of a great foreign policy, founder of a New American Century. Or maybe his motives are no different from those of ancient kings who had all their wives and servants buried along with them, or those dirtbags who kill their ex-wives and kids or go on shooting sprees at work before blowing their own brains out. He's scared to go out alone, and wants to take everyone else with him.

MY OTHER CRACKPOT THEORIES: Alito will prove to be a Fundamentalist authoritarian out to protect the civil liberties of zygotes and reinstate the Divine Right of Kings. The N.S.A. is regularly spying not just on suspected terrorists and their associates but on dissident groups, antiwar activists, environmentalists, socialists, Democrats, journalists, and anyone else they don't like the looks of. Nobody in power actually cares about the state of public education. If Pakistan's military junta is ever overthrown by an Islamic coup, we will nuke them within the week. The Chinese will get back to the moon before we do. We should not forget about the Russians. Industrial society as we know it will collapse within our lifetimes, either because of global warming or oil depletion. People are getting noticeably stupider. Everything is getting worse, except for stadium seating in theaters, which is unfortunately cancelled out by the ads before previews. *The Big Lebowski* is all about Vietnam. Pluto is a planet no matter what anyone says. There are sea monsters.

AT LAST THEY HAVE REVEALED THEMSELVES TO THE WORLD—

What Now for the Giant Squid?

PORN STAR IN JAPAN!

SENATE HEARINGS ON STEROID USE

DEPLOYED BY U.S. AS SECRET WEAPON IN IRAQ

ENLIST AID OF HUMANS TO HUNT DOWN AND KILL EVERY LAST MOTHERFUCKING SPERM WHALE!

As my regular readers know I am a vociferous and unyielding proponent of Pluto's permanent status as a planet in the solar system. The New Horizons probe, launched a few days ago, will be the first ever to photograph our mysterious but no-less-legitimate Ninth Planet. It is the fastest object ever launched by human beings. It reached the moon about three hours after it was launched (the Apollo rockets took three days to get there). It will arrive at Pluto in 2015.

I wish I'd had more space to get into all the wonky jerry-rigged embellishments scientists added to the Ptolemaic model of the solar system over the centuries to account for discrepancies between their perfect theory and the messy observational data, like the apparent retrograde motion of the planets; epicycles, deferents and equants, crystalline spheres within spheres. It was not unlike the desperate intellectual improvisation that now goes into explaining how the dinosaurs were fit on board Noah's ark (eggs). Neogeocentrists in the age of outer planetary exploration are no more ludicrous than Creationists in the age of genome sequencing.

It may be worth mentioning that this entire cartoon was conceived and drawn under the unexpectedly long-lasting effect of poppy tea. A friend of mine, who shall be given a pseudonym here to head off any potential legal hassles—let's call him "Nancy"—recently had to quit drinking for medical reasons and has since been exploring ever more exotic and out-of-the-way avenues to fucked-upédness. Nancy had bought the poppy heads on Ebay. What you do, he demonstrated, is to crush them up, pulverize them in a coffee grinder, and then make tea with them,

adding anything you can think of—lemon and ginger, instant eggnog flavoring, an altoid—to make the resulting concoction even slightly more palatable, since in its natural state it tastes like dirt. Nancy used ten or eleven poppy heads in each batch, of which we each drank two. This, I learned, was in the nature of an experimental dosage to gauge how much would be too much. It turned out that the amount that would be too much was exactly the amount we had.

Little by little Nancy let drop tidbits of information he'd gleaned about the effect of the drug from various internet sources after it became too late for me to do anything about them. For example, that it would totally shut down peristalsis for the next twenty-four hours, so I might want to take a laxative before going to sleep. And that our voices were hoarse because it also partly paralyzes your vocal chords. And, oh yeah, also that some sites had warned that the effect might last up to two or three *days*. Nancy hadn't bothered to mention this to me, he explained, because he hadn't believed it.

But indeed we remained incredibly high for the next forty-eight hours. As with many experiences in life, this was considerably less fun than it sounds. Being incredibly high gets boring after a while, and then annoying. It was as relentless as LSD. Waking up on Day 3 to discover: *yep, still incredibly high* is a little like that moment when you realize that what you had hoped was maybe just a stomachache is instead food poisoning. It is also inconvenient if you are on deadline. Suffice it to say it is hereby not recommended to aspiring cartoonists.

THE NEW HORIZONS PROBE, LAUNCHED LAST WEEK, IS DUE TO ARRIVE AT PLUTO IN 2015.
THE PAIN IMAGINES HOW OUR WORLD WILL HAVE CHANGED

By the Time We Get to Pluto

YOUR ADORABLE TODDLER WILL BE CALLING YOU AN ASSHOLE

YOUNG MAN, YOU ARE **NOT** GETTING A SEX CHANGE JUST BECAUSE THEY'RE "VERSIV"!

笨蛋.

CAN'T YOU JUST GET A NICE PRINCE ALBERT?

IRAQI INSURGENCY WILL BE IN ITS LAST THROES

TODAY MARKS WHAT THE ADMINISTRATION IS CALLING 'A MAJOR MILESTONE' IN THE RECONSTRUCTION EFFORT WITH THE RATIFICATION OF IRAQ'S THIRD

ALLAHU AKHBAR—

ALL THE PROBE'S "FINDINGS" WILL BE CHALLENGED BY NEOGEOCENTRISTS.

AS WE SEE HERE, NO PROBE COULD HAVE PENETRATED THE CRYSTAL SPHERES IN WHICH THE PLANETS ARE EMBEDDED.

PLUTOCRAT, HERITAGE FOUNDATION

TURNS OUT WE DIDN'T ACTUALLY NEED TO FLY THREE BILLION MILES TO EXPLORE A DEAD ICE PLANET.

I drew this cartoon during a week I spent in the Magic Kingdom. This is not a euphemism for some opiate stupor (see last week's regrettable poppy-tea episode); my mother, who turned seventy this week, issued a maternal fiat decreeing that our entire family—her, my sister and her husband, their two children, and myself—would celebrate the occasion in Disneyworld, in Orlando, Florida.

I had a better time at Disneyworld than those familiar with my work might expect. We were staying at the Wilderness Lodge, a kind of architectural fantasia on the theme of a Pacific Northwest lodge, with a vast wood-beam-construction atrium, massive, towering totem poles, and a stone fireplace five stories tall representing a cross-section of strata from the Grand Canyon. There was a fake waterfall and geyser. All day long ubiquitous invisible speakers played Western movie music—Copland, Grofé, the soundtracks to *The Magnificent Seven* and *Silverado*. Luckily I am a huge fan of this stuff or else I might soon have been driven mad by its incessant repetition. The grounds were plagued with grackles, who swooped at screaming young children to steal Cheetos out of their hands. After I discovered that the Territory Lounge had a bottle of Lagavulin, and that there were hot tubs outside, I fell into a pleasant nightly routine.

However, it's not an environment that's conducive to concentration. I took a day off from going to theme parks with my family and tried to work on my cartoon at one of those sad tables in hotel lobbies where you can tell nobody has ever sat, a really nice desk in the style of Frank Lloyd Wright. The vastness of the interior, the burnished wood and Indian design motifs reminded me strongly of the Overlook Hotel in *The Shining*, an association that did not ease my writer's block. All I accomplished was to drink a whole pot of room service coffee and read the *New York Times*, which made me angry and depressed. This is traditionally step I of my artistic process.

Apparently it was big news that Oprah Winfrey had given a televised dressing-down to the author of the purported memoir *A Million Little Pieces*. I for one was unshocked to learn that this self-celebrated drug addict and criminal was a liar. Is this the first occasion Oprah's viewers have had to realize that not everything they read is necessarily true? And since when did we decide to start holding anyone in public life accountable for lying? And why did we decide to start with *this* guy, instead of, I don't know, Donald Rumsfeld, or The President? Everyone's outraged because some writer claims to be a hardened criminal and really isn't, whereas the President claims to be a Godly man but has killed thirty thousand people?

I also learned that a slim majority of Americans polled support the government's illegal wiretapping program so long as they're eavesdropping on Americans they consider "suspicious." I cannot begin to express my contempt for anyone willing to give up any civil liberties in exchange for some illusion of security. If they could give up their rights without me having to give up mine, I'd say fine, go right ahead, you babies. Unfortunately their craven acquiescence means I have to lose my birthright as an American citizen as well, so instead I must say, over my dead body. You may only ever use your constitutional rights during hunting season, but I use mine every week.

Remember Patrick Henry? *Give me liberty or give me death*? He was not fucking kidding. These days our motto is more like the sort of thing you'd blubber to a mugger: "Take my liberty, please, take it, take *Habeas Corpus*, the whole Bill of Rights, anything, I don't care, just please don't let me die!" The fear of death— the code word for which, in current political rhetoric, is *Security*—has become the central value in American society. But freedom *is* danger. These cowards who are willing to give up their civil liberties—the rights for which our founding fathers pledged their lives, their fortunes, and their sacred honor—don't deserve to call themselves Americans. We're the distant grandchildren of the frontiersmen; have we already grown so fat and uncalloused that we're only at home in a sanitized, litigation-proof plastic wilderness?

AN INTRODUCTORY GUIDE TO YOUR NEW HOMELAND, 'MURIKA

FACTS AT A GLANCE

CAPITOL: UNDISCLOSED LOCATION
FORM OF GOVERNMENT: UNITARY EXECUTIVE
MOTTO: "SUPPORT OUR TROOPS"

OFFICIAL LANGUAGE: 'MURIKAN!
OFFICIAL RELIGION: JESUSISM
CHIEF IMPORT: OIL
CHIEF EXPORT: DEMOCRACY, A.K.A. WHUP-ASS!

FROM THE SACRED PIT OF GROUND ZERO TO THE BARBED-WIRE FENCE AT THE MEXICAN BORDER TO THE GATED COMMUNITIES OF SUBURBIA, MURIKA IS A LIVING MONUMENT TO ITS PEOPLE'S DEAREST VALUE: SECURITY.

HER CITIZENS CAN BE SPIED ON WITHOUT WARRANTS AND IMPRISONED WITHOUT CHARGES, BUT MURIKANS HAVE GLADLY FORFEITED THESE LIBERTIES BECAUSE THEY KNOW THAT SECURITY IS FREEDOM.

ANY THREATS TO MURIKANS' SECURITY ARE DETERRED BY THEIR REPUTATION FOR TORTURE AND UNPROVOKED ATTACK!

A THOUSAND YEARS FROM NOW, PEOPLES THE WORLD 'ROUND WILL STILL REMEMBER THE NAME... MURIKA!

It was after reading this poll that I gave up (for neither the first nor, probably, the last time) any hope that our current infatuation with authoritarianism might just be a passing spasm, a kind of mass hysteria or psychotic episode from which America would soon recover. It seems clear that we have a far-right, warlike theocratic junta in charge of our country not because most Americans have been temporarily duped but because that's what they want. Horrifying as it is to contemplate, I fear the policies of the Republican party may actually reflect the will of the people.

It's time for me to accept that this is no longer the country I grew up in, where it was socially unacceptable to be bigoted, where something like the Freedom of Information Act could get passed, and an antiwar comedy was the most beloved show on TV. This isn't America anymore; it's 'Murika. I used to imagine that a thousand years from now, if people remembered nothing else about the ancient Americans, they would know that we had walked on the Moon, the way we remember the Egyptians for the building the Pyramids. Lately I'm starting to worry the word *Americans* might someday have the same sort of monstrous connotation, stinking down through the centuries, as the names *Mongols*, *Huns*, or *Nazis*.

On my last day in the Magic Kingdom my mother and I went to the Hall of Presidents. Mom and I had been there together before, long ago, when I was a little boy and my father was with us. Apparently The Hall of Presidents is one of the more antiquated, unhip attractions at Disneyworld; the great hall was almost deserted. There, to my horror, I learned that the animatronic George W. Bush now gives a speech about freedom and equality. This was the only time in my life I am ever likely to listen voluntarily to an entire speech by George Bush. The Robot George was a lot more eloquent than the real one. He said that any time someone tries to take away people's rights in this country, someone else always speaks up against it and things are eventually set right—"Until recently," I hissed. It was the kind of casual, oblivious hypocrisy that always reduces me to apoplexy whenever I hear him speak in real life.

He was followed by Abraham Lincoln, who even in robot form is a much better speaker. His words calmed me down and renewed my dedication to the struggle. "Our fight is not just for today," he reminded me, "but for the vast future." Yes. Right. I stand with Robot President Lincoln, even if we speak to an empty auditorium, until the day we're shut down for good.

HEY DID ANYONE NOTICE HOW, IN THE STATE OF THE UNION ADDRESS, PRESIDENT BUSH MADE A REFERENCE TO

Human/Animal Hybrids?

FOLLOWING THE MOREAU SCANDAL, PRESIDENT BUSH ANNOUNCED AN AGGRESSIVE CRACKDOWN ON HYBRIDS.

EVEN SOME *SEEMINGLY* HUMAN AMERICAN CITIZENS WOULD HAVE TO BE DETAINED AND INTERROGATED IN THE HUNT FOR HYBRIDS.

AMERICA WOULD GET TOUGH WITH NATIONS THAT NOT ONLY HARBOR BUT REVERE THESE MONSTROSITES.

INEVITABLY, AN INSURGENCY AROSE.

February 8th, 2006

I've been consumed with envy and self-doubt over the Danish cartoons that have provoked riots, kidnappings, and stone-throwing throughout the Arab world. Not that it's any feat to provoke rioting in the Arab world, where it seems retirements, anniversaries, and children's birthdays are celebrated with angry chanting and flag-burning. But I do my very best to cause a furor every week, and every week: nothing. American Christians are a bunch of pussies. All they ever do is call for boycotts; they never demand anyone's *head*.

I'd intended to draw a cartoon about fundamentalist Islam years ago, not long after 9/11, but my colleague Megan talked me out of it, rightly warning me that I'd be jumping on a bandwagon on which I'd find myself in the company of some very unsavory wagonmates indeed. Nonetheless, I now regret showing them any special deference. Their religion is at least as silly as Christianity, and, unlike most Christians, they still take it seriously enough to kill people over it.

I wish religious people would get used to being offended. I'm offended daily by almost everything I read and hear. That's what it means to live in a pluralistic society: being constantly offended by other people's stupid ideas and wrong opinions. I get tired of waiting for the Muslim world to catch up to the freaking Enlightenment already. Notice how these things don't seem happen so much in the West—the angry chanting in the streets and setting of things on fire and the attacking of embassies and kidnapping of innocent aid workers? Is this just because we are a Godless people who believe in nothing fervently enough to lacerate ourselves and trample each other and behead foreigners for it?

There's something pathetic, almost poignant, about the footage of furious Arabs whapping American and Danish flags with shoes and setting them on fire, as though this could hurt us in the same way that the cartoons of Mohammed have hurt them. They have, as one of our American folk sayings has it, obviously mistaken us for someone who gives a shit. They seem to be operating on an entirely different cognitive level, imbuing concrete symbols with life, seeing images as reality. I'm not entertaining some 19th-century theory that Arabs are less evolved than Westerners—most of my fellow Americans seem to be operating on the same level, far more concerned with the actual cloth (or decal) Flag than with the liberties it represents, passionately interested in the lives of people seen only in tabloids, believing that TV is real.

John Ralston Saul's indispensable critique of rationalism, *Voltaire's Bastards*, devotes an entire chapter to the decline of the psychic power of imagery in the West and art's loss of utility in society. "And yet it is improbable that the image, which has played a fundamentally religious or magical role for more than fifteen thousand years, could simply be freed of itself in the space of a few centuries to become a mere object of art," he writes. "This is where Western experience parts company with that of other civilizations." The bemused incomprehension I feel for those outraged rioters is that of a culture that no longer believes in imagery as real or meaningful regarding one that still does, passionately and literally.[1] Of course it's also that of someone who's enjoyed relative safety, privilege, and luxury his whole life rolling his eyes at the paranoia and rage of people who've always been threatened, oppressed, and impoverished.

All of which makes their reaction more understandable, but I'm not sure it makes it any less stupid or wrong. As R. Crumb famously said: "It's just lines on paper, folks."

---

1   Also, because images of Mohammed are interdicted in Islam—and what is repressed always grows more powerful—those unabashed caricatures of the Prophet may have had the same sort of deranging impact on the Arab psyche as the exposure of those last dwindling areas hidden by bikinis has on the mind of the Western male.

Scientists Riot!

SCIENTISTS WORLDWIDE ARE RIOTING IN PROTEST OF A CARTOON RELIGIOUS PAMPHLET.

THESE EMPIRICAL EXTREMISTS ARE OUTRAGED BY THE CARTOONS' BLASPHEMOUS MOCKERY OF THE BIG BANG THEORY AND EVOLUTION BY NATURAL SELECTION, TWO CORNERSTONES OF THE SCIENTIFIC WORLDVIEW. THEY ALSO CITE NUMEROUS OTHER HERESIES, INCLUDING:

- FALSE DICHOTOMIES
- CHERRYPICKED DATA
- POSTULATING FROM IGNORANCE
- INVOCATION OF SUPERNATURAL CAUSES
- APPEALS TO AUTHORITY
- TAUTOLOGIES
- NON SEQUITURS
- INACCURATE ANATOMY AND PERSPECTIVE.

A MILITANT GROUP CALLING ITSELF "THE FIFTH FORCE," BELIEVED TO BE AFFILIATED WITH THE RADICAL SCIENCE NETWORK "J.P.L.", KIDNAPPED A CHRISTIAN AT RANDOM AND AIRED A VIDEO ON PBS THREATENING TO DISEMBOWEL HER.

PRESIDENT BUSH CLAIMS THE RIOTS ONLY DEMONSTRATE THE NEED FOR STEADFAST RESOLVE IN THE WAR ON SCIENCE.

"Silver Linings of the Holocaust," February 22nd 2006

It was my colleague Emily Flake who first brought the Iranian's newspaper *Hamshahri*'s Holocaust Cartoon contest to my attention. We immediately agreed that any self-respecting cartoonist could only take this as a challenge. The Persians have thrown down the gauntlet.

"Obviously," I said, "the premise must be, 'The Best Things About the Holocaust.'" Without missing a beat Emily brightly said, "Well, it got rid of all those Jews!" (Tragically, this could not be transposed into cartoon form because it depends on the cherubic, blue-eyed ingenuousness of Emily's delivery. For the record, she was kidding.) This confirms my suspicion that Emily is secretly a worse person than me, but censors herself more in print. She dared me to draw this cartoon, egging me on to infamy, although there was no way in hell she was going to do it herself.

My goal was to demonstrate to the world that Freedom of Speech is not just a convenient pretext to bash Mohammed. Nobody needs any pretext to insult Muslims. Shit, our government didn't even need a pretext to bomb them. I wanted to show them that Americans are ballsy and funny and free enough to laugh at anything, even in the face of death.

Also, of course, I wanted to meet the challenge of drawing a cartoon about the Holocaust without being anti-Semitic, one that would be shocking and outrageous without being offensive, that would be, most importantly, authentically hilarious. It was something of a trick, let me tell you. All week I teetered and windmilled on the treacherous, invisible line between clever and stupid. I had to rule out, with regret, some brilliant ideas because they might've tipped over the line into a kind of humor to which I, as a non-Jew, have no rhetorical right–like "Gave the Jews Something to *Really* Kvetch About." I had to ignore Boyd telling me that I was a pussy because I resolutely resisted his pleas to draw "The Diary of Anne Spank." Panel #1 was inspired by a story Ben Walker told me about a girl he'd fucked on my neighbors' dock who deployed a novel sexual technique which, infuriatingly, he could not adequately describe but which he claimed was so devastating in its effect that, he sighed, "Even thinkin' about the Holocaust wasn't helpin'." It may be worthy of note that the only panel that gave me any qualm at all was #3, because I apparently have more genuine reverence for works of literature than for any faith or ethnicity.

The letter I sent to *Hamshahri* to accompany this cartoon follows:

I hesitated to enter your contest because your choice of the Holocaust as a subject seems to reveal more about your own bigotry than about Western taboos. Being offended by Danes and retaliating by insulting the Jews seems suspiciously misdirected—sort of like being attacked by al Qaeda and invading Iraq. As I hope you can see from my entry, I do not share in the mean-spiritedness of your contest. My intention in drawing this cartoon was to call your bluff—to prove that we in the West can, as we say, take it as good as we dish it out. We are not kidding about Freedom of Speech. We truly believe that nothing is off-limits to question or ridicule. We can find the punchline in anything—the Holocaust, 9/11, the Bush administration. As an American humorist and heir to the greatest comedic tradition on Earth, I believe there is nothing so sacred that it cannot be further consecrated— nor anything so monstrous it cannot be redeemed—by laughter. Laughter is sanity; it is strength; it is fearlessness in the face of hatred and death. Laughter is how we get through this life without faith. It's the wine we make from rage. We Americans are braver and freer and funnier than you can begin to understand. I genuinely pity your humorlessness. We have a saying that I offer you not as a rebuke but as friendly advice: "Lighten up."

I do not actually believe *Hamshahri* will run this cartoon, if for no other reason than the same one most American newspapers wouldn't: there are people fucking in it. (For all their differences, both our cultures agree that some things are too monstrous and offensive to print.) If there were any justice in the world, which there isn't—and if there is it's definitely not in Iran—I would win this contest. Ideally I would get to attend an awards luncheon in Iran. Maybe a luncheon and beheading! I am told the prize money is to be given out in the form of gold coins, a unit of currency I have not used since playing Dungeons & Dragons. If I do win it I intend to either donate the money to the Holocaust museum or blow it all on beer.

IN RESPONSE TO DANISH CARTOONS OF MOHAMMED, AN IRANIAN NEWSPAPER ANNOUNCED A CONTEST FOR THE FUNNIEST CARTOON ABOUT THE HOLOCAUST. The Pain PRESENTS OUR SUBMISSION:

Silver Linings of the Holocaust

EXCELLENT SEXUAL ENDURANCE AID

FIFTY YEARS OF FORCED CONTRITION HAVE REDUCED A RACE OF RAPACIOUS SUPERMEN TO HARMLESS ELECTRONICA HIPPIES

WITHOUT IT, WE WOULD HAVE BEEN ROBBED OF COUNTLESS ARTISTIC TREASURES.

THE MOST IMPORTANT LESSON OF ALL: THE WORLD RESOLVED THAT THIS WOULD NEVER AGAIN HAPPEN TO WHITE PEOPLE.

I had come across your cartoon on the Holocaust, and I must say that it was a well-done statement. I had read your statement about the cartoon, which was well said and well pointed out, except for a few things.

Before I state any what's wrong with your statement, I would like to say what's right (in my opinion). First, the idea of "never again!" being associated with only that tragedy should not strike the industrialized (or as you put it, white) societies, is very true, the examples are numerous from the situation of Rwanda to Cambodia (etc...). Also it is true with the statement that there are moments in which the Arab media singles out Jews for the actions of Zionist (which is entirely unfair, it is like equating Muslims to the actions of the idiots of Al Qaeda).

Here is where I disagree with you. We Arabs have an excellent sense of humour, which, I may say, is not entirely noticed by the Americans. We do make fun of our religion, we do make fun of our situation, in fact if you read up more about our society and our culture, we are a vibrant race, cultured and extraordinarily funny in many cases...the issue of the Danish cartoons, is not entirely on the depiction of the prophet (which although is an issue, is not what caused outrage) it is how the Prophet was depicted (come on, a bomb for a turban, or evil eyes, are not looking for a laugh), and it is the excuse of freedom of speech to justify the depiction, especially when the West (and i mean both Europe and America) are not completely true to the issue of freedom of speech. Look at the case of the continual attacks and censorship of Al-Jazeera because its a "medium for terrorists" , or the censorship of anti-war personal for being anti-American, and etc etc etc.

See the point here is that every society has freedom of speech but it is relative to the limitations associated by the society itself. One can not generalize and say a group of people lack the vaules of liberty, or the understanding of freedom of speech, it all relates to the context of the current situation and obstacles faced by the society at the time. Saying Islam as a unit is against freedom of speech is silly, the historical example of the Muslim empire in India during the European dark ages (the time of the Inquisition, and witch burning) was a model of freedom of speech in which the court had members of all religions (including atheists) debating the existence of God...

anyways, just thought of adding my two cents,
hope you win the contest

take care
Yazan Al-S.

Yazan Al-S.,

Thank you for your thoughtful response to my artist's statement, and for taking a tone more moderate than my own.

Your point about Western hypocrisy concerning free expression is astute. *Hamshahri's* citing the prosecution of Holocaust deniers is a bad example of this, but your citing the harassment of al Jazeera is a good one. I did take on a somewhat jingoistic tone, it's true. I am proud of the American comedic tradition of which I am a small and marginal part, but I guess I really ought to have spoken instead on behalf of the humorous against the humorless.

I also agree that the cartoons about Mohammed weren't funny—except for the one showing suicide bombers arriving in heaven and being told they were out of virgins. Come on. That's pretty good.

You're right that my line about the Arabic sense of humor was written out of ignorance. Of course broad, unfair generalizations are one's stock in trade as a humorist, but in this instance I was indeed subscribing thoughtlessly to a stereotype that's all too pervasive in the U.S, and for this I apologize.

I know that the media only ever shows us angry chanting fanatics as though they were representative of the whole of Islam (just as the only Christians you ever hear about are ignorant bigots). I also know that Islamic civilization was the one keeping it together throughout the Middle Ages when Europe had dropped the ball.

I appreciate your calling me on my blanket dismissal of a whole culture and will bear in mind that there are humorless dogmatists in all cultures, as well as funny and thoughtful people. It's too bad the former so often drown out the latter. I consider all funny and thoughtful people, regardless of their race, religion, or nationality, to be my allies in the war against seriousness and stupidity, and I am grateful to have you as one.

Sincerely,
Tim Kreider

"In the Parallel Universe," March 8th 2006

I tend to think about parallel universes a lot—too often, probably, since it keeps me from grappling with the realities of the cruddy and lusterless one in which we're all trapped. I'm tormented by the suspicion that the Tim Kreiders in all those other parallel universes are doing better than me, that they're winning. I worry that ours is the worst of all possible universes. (It would certainly be appalling if it were the best one.) At least we're not in one of those shithole universes where the Charles "the Hammer" Martel failed to repel the Moslems, or the Axis won the Second World War, or Ronald Reagan was cast as Rick in Casablanca.

It was during my weekly Thursday night Belgian ale at Burp Castle with my colleague Tom Hart that we got to thinking, with wistfulness and rue, about the parallel universe where Al Gore won the 2000 election (or, rather, where he was awarded the Presidency by the Supreme Court). I don't really imagine that the Gore administration would've been any more successful at preventing the 9/11 attacks than the Bush administration… but, then again, who knows? The Clinton administration tried to warn the incoming Bush administration about al Qaeda, and told them that this would be their number one foreign policy problem. As has been well documented, the Bush administration ignored this and all other warnings about Osama bin Laden and instead devoted their attention to gutting environmental regulation and giving out tax cuts to their campaign donors. Subsequent events have demonstrated, again and again, the Bush administration's incapacity to foresee or cope with any crisis at all. How many times have you heard George Bush bleat, "I don't think anyone anticipated…" or "No one could have predicted…" about something that had been repeatedly and publicly predicted (flying commercial jets into skyscrapers, the levees of New Orleans breached by a flood)? As if this would be an acceptable excuse anyway? It seems like one obvious retort would be: Why didn't you? I still don't understand why Bush isn't more generally held accountable for his failure to prevent the terrorist attacks. If it had happened on a Democratic President's watch the right-wing *spittlerati* would've demanded his immediate impeachment, if not his execution.

It was Tom who told me that Bush once wanted to be Baseball Commissioner. I am reminded, not for the first time, that all Adolf Hitler originally wanted was to go to art school. If we have learned nothing else from World War II and the Holocaust, we have learned this bitter lesson: *let everybody into art school who wants to go.* Why couldn't they just have let Bush be baseball commissioner? He would've been a disaster, of course, just as he was a disaster as a baseball team owner and an oil company executive before that. The man's a chronic failure. But so what? Destroying major league baseball would've been relatively harmless. Nobody would've *died*. Maybe we could still offer him the position in exchange for resigning the presidency. I'd certainly sleep easier with President Steinbrenner in the Oval Office. But I may be an exception. It's funny—not funny ha-ha, but funny end-of-democracy—how much more passionate and better informed most people are about sports than politics. Imagine how much more fiercely critical of George Bush the Fox-watching audience would be if he'd brought his signature lack of experience and poor judgment to professional baseball instead of the governance of the nation.

Colleague Jason Little helped me resolve the problem of illustrating the last panel. All I could envision was something unacceptably clichéd and Rockwellian—a dad barbecuing with his family or some such horseshit. I love the image of these guys doing something stupid and loutish but basically harmless. It keeps the drawing from being sentimental even though it's essentially an unironic celebration of life—any life, no matter how sordid or squandered. These are the real heroes—not those poor saps shooting people and getting shot at in Iraq, but the men and women who loyally patronize our nation's strip clubs, who are downing shooters and folding dollar bills in half lengthwise to slip through garters and G-strings and hooting and cheering over "Wild, Wild West" and "Welcome to the Jungle." O shake the tits of liberty, ladies! Shake them for America! Waggle the ass of happiness! Waggle it for us all.

EVERY ONCE IN A WHILE I WONDER HOW THINGS ARE GOING

In the Parallel Universe...

PRESIDENT GORE'S POLL NUMBERS FALL AND REPUBLICANS CALL FOR IMPEACHMENT FOLLOWING THE ATTACK ON THE PENTAGON.

COMISSIONER GEORGE BUSH IS VOTED 'THE MOST HATED MAN IN BASEBALL' AFTER INEXPLICABLY MOVING THE WORLD SERIES TO DUBAI.

...AND CARTOONIST TIM KREIDER HAS CAPTURED AMERICA'S HEARTS WITH HIS WACKY AND WUVABLE WAMINALS!

CASUALTIES IN IRAQ: 0

It's hard to escape the conclusion that, in the same sense that Germany and Japan ultimately came out on top after World War II, emerging as economic giants without the crippling burden of maintaining military empires, the South really did win the Civil War. Their victory was cemented after the struggle for civil rights in the Sixties. This was the last time the Democratic Party fought for anything unpopular because it was right, and because of it they lost the South forever and vowed that they would never stand up for any principle again. They haven't gotten a northerner elected President since Kennedy. This would be a civilized country by now if we weren't still handcuffed to the bellowing idiot manchild of the Slave States. Instead of having free health care we have to listen to these dumb hicks bellyache about their beloved guns and unborn babies, Traditional Marriage and Intelligent Design. A supreme court packed with pro-life stooges is set to overturn Roe v. Wade. Tennessee wants to join Alabama in outlawing vibrators. *Exterminate all the brutes!*

Some of my rancor toward the South would be mollified if they'd just acknowledge that the Civil War was about slavery, that they were wrong, and that they lost. You know who would be a good model for the South? The Germans. The Germans, like the South, had to get their country razed flat for them and, unlike the South, they were honest and contrite enough to admit that, you know what, we lost it there for a while. Thanks, we needed that. The Germans are still apologizing for the Holocaust sixty years later, haunted by collective guilt, while the South remains in defiant denial about the Civil War a hundred and fifty years after Appomattox. They're proudly flying the Stars and Bars over their state capitols, like Germans innocently displaying the swastika and ingenuously defending it as an historic part of their cultural heritage. I know most Southerners believed they were fighting to defend their land; the Germans were fighting for their homeland, too. Who cares? Their cause was evil; they deserved to be destroyed. So take down the goddamned Confederate flags already. Don't make us come down there again. Remember what happened last time? We had all the foundries, and you realized that you can't make Gatling guns out of cotton. We whupped you good because you had it coming, and we'll do it again if you're too dumb to know when you're beat.

This venting may be part of the yearly sigh of relief I let out whenever I move back to New York City from rural Maryland. Although Maryland was, of necessity, a Union State (Baltimore was literally held at cannonpoint by Federal troops), it is south of the Mason-Dixon line, and was, I am sorry to say, a slave state. These days it is, except for Baltimore, solid Red country. There is still rumored to be a Klan chapter in my county. In order to run any errand I have to brace myself for an emotional gauntlet of bumper stickers advertising every brand of ignorance, bigotry and bad idea imaginable: the ubiquitous yellow-ribbon magnets, the stars and bars displayed alongside Old Glory, "FREEDOM ISN'T FREE," "MY PRESIDENT IS CHARLTON HESTON," "VOTE YOUR SPORT," "EVOLUTION ISN'T SCIENCE," "THE BIG BANG THEORY: GOD SAID IT… AND BANG!— IT HAPPENED!" (You don't see a lot of anti-Big Bang bumper stickers since all the Steady State proponents sullenly peeled their off in the sixties.) By the time I get home with a bag of groceries I'm often dazed and fatigued with rage.

The three characters on the left in panel 1 were copied faithfully from photographs of a local Southern Rock festival. The guy in the center, in particular, is an archetype of the area; something in the inbred, suspicious squint of the eyes, the protuberant ears and thin, filmy pubescent moustache. To my dismay I found that, having drawn the guy on the far right, I did not hate him; in fact, I kind of pitied and loved him. He doesn't mean any harm. He's just a big ole doofus. This always happens when I draw George Bush, whom I also despise in real life. Empathy is an occupational hazard. As the priest in Grahan Greene's *The Power and the Glory* muses, "When you visualized a man or woman carefully, you could always begin to feel pity."

NOW IS THE TIME! SUDDENLY AND WITHOUT WARNING WE MUST PREEMPTIVELY LAUNCH—

THE CIVIL WAR II

WHY?

IT COMPRISES A GEOGRAPHICALLY AND ETHNICALLY DISTINCT REGION WITH ITS OWN HISTORY, CULTURE, DIALECT AND CUSTOMS, WHOSE CORE BELIEFS ARE FUNDAMENTALLY INCOMPATIBLE WITH AMERICA'S.

OUR STRATEGY:

1.) CLONE WILLIAM TECUMSEH SHERMAN.[1]
2.) INTRODUCE HIM TO NUCLEAR WEAPONS.

[1] IF CLONING PROVES IMPRACTICAL, RETRIEVE GEN. SHERMAN USING *TIME TRAVEL*.

INSTEAD OF A SOLEMN SURRENDER AT APPOMATTOX, VICTORY WILL BE CELEBRATED BY PRESIDENT WINFREY *WIPING HER ASS* WITH THE CONFEDERATE FLAG.

INEVITABLY, THERE WILL BE SOME UPHEAVALS OF THE SOCIAL ORDER.

Webmaster Dave once wrote a song about how well science-fiction films have prepared us for every conceivable dystopian and apocalyptic contingency, if only we pay heed to their lessons. We all now know, for example, that any worldwide pandemic carries with it the risk of widespread zombiism. For some reason I invariably seem to associate my friend Jim with post-apocalyptic scenarios. I suspect Jim will thrive in the post-apocalyptic environment, if for no other reason than because of his oft-stated readiness—verging on eagerness—to resort to cannibalism.

It does seem, at this point, like sort of a horse race between the four horsemen of the Apocalypse: global warming, peak oil, pandemic, and don't let's forget nuclear holocaust. What, you think they took apart all the nuclear warheads and buried all that uranium back in the ground? No. They are still out there, in their silos, many of them in what's left of the Soviet Union, in the hands of badly disillusioned men with dramatically decreased life expectancies who haven't gotten a paycheck in a decade, blind drunk on cheap vodka. Think about that sometime when you're trying to fall back asleep.

The flunkies of the Bush administration are the very last people on the planet still in denial about global warming, just as they are about Iraq. Even *USA Today* and *Time*, those big color picturebooks of the news, have finally come out and announced to their readers, several decades belatedly, that the debate about global warming is over. But George famously doesn't read the papers; he gets his information about such matters directly from the experts, former CEOs of oil companies. There are days when I think that our government's official refusal to acknowledge or do anything about global warming—their willingness to forfeit the future of our species for the sake of short-term profits—may be not only the most evil thing happening on the planet right now, worse than Iraq or Dafur, but the most evil thing that's ever been done in human history. It depends on whether or not it eventually causes the extinction of humanity. We will have to wait and see. If it does, both the Bushes, father and son, will have some explaining to do.

My friend Ken has offered to pay for me to attend a conference on Peak Oil in New York later this month. A Google search of the term "peak oil" will instantly tell you far more than you ever wanted to know about this subject and immerse you in a subculture of tediously well-informed people who believe, with alarming certainty and unanimity, that modern society is going to go to all to hell in the very near future. "Peak oil" refers to that historical moment at which depletion of the resource exceeds production. We won't run out of oil; after a point, the cost of extracting the stuff will no longer be worth any possible profit. Exacerbating the crisis is the fact that the Indians and the Chinese have just learned that cars are fun to drive. The most easily grasped and chilling analogy I've read is that, in party terms, we are down to one six-pack, of which we've drunk four cans, a bunch of new people have just shown up without bringing beer, and it's after two. After we pass the Peak, energy prices will continue to rise and never come back down, massive shortages and crises will become commonplace, and eventually the infrastructure of industrial civilization will collapse, after which we will descend into Mad Maxean savagery and the reign of terrible warlords such as Lord Humongus, the Ayatollah of Rock and Rollah. I am paraphrasing somewhat. Estimates on when this will begin happening range from fifteen or twenty years from now (according to most petroleum geologists in speeches at conferences) to one or two (according to the same scientists later on at the hotel bar).

The most worrisome part is, western civilization has no fallback plan. Many of those in positions of wealth and power in this society coincidentally also seem to have a lot personally invested in the oil economy, and not much incentive to risk any capital exploring other options. Our current contingency plan for what to do when the oil runs out is: we're fucked. Ken is preparing for this eventuality by buying gold and moving to New Zealand (a questionable choice, as it falls well within Lord Humongous's sphere of influence). He's also tirelessly proselytizing to his friends, which is why he's offered to pay my way to this conference. I keep trying to gently explain to Ken that in the event of a global collapse my contingency plan is: to die. I am a frivolous person and will go the way of all extravagances when the shit hits the fan.

Jim, philosopher-king of the post-apocalyptic world, assures me that Ken has always been a crackpot and a pussy so good riddance to him, not to worry, there's plenty of oil, we'll figure something out before it all runs out, so just relax and take

THE FUTURE
According to...

CLIMATOLOGISTS

PETROLEUM GEOLOGISTS

EPIDEMIOLOGISTS

THE BUSH ADMINISTRATION

another half a Xanax and why not get myself a beer from the fridge and get him one too while I'm at it. I would like to be comforted by this advice but the fact that it is roughly identical to the official position of the Bush adminstration RE: oil and alternative energy sources (except for the Xanax and beer) disquiets me.

I've proposed to Jim that he join me at the Peak Oil conference. While I was on the phone with him pitching this trip he dismissed my concerns with the following argument: "It's like a few years ago, environmentalists were all worried about the birds, like, 'oh, we have to protect their migration patterns.' Now look what we got coming: the bird flu. If we'd just let those migration patterns go to hell we wouldn't be worrying about the bird flu now." In the background I could hear Jim's wife Sarah say: "You're killing me."

I am less worried about a pandemic than about Peak Oil only because I know even less about it. I am sure if I conducted even the most cursory research into the possibilities I would immediately barricade myself at my undisclosed location on the Chesapeake Bay with a face mask and gloves on, a decade's supply of canned Italian wedding soup and Juicy Juice, and a Thompson gun to mow down the inevitable waves of zombies.

Of the alternatives depicted in this cartoon, my money's on global warming. Even if Ken's right and industrial civilization does collapse and millions like me die because they never learned how to catch a rabbit or build a lean-to, there are still hundreds of millions more who never had a toaster oven or central heating who'll get by living in what we would consider squalor just as well as they always have. Humans lived as hunter-gatherers for hundreds of thousands of years. We'll be fine. And in every epidemic, even horrifically virulent ones like the Black Death,

or the Flu pandemic that killed millions of people at the turn of the century, there are always people whose immune systems are resistant. The race will survive. But if the global average temperature rises by even a few degrees, we are all going to die. Anyone taken a look at Venus lately? Real estate values there are the lowest in the solar system.

Inevitably the end of the world will instead be brought about by some freakish dark-horse disaster, like the double-whammy of a meteor shower that blinds everyone and walking killer plants in *Day of the Triffids*. Of only one thing can we be sure: whichever calamity brings an end to humanity, no matter how long, how often, how urgently, and how publicly scientists have been warning us about it, if George Bush is still in charge, he will say: "*No one could have predicted* that [global warming, oil depletion, a pandemic, zombies] could have posed such an imminent, serious threat."

In the meantime George, who is not only indifferent but actively hostile to science, since its findings are so often impious and unpatriotic, keeps his fingers jammed firmly in his ears singing an hysterical hymn of denial and rolling his eyes Heavenward, confident that in the very near future he and all Righteous God-fearing folk will be lifted bodily into the clouds, there to dwell with Jesus forever and ever while us sinners and liberals back on Earth get smitten hard by flaming hail and locusts and lepers. The President of the United States believes this, literally. Louis the XIV believed that he was the Sun King, with a divine right to rule. Moctezuma believed that Cortez was the return of Quetzalcoatl. Caligula believed he was a god. They were all executed, and their empires are gone now.

Tim,

Being a near-death survivor I figured you would know better than to worry about all this fatalistic crap. Please, for God sakes go fuck some pretty girl and have a few oysters with drinks. Yes, the world is going to crap, it has always been doing this. Do you even bother to watch White Christmas *every year? You should, then you would learn to go to sleep counting your blessings. Those poor fuckers who survived WWII didn't come home and say "holy shit we almost blew it that time, we better clean up our act." Fuck No! they went home and fucked their girl friends and built cars the size of city blocks, so that they could fuck in bigger cars. If you are really worried about this stuff, you should buy a gun. Does Ken own one? A gun is the only thing that has a small chance of protecting you.*

Worrying about all this stuff is just not worth the trouble. If the world goes to shit, it doesn't matter where you are if you're old, which we will be by the time this becomes a worry. Cheer up, I am sure it won't be long til' my father's prediction of "Sabrina" [Melissa Joan Hart, a.k.a. Sabrina the Teenage Witch*] being in* Playboy *comes true.*

Your unworried pal,

Jim

P.S. I love you.

The initial inspiration for this cartoon was a story in the *New York Times Magazine* about the Christian effort to ban not only abortion but contraception. There really is a faction of American dingbat fundamentalism that believes that anything other than sex within the sanctity of marriage for the divinely ordained purpose of begetting children—what Hunter Thompson called "a quick dutiful hump in the missionary position"—is dehumanizing and evil. (Sex can be dehumanizing and evil, of course, but only if it's done very well indeed.) Hence their insistence on abstinence-only education, not only here in America but in countries decimated by AIDS. This seems somehow related to the syndrome I discussed in "Conservative Christians' Guide to Compassion"—Fundamentalists' sentimental love for unformed fetuses and babies and their hatred of adult human beings.

My totally unverifiable personal suspicion is that the most vociferous such people were probably raped or molested as children (a traditional red-state pastime), which might account for their unwholesome associations with sexuality and their creepy fixation, in particular, on homosexuality and other forms of "deviance." Of course there are historical as well as psychological explanations—the hatred of sex goes way back in Christianity, inextricably associated with the Church's disgust for the corporeal body and the physical world—its enmity, in short, toward everything that actually exists. The Bush administration's entrenched hostility to empiricism, or what we who live there call 'reality," is an extension of this philosophy as state policy.

I learned about the firebombing from CNN. A twenty-year-old student at Crown College, a Baptist institution in Powell, Tennessee, disguised himself as a ninja and used a fake gun to drive employees out of an adult bookstore before dousing the place with gasoline and setting it on fire. He later experienced an attack of conscience after getting into a car accident, which he interpreted as a sign from God, and his college President,

to his credit, called the police and urged the confused youth to turn himself in. The owner of the bookstore, on learning it was torched for religious reasons, wanted to charge the boy with a hate crime. This is a great country.

My colleague Emily Flake, who is way eviler than I am, suggested a fourth panel that would've provided the perfect punchline to the whole cartoon: "BRING RAPE BACK TO MODERN WARFARE; THE RIGHT WILL HAVE TO SUPPORT IT." It just turns out to be very challenging to make rape funny, especially for a male cartoonist. In the end I had to throw out the whole premise when I did a little research and learned that American soldiers really are raping Iraqi women. This really ought not to come as a shock; whenever there is war there is always rape. I read in the U.K. *Guardian* about a letter smuggled out of Abu Ghraib in 2004 that disclosed that women prisoners there were being forced to strip and were raped, and that several had become pregnant. The note ended by begging insurgents to bomb the prison to end their disgrace. I guess the U.S. media felt it would've been unpatriotic to report this here. Members of the U.S. Congress have seen photographs from Abu Ghraib documenting these abuses, but they haven't been released to the public, supposedly for fear of reprisals against Americans in Iraq. Not many Iraqi women are likely to come forward with such stories, either, since the Islamic world is an even more virtuous society than Christendom, where rape is such an unspeakable sin that its victims must often be killed.

It may be worthy of note that two of my recent cartoons—"My Rejected New Yorker Cartoons" (which included the infamous "Graveyard Shift at the Pussy Juice Factory") and this week's "War on Sex"—have interfered with my own sex life. The former actually caused a girl to flee my apartment a couple of weeks ago. She claimed that "it would be a betrayal of my family and everyone I grew up with for me to stay here." Wow! I have

WHAT *YOU* CAN DO TO FIGHT AGAINST

THE **WAR** ON *Sex*

DISPATCH ELITE CADRE OF GUERRILLA FUCK TROOPS TO THE HEARTLAND TO CORRUPT ABSTINENT YOUTH.

MASS MAILING OF SEX TOYS TO THE WIVES OF PROMINENT REPUBLICANS

IF YOU'RE NOT ALREADY HOMOSEXUAL, PLEASE CONSIDER AT LEAST GOING BI.

been told some memorably unflattering things by women—an insane German neuroscientist once told me that I personally epitomized the moral failings of my country ("This is the problem with America, everybody fucks each other and lies!")—but this is the first time anyone's suggested that associating with me would bring *disgrace* upon their entire family. I blame Michael Kirby, who dictated this cartoon to me a decade ago.

Then, a couple of days ago, I happened to find myself at the same bus stop as a young woman I'd recently asked out. She had accepted, but we had yet to go out on the proposed date. I unfortunately had my folder of work-in-progress with me, and she asked if she could see some of my drawings. Alas, the only thing I had with me was panel #1, the one with the word balloon about "...a tongue in your ass feel[ing] one million times better than Jesus in your heart." I didn't even attempt to explain the context. I figured, better to be boldly unapologetic than defensive. She laughed, or pretended to, but she never called me again. Even by the degraded standards of contemporary urban dating etiquette, the whole subject of tongue/ass contact isn't customarily broached before the first date. However, in general my cartoons

have proved an efficient filtering device for screening out the humorless, literal-minded, and thin-skinned, and attracting the deviant, so I'm not about to start making a secret of them.

I drew the panel of the Republican lady tentatively fingering the enormous black dildo while sitting about a foot and a half away from a couple of underwear models in Chumley's in Greenwich Village. I eavesdropped in horror on these women for about forty-five minutes. I was cruelly disillusioned to learn that the women we ogle in underwear catalogs may not actually be smart or interesting or the kinds of people we would like to spend time with in real life at all. All they talked about was going clubbing and dancing, exotic locales they'd been flown to, and what a creep such-and-such a celebrity was. (Apparently one of them had had some sort of altercation on a dance floor with Mary-Kate of Mary-Kate-and-Ashley.) They had bland unbeautiful generically attractive faces, the faces of dumb spoiled cheerleaders, but the juicy, aching-hot bodies of underwear models. Seldom have I experienced such powerful attraction toward anyone for whom I felt such intense repulsion. Which paradox, come to think of it, may offer some insight into Fundamentalists' hatred of the flesh.

Hello Ms. Phelatia Czochula-Hautpanz!

I was wondering what the requirements were for becoming a groupie for Tim Kreider? Other than being female of course (as seems to be his usual sexual preference) and luckily that I'm young but still legal?
    Also, please send Tim my gratitude for his comics, and especially the "artistic statements" that go along with them. I'd say "yay for cynicism" but somehow it seems a bit ironic, but hey, irony is a great thing. So, "yay!"

from one supposed artist to another,
Karin

PS: I sincerely apologize for my not including pictures of my "boobies," though obviously not quite enough to include said pictures anyways, but hopefully this will not hurt my "groupie" application, as I can assure that they are quite nice.

Karin,

Mr. Kreider often wonders that people find his drawings cynical. With him they seem simply realistic. He will appreciate your cheers.
    It is an ideal time for Mr. Kreider to receive new a groupie as he is currently "down in the dumpster" for a variety of reasons, extending from the failure of his book To the Cold of Encroachment. He will be very eager to hear that you are a young person as many women that are his own age are rabid for the babies. Photographs of the breasts are not necessary (Mr. Kreider he is a man of ass of the higher order).
    Please do not be an alienated person as Mr. Kreider has resolved no longer to liaise with the mentally unsound. He has sure had some unhappy romantic tangles with the lunatic.

Respect,
C.-H.

I recently experienced yet another of those increasingly frequent moments of surreal and terrifying lucidity when I realize how far we've come from anything I recognize as the America I grew up in. It occurred to me that we've started thinking of the hawkish and anti-choice John McCain as a reasonable moderate because he's opposed to torture.

A few years ago "anti-torture" wasn't even a political position; it was like being "anti-rape" or "anti-genocide"—it pretty much went without saying, unless you were an out-and-out monster. A national politician being referred to as "anti-torture" would've been one of those clever background details that a science-fiction novelist would drop to clue us in to the fact that we're in some brutal fascist dystopia of the future or a nightmarish parallel history where the Nazis won the war. I can no longer pinpoint the moment when supposedly respectable people were no longer ashamed to debate the merits of "torture" in public, when we became an unapologetically evil nation; it's like trying to identify exactly when you ceased to be a basically decent if flawed person and drifted over some unnoticed line into irredeemable depravity.

The scenario routinely invoked to justify torture—a nuclear device about to be detonated in Times Square, only an hour until it goes off, and we have one terrorist in custody who knows where it is!—is such a ludicrously unrealistic James Bond fantasy I can't believe anyone takes it seriously. If 9/11 and Hurricane Katrina have shown us anything, it's that the first time the Bush administration will hear about a nuclear weapon being detonated in America will be when some reporter tells them about it. George Bush will still be obliviously joshing around with billionaire donors at a campaign fundraiser while the rest of us are weeping in horror at footage of children's skin peeling off in East Orange. Besides, didn't we manage to beat Nazi Germany and Imperial Japan while observing the Geneva conventions? This delusion that torturing people is going to make us safer or tougher in the War on Terror is a fantasy that has more to do with fear and hatred than with real security, like the craven adolescent fantasy that owning a gun will keep you safe from all those gangstas and serial killers and child molesters you hear about on Fox News and in the *New York Post*.

A few days ago my colleague and old comrade-at-arms from the war-protest days, Megan, sent me an "action alert," urging me to write my representatives and the President asking them not to nuke Iran. It's hard to believe the phrase "don't nuke Iran" is even necessary. It seems to me we really ought not to have to beg our government not to nuke anyone, just as in the ordinary course of events I don't have to talk my friends out of raping anybody. But, as Batman once said, "It's isn't exactly a normal world, is it?"

A GUIDE TO OFFICIALLY SANCTIONED
American Torture Methods

FORCE-FEEDING

SENSORY DEPRIVATION

SEXUAL DEGRADATION

PSYCHOLOGICAL

"Everything I Know I Learned from the Bush Administration," April 26th 2006

I have learned so much about the art of brazen deception from this administration that I ended up with this six-panel extravaganza and still had to discard several ideas due to space limitations. One I still wish I'd had room and time to include is: "WHEN YOUR FRIENDS FUCK UP, REWARD THEM LAVISHLY." This referring to a particularly galling move of Bush's whereby, whenever one of his cronies comes under fire for exceptionally appalling incompetence or criminality, he promotes them or gives them a medal as a defiant fuck-you to public opinion. It epitomizes his President's-kid attitude of blithely flouting the ethics and consequences that apply to everybody else in the world. The drawing would've shown my beloved cat sulking after having clawed out someone's eyeball and me coddling her, cooing, "Are you an unhappy cat? Bist du eine unhaplische këtzle? I want you to be happy. That is what we all want: a happy, happy cat. Who would like some catnip? Would you?" even as her victim clasps a hand in shock over the bleeding socket.

On the subject of the "meaningless re-shuffling of associates," let us take this opportunity to bid a contemptuous farewell to Press Secretary Scott McClellan. He reminded me of a child smeared with chocolate earnestly insisting that he does not know who ate the mousse, or a suspect soaked in blood doggedly insisting that the true culprit was "some other dude." His standard rhetorical tactic was to obstinately recite his single scripted line—"we cannot comment on an ongoing legal case," for example—over and over, robotically, maddeningly, in response to increasingly specific and pointed variations on some perfectly straightforward question. It was good sadistic fun watching him straining to draw a fine, convoluted distinction between the treasonous crimes of the administration's critics and the President's identical but necessary and virtuous actions. Also, he was fun to draw: that tiny, clammy face peering nervously out, as if trapped, from the center of a broad, doughy bowlful of head; the soft, plump little white hands held up as if to tamp down the barrage of charges. He couldn't handle the one simple job he'd been given of stonewalling the press while the administration did whatever the fuck it wanted. If he'd been a front man for the Mafia instead of the White House they'd've put a couple of bullets in the back of his head and dumped his body in Jersey. Instead he goes on to corporate flakdom, to deny less glamorous crimes.[1]

After I finished this cartoon, I went out for a cocktail with someone who told me an extraordinary story. (Since I am not a journalist but a cartoonist, I feel no obligation to attribute or confirm this story. I'm just repeating what somebody told me in a bar, one of the few places on Earth where the truth is ever uttered.) The story concerns Karen Hughes, counsel to the President and one of that celibate harem of brittle, fawning women with whom George Bush likes to surround himself. Hughes invited the head of a well-known P.R. firm to Texas to advise her on the administration's "P.R. problem." For a long time they didn't acknowledge that they even had one, she admitted, but now they did, and they needed to know how to fix it. The head of this firm warned Hughes that if she was really asking, he was going to tell her the truth, not what she wanted to hear. She said that was exactly why she had come to him; they'd been hearing what they wanted to hear for too long.

Well, first of all, he told her, you don't have a P.R. problem—you don't even have a P.R. department. What you have is an attitude problem. You're arrogant, and you don't listen. Also, you should've changed the White House staff in your second administration. It would have been a perfectly acceptable time to fire a bunch of people and bring in new blood. And the first person you should've fired, he said, is Dick Cheney. Hughes agreed with all of this. She already knew it; everybody knew it. But she was afraid to tell it to the President. Everyone around him was afraid to tell him anything he didn't want to hear. She told him an incredible story: George's own father, Former President George H.W. Bush, had called him around Thanksgiving to tell him that Dick Cheney was horrible, he should be fired immediately, and George Bush *hung up on him*. (Lesson #8: *Show the Old Man Who is Boss*.)

This story not only confirms all our worst fears about Bush's willful insularity from reality but also lends credence to the chilling hypothesis that the last six years of American history have been a one-man psychodrama played out on the world stage, with a cast of millions, a budget in the trillions, and real blood.

---

[1]   In fact McClellan went on to write a belated *sua culpa* called *What Happened: Inside the Bush White House and Washington's Culture of Deception*, in which he asks us to believe one last prevarication so insultingly implausible it may actually be true: that Scott McClellan was the very last person in America to realize that he was lying.

Everything I Know I Learned from the Bush Administration

PREEMPTIVE STRIKES!

PLEAD IGNORANCE

BALDFACED LYING.

FLAT DENIAL.

MEANINGLESS RE-SHUFFLING OF ASSOCIATES

NEVER ADMIT ERROR.

Last week my friend Ben and I, our judgment impaired by painkillers, made a pact to abstain from alcohol for the entire month of June. In the last few days I have received several high-strung and vengeful phone messages from Ben suggesting that he may be having second thoughts about this experiment.

To quote *Airplane!*, "Looks like I picked the wrong week to quit sniffing glue!" American soldiers massacred women and children in Iraq, raping and torturing and generally behaving indistinguishably from Nazis. The Republicans trotted out their usual fag-bashing platform in a desperate attempt to suck up to the bigots who constitute their base. Even some Republicans, who are normally as sensitive to the pangs of conscience as a pack of hyenas hungrily digging their snouts into the anus of a bloated antelope corpse, seem embarrassed by the transparency of this tired old pandering tactic. But not even the sorts of people who usually start frothing as reliably as Pavlov's dogs at the mention of the homos seem to be buying it this time around.

As I've said before, I do not credit the officially sanctioned myth of George Bush's giving up alcohol on his fortieth birthday— something about a bad hangover, an ultimatum from the wife, and a long walk on the beach with Jesus. My best guess is that his parents made a deal with him not unlike the offer depicted here: if you can stay off the sauce, we'll let you be President. Whether he's really quit or not is a matter of some national interest. I've read analyses of his behavior as exhibiting all the symptoms of a "dry drunk," someone attempting to quit drinking without the support of a recovery program. I know it'd be hard for me to face national poll numbers in the low thirties without a stiff one, but perhaps George's ego is healthier than mine.

Most of the drawings of George's henchwomen that appear in his fantasy balloon are culled from earlier cartoons of mine, except for that cowtown Machiavelli and Counsel to the President Karen Hughes, whom I depict here for the first time. She really is pretty much the Mannerist nightmare seen here, with stenciled-on whiplash eyebrows and a wattled saurian throat. Drawing these horrible women has brought home to me that George really does have a consistent "type": bony, desiccated, hard-faced women with brittle hair, glassy eyes, and thickly applied black eyeliner. (What's *with* that eyeliner, anyway? Is it just that most of them are from Texas, where women don't know any better than to keep slathering on the tacky middle-school makeup well into late middle age? Am I forgetting some Biblical passage in which Jesus commands women to smear their eyes thickly with kohl as a sign of reverence for Him?) They also tend to have an unwholesome nunnish quality to them, as though they'd renounced all other men to devote themselves wholly to the cultivation and advancement of this ungifted but well-born manchild.

Since drawing this cartoon events have overtaken me: U.S. forces have "eliminated" al Qaeda's leader in Iraq, al Zarqawi (at least he's been al Qaeda's leader in Iraq ever since Colin Powell inadvertently appointed him to the position that in his infamous U.N. speech). You know what this means—the insurgency is over! I guess this shows me and all my defeatist liberal pals. At last democracy will be restored to these freedom-loving people. Victory in Iraq!

George & Me in Sobriety

GEORGE QUIT WITH THE HELP OF JESUS.

I QUIT WITH THE HELP OF BEN WALKER.

FACING GRIM REALITY OF FUCKING LAURA

FACING GRIM REALITY OF FUCKING NO ONE

STILL HAS A LI'L NIP NOW AND AGAIN

STILL STICKING WITH IT AS OF DAY 8!

It was hard to make this cartoon funny. I got so angry and despairing last week when I heard about the massacre of civilians in Iraq. It shouldn't be shocking that such things happen in war, especially wars of occupation in which the enemy insurgency is invisible and the civilian population is hostile to the invaders. I blame our civilian leaders (most of whom evaded military service) who sent teenagers into this baking hellhole and have kept them there for three years. If I'd been over there this long and someone blew up one of my friends in front of me I'd probably start shooting women and children, too.

There were also three simultaneous suicides at Guantanamo this week. Rear Admiral Harry Harris, the commanding officer of the base, said of his dead captives: "They have no regard for life, either ours or their own. I believe this was not an act of desperation, but an act of asymmetrical warfare waged against us." Reading this line brought me that piquant mixture of incredulity, disgust, and perverse satisfaction at seeing one's blackest, most cynical expectations exceeded—it's a reaction not unlike the slow, sarcastic, but also sincere applause a character in a *noir* might give his *femme fatale* after an especially transparent and manipulative performance. It's a delicacy increasingly available to us connoisseurs of human hypocrisy under the Bush administration. Like cigars and single-malt scotch, it's an acquired taste, and not especially good for you in daily doses.

This story reads like a *reductio ad absurdum* of the pathological right-wing need to position themselves as victims and underdogs, besieged on all sides. (Even the admiral's name, Harry Harris, sounds like the stuff of parody, an echo of Heller's Major Major.) It's bizarre enough when demagogues bewail the marginalization and oppression of the straight white American male, but grotesque when an admiral accuses prisoners he's tortured to the point of suicide of unfair tactics. Hanging yourself in your cell is about as asymmetrical as warfare gets. Help, someone—America is under attack by suicide hangers! O the humanity! Will no one save us from these monsters?

Further complicating matters, the World Cup is in progress, which, since I am oblivious to the world of sports, has occasioned me the odd jarring moment of surreal shock while reading the morning paper. How to tell, at a glance, which is sports and which is international news when you see headlines like "SRI LANKA, TIGERS CLASH" and "ARGENTINA CRUSHES SERBIA"? For a second I was like: holy shit—*Argentina* crushes *Serbia*? What in hell do the Argentines want in the Balkans?

It at first seemed too heavy-handed to put Hitler's rationales for invading Poland into Bush's mouth. (I realize this whole cartoon is an illustration of what is known in online circles as "Godwin's Law," or the argumentative fallacy of *reductio ad Hitlerum*.) But when I looked up his actual speeches I was impressed by their uncanny appropriateness. They are all but indistinguishable from George Bush's speeches preceding the war in Iraq, except for the place names and Hitler's superior rhetorical style. (Hitler would've mopped up the stage with George at forensics.) I think the basic template for this speech has remained unchanged since about 250,000 B.C. Nation-states' pretexts for launching wars are pretty much the same from one millennium to another; always the invader poses as rescuer, attacking in self-defense or to protect an oppressed minority, always claiming that their enemy is not the country but its leader, who is called a madman and a tyrant. This is one of several reasons why it might be helpful if Americans knew any history; the propaganda might start to sound suspiciously familiar. But to most products of our public school system the Gulf of Tonkin is as obscure and meaningless a reference as the U.S.S. *Maine*, Jenkins' Ear, or Helen of Troy.

My comparison here is facile and hyperbolic: the Nazis were killing millions of civilians on purpose, as part of a deliberate, calculated campaign of genocide, whereas we're only killing tens of thousands of civilians by accident, as part of an invasion of a strategically valuable country rich in resources, and we officially regret it. Though I'm not sure this is anything to be proud of. If

ARRESTS AND DETENTION WITHOUT TRIALS, SECRET PRISONS, TORTURE, UNPROVOKED INVASIONS, CIVILIAN MASSACRES: STILL NO ONE WANTS TO SPEAK THE FORBIDDEN

N-Word

THE GOVERNMENT ASSURES US WE ONLY PUT VERY BAD PEOPLE IN OUR CONCENTRATION CAMPS.

WE ONLY EVER ATTACK COUNTRIES THAT THREATEN US.

"WE HAVE NO INTEREST IN OPPRESSING OTHER PEOPLE... IT'S NOT SO MUCH THE COUNTRY; IT IS ITS LEADER. HE HAS LED A REIGN OF TERROR... THE MAINTENANCE OF A TREMENDOUS MILITARY ARSENAL CAN ONLY BE REGARDED AS A FOCUS OF DANGER. WE HAVE DISPLAYED A TRULY UNEXAMPLED PATIENCE, BUT I AM NO LONGER WILLING TO REMAIN INACTIVE WHILE THIS MADMAN ILL-TREATS MILLIONS OF HUMAN BEINGS." *

*ADOLF HITLER, 14 APRIL 1939, ON THE INVASION OF CZECHOSLOVAKIA.

WHEN WE COMMIT ATROCITIES WE APOLOGIZE AND REPRIMAND ANY ENLISTED MEN INVOLVED AS SOON AS THE PRESS FINDS OUT ABOUT IT.

IF IT AIN'T HITLER, IT AIN'T FASCISM!

we've reached the point where we have to go out of our way to trumpet our moral superiority over the Nazis we might want to stop and retrace our steps and try to pinpoint where we went wrong.

Michael Berg, father of Nicholas Berg, who was beheaded by al-Zarquawi, said in a recent interview:

> "I'm not saying Saddam Hussein was a good man, but he's no worse than George Bush. Saddam Hussein didn't pull the trigger, didn't commit the rapes. Neither did George Bush. But both men are responsible for them under their reigns of terror... Under Saddam Hussein, no al Qaeda. Under George Bush, al Qaeda. Under Saddam Hussein, relative stability. Under George Bush, instability. Under Saddam Hussein, about 30,000 deaths a year. Under George Bush, about 60,000 deaths a year. I don't get it. Why is it better to have George Bush the king of Iraq rather than Saddam Hussein?"

Whenever I get into impassioned imaginary arguments with pro-war politicians and pundits, I always want to pose the rhetorical question of whether they'd be willing to accept their own families' deaths as "collateral damage" in this great mission to bring peace and freedom to the Middle East. Would Bill Kristol consider his children acceptable casualties if it meant the success of the mission? How about only one of his children? In fact, if I ever got to attend one of Bush's press conferences (admittedly a long shot at this point) the question I'd want to ask would be: If sacrificing your two daughters' lives would ensure stability and democracy in Iraq, would you do it? Follow-up question (not that I'm likely to get one): If so, why don't you make the offer? Because it seems like al Qaeda might possibly go for this. It would speak to their medieval sense of justice. Plus it'd make you an Old-Testament-style hero at home, giving the lives of your own daughters to save the lives of thousands of American soldiers! Quote the Biblical story of Isaac and then cut their throats yourself on live TV! It would definitely appeal to the Base.

It was this week that I finally accepted that I don't care what happens in Iraq. All I want is for people to stop getting killed there. This endless ghastly disaster is entirely the fault of George Bush and everyone who supported the invasion. I'm not sure whether I'll even be able to force myself to vote for Hillary Clinton or anyone else who authorized the use of force in Iraq. I'm tired of our elected officials being cowards and fools. I'm tired of being ashamed of this country. I'm tired of being lied to and spied on and intimidated, and of Americans being seen around the world as invaders and torturers and killers. I won't feel like we've begun to atone for the atrocity of Iraq until George Bush and Dick Cheney and Donald Rumsfeld and Colin Powell and Condoleeza Rice and yes, even that bowtied academic Paul Wolfowitz have all been tried for war crimes and hanged like Eichmann.

Today's headline from the World Cup: "Scoreless in Nuremberg."

Tim,

You'll likely never read this comment, but I would like to correct you on your artist's statement for the current comic, "The N-Word" of 06/21/06. In the comment, you discuss the importance of being familiar with History but reiterate the common misconception that Hitler killed more people than Stalin or Mao. In actual fact, Stalin's Purges killed in excess of 20 million people between 1929 and 1933, averaging at 5 million deaths per year. Similarly, Mao's Great Leap Forward is said to have caused the deaths of at least 30 million between the years of 1959 and 1962—an unbelievable average of 10 million per year. 6 million Jews slaughtered in five years? Tragic, yes, but not as unique or as astronomical as most people seem to think.

Chris

Chris,

So much information Mr. Kreider has received about the respective scales of the mass murders of the twentieth century in this week! His readers seem disturbingly quite informed on this subject. Consequently Mr. Kreider must constantly update his opinion of Hitler. After reading your message he must admit that Hitler is not so bad after all. He now arranges the dictators by evilness: 1.) Mao 2.) Stalin 3.) Hitler 4.) Pol Pot. He hopes that this will be considered precise and that these proportionate hatreds will make him the decent man at last.

This information has also given Mr. Kreider much more agitation about ordering the beans of mung and the pig sournesses beloved by Mao at Grand Sichuan.

Respect,
C.-H.

The idea for this cartoon came to me in a dream, in which I was a third-party candidate for president in a debate among all the third-party candidates. The candidates were speaking in alphabetical order, so my fellow cartoonists Megan Kelso and John Kerschbaum preceded me. (Why all the candidates happened to be cartoonists was not clear, nor was why their names all began with K, unless it was to emphasize the Kafkaesque aspect of the dream.) The press was there getting footage of Megan, who happened to be the first speaker, to edit into their bemused end-of-the-newscast look at some of the also-rans.

Megan was killing us. Her opening statement was intelligent, funny, down-to-earth, genuine and engaging. She had the crowd eating out of her hand. As she was speaking, I glanced over my own speech, which, in my cockiness about public speaking, I hadn't even looked at in some time. As I read it over, I realized it was almost totally obsolete and irrelevant now. For one thing, my stance on Iraq had changed since I'd written it. Fuck! What to do? I didn't want to misrepresent my position, but I also thought I probably shouldn't, like, wing a whole new foreign policy statement live on national TV. While Megan was still talking I ran downstairs to the bathroom to try to collect my thoughts and formulate a strategy, but when I tried to get back to the debate I found my way blocked by the crowd. I was going to be late for my own speech! Everyone was waiting for me. Also, I suddenly realized, I had forgotten my suit jacket in the bathroom. A fiasco.

Anyway, in the dream, my new foreign policy in Iraq was essentially the one presented here: let's maybe try to win! Reinstate the draft, send another hundred thousand guys over there, get the country locked down, and then bring 'em all home. I mean, it's either a war or it isn't, right? If we're not going to withdraw, why not actually fight it? Instead the Bush administration just keeps muddling along, vaguely hoping, like all addicts, that doing the same thing they've done so far will somehow produce dramatically different results, which policy has been getting a consistent hundred-or-so men killed per month. Nobody in power seems to have any ideas except for staging P.R. stunts—trumpeting the killing of "the head of al Qaeda in Iraq," or sending the President over there to do one of his pop-in-for-a-couple-hours-then-hightail-it-home photo ops. Just more spin. Currently they're crowing over the President's "bounce" in opinion polls—up to a merely dismal 40%, back from the near-Mansonian levels to which they'd sunk—as if the President's poll numbers were the strategic aim of the war.

If the Democrats really wanted to do an end run around the Republicans and blindside them in this election, this is the way they'd go: call for a draft, the escalation of the war, nuking Fallujah if necessary, total victory inside a year. The Republicans would be utterly confounded and helpless faced with the unprecedented spectre of hawkish and bloodthirsty Democrats calling them a bunch of pussies. Also, maybe they'd start taking this war seriously if rich people's kids had to go.

It's surprising how easy it is to call for a draft once you're safely over the draft age. The aging hate the young; they're undeservedly attractive, pugnacious, stupid, and loud, they affect a blanket cynicism but they'll buy anything, and the whole culture has to pander to their puerile tastes. It must be obscenely life-affirming and fun to dispatch thousands of them to an early grave. You can see how someone like Dick Cheney, who was born fifty, could develop an insatiable taste for it.

I am not some America-hating leftie who's secretly rooting for the people of the Middle East in their fight against our imperialist aggression. It's self-defeating to pretend that our enemies are inhuman and incomprehensible rather than people like ourselves driven to extremist beliefs by desperate circumstances, but this is not the same as having any sympathy for them. It's true that the people of the Middle East have been impoverished and oppressed for a long time, and America has kept their despotic ruling families in power while occupying their sacred lands, crippling their economies with debt, and corrupting their children with our vulgar and Godless pop culture.

However: who cares? That's supposed to be a good excuse for 9/11? Al Qaeda, the Taliban, the jihadists in Iraq—these are the same kind of assholes we're at war with here at home, the ones who firebomb abortion clinics and want to ban contraception and hold up **"GOD HATES FAGS"** signs at soldiers' funerals. I find no more to admire in fundamentalist Islam than I do in fundamentalist Christianity—even less, in fact, since even most dingbat Christians in this country have been semicivilized and can't quite believe in their own delusions wholeheartedly enough any more to kill anybody.

If it's to be a war between totalitarian theocracy and pluralist democracy—even democracy in its current corrupt and decadent corporate-owned form—hey, I'm on our side. I like being able to call the president a liar; I enjoy Hollywood

OKAY: AS LONG AS WE'RE NOT PULLING OUT, MAYBE WE SHOULD ACTUALLY TRY TO WIN.

My NEW Iraq Policy

REINSTATE THE DRAFT. THERE ARE 1.8 TRILLION DUMB, ABLE-BODIED FRAT BOYS IN THIS COUNTRY DOING JACK SHIT BESIDES BEER BONGS AND FLAMING SHOOTERS. LET'S SEND THEM ALL OVER THERE AND GET THE COUNTRY UNDER CONTROL.

HERE | THERE

AND HOW ABOUT MAKING SOME SACRIFICES ON THE HOME FRONT— LIKE, OH, I DON'T KNOW, SAY, *RATIONING GAS CONSUMPTION?*

I ONLY REGRET THAT I AM TOO OLD TO SERVE.

movies and Motown; I appreciate not having polio and seeing photos from the Hubble. And I thank God every day that our Western women dress and conduct themselves like shameless whores. Conservatives are right in saying that there can be no compromise or détente with an enemy that doesn't believe in tolerance or pluralism. (Not that conservatives themselves have historically been on the front lines of tolerance or pluralism.) But I'd be a lot more enthusiastic in my support of this war if it didn't look, under the current administration, so much like a war between one faction of totalitarian theocracy and another— what the media refers to, when things get too complicated and boring to follow, as "sectarian violence."

Whenever I read Christopher Hitchens's or listen to Tony Blair's eloquent, forceful arguments in favor of the Iraq war, I think, almost wistfully, that if Bush had been half as articulate, or had tried to appeal to my reason instead of to chauvinism and fear, I might actually have supported it. It makes me worry that I'm just as gullible as anyone else, but that Bush just pandered to the wrong sensibilities and signifiers. Maybe I just mistrust him because of his affected shitkicker accent and swagger, his Yalie anti-intellectualism and born-again act. Like my old dance instructor used to tell us between whacks with the rod, "One often contradicts an opinion when it is really only the tone in which it has been presented that is unsympathetic." In truth, the main reason I've opposed this war from the moment I heard the first ominous rustling of propaganda back in spring of 2002 is simply because I don't believe anything the Bush administration says and reflexively oppose anything they want to do. This instinct seems sound in principle; the question is whether it's right in this case.

To quote my dance instructor again: "At times one remains faithful to a cause only because its opponents do not cease to be insipid." It's often easiest to decide which side of a complex debate you belong on by just looking around and seeing who's where. Oh look, over there: all the same guys who call you a faggot and beat you up in dive bars, plus George Will. On this side: all the cute girls. Even if I were to decide that the war in Iraq was in the best interest of this country and civilization in general, could I actually bear to ally myself with the likes of George Bush, Bill O'Reilly, Rush Limbaugh, Ann Coulter, the whole Ministry of Propaganda of professional liars and slanderers and apologists for torture, the homicidal Jesus freaks and NASCAR rednecks who think Saddam was behind 9/11 and complacent fatassed suburban Republicans driving Hummers with flag decals, all those angry, smug, priggish, sneering people of the right, the heartless, the sexless and humorless, so self-righteous and complacent about killing?

Naw. But it does me good to acknowledge some validity in my opponents' arguments, and to be given pause to reconsider my own opinion. Everybody on all sides of the American dialogue has become too strident and sure of themselves, isolated inside their own ideological echo chambers, dismissing anyone who disagrees with them as a fool or a traitor. It is a characteristic failing of the Bush administration that they would rather cling desperately to their bad ideas at the expense of thousands of lives and billions of dollars rather than admit to error. Let's make sure we don't share it.

H.L. Mencken once described the kind of man he admired in public life:

> When he fights he fights in the manner of a gentleman fighting a duel, not in that of a longshoreman cleaning out a waterfront saloon. That is to say, he carefully guards his amour prope by assuming that his opponent is as decent a man as he is, and just as honest—and perhaps, after all, right.

I cant spell to save my life but im sure as hell not going to get drafted either damn bastard lets raise the age for the draft and send in the old guys first to find out where the their shooting before the guys that are NOT halfway to death go in. Fricken Bastard. Love your comics still but your a bastard. If there's a draft they should take at least one family member from each politician and their the first in. And women should be drafted too bastard. I get drafted any time in the future ill track you down yell at you then run for the nearest border. Seriously that's the best inequality chicks have going for them equality but not for the draft. Hell half the chicks I know are homicidal and sneaky as hell perfect for the army sorry im rambling.

YOUR A BASTARD
a bum that could get drafted if there is one.

Mr. Kreider approves of the heart of your suggestions concerning a restored policy of drafting. (It is appropriate that the women are primarily the wilder kind.) It is true he is a bastard. However, he jokes only by suggesting a replaced draft. He certainly would not wish to see the increased age, as he is adapted little to the discipline and the poor life-style of the armed forces, as well as to fear their tendency to be killed.

Respect,
C.-H.

...great way to falsify the facts in order to push your anti-american, anti-military agenda through rubber-stamped cartooning! Go you! You're really going places.

PS: Why don't you talk to a US Soldier (who is, by the way, unselfishly fighting for your right to continue to spew this diahrrea unabaited and uncensored) who would perhaps give you a little bit of insight on what this war is -really- about? Lets start with my brother — tell him how you like to piss on his sacrafices with lies that have been spoon-fed to you from your friends George Soros and Michael Moore?

Please educate yourself. How about starting with the Persian Gulf War? After, research your way though the Operation Iraqi Freedom Documents on their government website. The answers to why we're still fighting terrorists today all over the middle east lies within those pages.

Actually, nevermind. You go on making these webcomics for your 14-22 year old demographic. I don't know why i'm trying to dissaude you. It's best you make a jackass out of yourself :) Kill babies! save homosexual marriage!

Yay!

Love,
A mother, wife, and a conservative

A.M., W., A.A.C.,

As I said in the artist's statement accompanying my cartoon, my only position on Iraq at this point is that I wish people would stop dying there. My opinions aren't formed by the mass media; I was an adult during the first Gulf war, and I've read a fair amount about the history of this one. I think this war was unnecessary, and I doubt that perusing the administration's propaganda on the subject would change my mind. (I certainly don't believe Saddam Hussein was endangering my First Amendment rights.)

For whatever it may be worth to you, which I suspect isn't much, I do believe that individual altruism, courage, and honor are admirable even in the service of a misguided cause. It's obvious you and I wouldn't agree on many issues, but I'm with you in hoping your brother comes home safely, and soon.

As for the babies and homosexuals, I once drew a cartoon proposing the following compromise: outlaw abortion, legalize gay marriage, and then let gay couples adopt all the unwanted children. What do you say?

Sincerely,
Tim Kreider

TIM KREIDER BREAKS HIS HIATUS TO ADDRESS
THE URGENT CRISIS UNEXPECTEDLY FACING US TODAY:

Planethood for Pluto

AT THE UPCOMING GENERAL ASSEMBLY OF THE INTERNATIONAL ASTRONOMICAL UNION IN PRAGUE, SCIENTISTS WILL VOTE ON THE PRECISE DEFINITION OF A "PLANET" — A VOTE WITH THE GRAVEST IMPLICATIONS FOR THE FUTURE TAXONOMICAL STATUS OF OUR FARTHEST-FLUNG BUT NO LESS BELOVED NINTH SISTER WORLD.

EVERYONE KNOWS THE RULE IS: NO TAKEBACKS. ONCE YOU'VE LET SOMETHING IN, IT'S IN, NO MATTER HOW UNQUALIFIED IT MAY BE.

HAWAII

"Y"

...WELL, SOMETIMES.

NORTH AMERICA 3,000 MI.

CLARENCE THOMAS

AND WHAT ELSE THAT WE LEARNED IN GRADE SCHOOL ARE WE SUPPOSED TO UNLEARN?

THE FOOD TORUS

CHIP GROUP / PIE/TART GROUP / FOREIGN / IGNEOUS / CRUSTACEAN FUNGI / COLLOID GROUP / COW GROUP / CARBONATED GROUP

THE THREE TYPES OF ROCK

VOCIFEROUS

ABEDNEGO

PAREGORIC

GEORGE WASHINGTON:

· NOT OFFICIALLY PRESIDENT: TECHNICALLY A *TRANS-JEFFERSONIAN* OFFICIAL

· CATTLE RUSTLER

· INVENTOR OF THE BULLWHIP, PARKING METER

· ASIAN-AMERICAN

· FLAMENCO DANCER

REMEMBER: IF THEY CAN DO IT TO PLUTO, THEY CAN DO IT TO ANYONE. WHO'S NEXT?

What I Did On My Summer Vacation

SNAPPED OFF THE RADIO EVERY TIME I HEARD THE WORD 'HEZBOLLAH.'

VISITED THE GRAVE OF H.P. LOVECRAFT

FAILED TO SAVE PLUTO

TRIED OUT NEW *INVISIBILITY GOGGLES.*

As a senator, Joe Lieberman was merely contemptible rather than hateful; it's his refusal to go away that's made him infuriating. I had been looking forward to scraping whatever was left of Joe Lieberman off our shoes after Election Day and not looking back at it. But instead it's still clinging there and following us like expectorated gum or a ragged streamer of toilet paper. In truth he's less like a zombie than a gnat that you absent-mindedly try to smush but which keeps evading you and flying around your head in erratic squiggles as if in deliberate, gleeful defiance and gets into your ear canal where you can hear the maddening high-pitched whine of its wings filling your brain and you finally leap up screaming with murderous rage.

Lieberman is reportedly dismayed by the level of vitriol being directed against him on the web. Gosh, that must be a real bringdown, Joe. It's too bad, but you picked the wrong side of history to be on. Under the Bush administration, in this current dark age of illegal war and imprisonment and torture and spying, Democrats who work with the Other Side aren't "bipartisan"; they're collaborators. And all Vichy Democrats go up against the wall in this election. If it offers any perspective on the situation, Joe, you might want to stop and reflect that your political career has not been the only, or even the most important, casualty of this war.

For reasons to which I'm resisting the impulse to assign any conspiratorial agenda, our national pundits seem unable to accept that the ousting of Lieberman was not a coup by a few far-left bloggers and activists but the legitimate, mainstream rejection of a pro-war, Bush-friendly Democrat. I'm not sure why the Far Right, which believes that dinosaurs are fake and Christians will be beamed up into Heaven, has to be taken seriously as a political constituency whereas the Far Left, which believes that invading Iraq was a mistake and we should maybe

have national health care, is dismissed as a bunch of loonies. What kind of sense does it make for Democrats to treat their core constituency of progressives, African-Americans, labor, and the poor with contemptuous indifference (like, who else you gonna vote for—*Nader?*) and feebly try to sell themselves to NASCAR dads while the Republicans pander shamelessly to their base of fag-bashing Creationist sandwich-board fanatics in every election? How about the Democrats pandering to their own base for once? I for one, having been taken for granted and marginalized and ignored by the party I've voted for my entire adult life, would not say no, at this point, to a little pandering.

Listening to the punditry struggle to frame Lieberman's defeat this week, it occurred to me that when journalists strive for what they call "objectivity," this consists not in accurate, balanced, unbiased reportage, let alone "the Truth": what it means is not having any consumers complain. (This is only one among several objections to information being treated, like education and health, as a commodity.) So that as the political zeitgeist in America has skewed farther and farther to the right, so has what's considered "objectivity." You quote one scientist who supports anthropogenic global warming and an oil industry shill who challenges it, and conclude, "Well, who knows?" leaving viewers with the impression of a 50/50, up-for-grabs debate, even though 99% of the climatologists on Earth accept global warming as a reality. Similarly, you find one pundit to call antiwar activists and bloggers "a leftist jihad" who orchestrated some sort of sneaky unfair internet assassination of poor Joe Lieberman, and another who merely attributes his loss to a vague and mysterious "wave of anti-incumbency" having to do with everything from Katrina to Jack Abramoff, and no one notes that opposition to the war in Iraq has now become the majority position in America.

TWILIGHT OF THE ASSHOLES

Contributions of the World's Religions

"Part I: Christianity," October 4th 2006

This week begins a series of "Contributions of the World's Religions," which will likely culminate in my execution. Would-be assassins, please take note: webmaster Dave is no longer formally affiliated with this website.

First of all, a disclaimer (not to be misconstrued as an apology): I am aware that it is only the fringe dingbats in any religion who ever get airtime—the Creationists and fag-bashers, the militant Zionists and Jihadists, the angry chanting mobs. Most religious people are neither fanatical nor cruel, and most of the world's religions have produced great philosophers, scholars, humanitarians, and patrons of the arts. My own mother is an elder in the Presbyterian Church and does such useful work as nursing in Guatemala and Columbia. But I believe that well-brought-up people behave decently without any metaphysical carrots or sticks to bribe or threaten them. And congenital assholes would find some other dogma to be homicidal fanatics about without religion (see, for persuasive illustration, the body counts of noted atheists Mao, Stalin, and Hitler). But I still maintain that nothing fills people with such dangerous (and annoying) certitude as the illusion that they have some inside knowledge of the Will of God. Religion may well be an ineradicable aberration of the human mind, like war, something that we'll always have with us. But then that's what people have thought about most great evils in history, from smallpox to slavery. I'd just like to try doing without it for a while and seeing how it goes.

Regular readers will know of my longtime antipathy to Christianity. I must hasten to emphasize that this is not because Christianity is any more pernicious than most of the other world's religions. I single it out for scorn most often because it's the one I know best from personal experience and because, more importantly, it's the one that dominates the culture I live in. I make fun of it more than I do of Hinduism for the same reason I make fun of America more than Pakistan, and men more than women. My own religious upbringing wasn't traumatic or damaging, as it seems to have been for a lot of children of Protestant Fundamentalists or Catholics, many of whom seem to turn into Satanist death-metal musicians or promiscuous self-mutilating Wiccan priestesses, respectively, in reaction. My own most damning complaint about Christianity is that it was so boring. I had to go to an hour of church followed by an hour of Sunday School every week of my life until I left for college, and I never sat through another minute of it after that if I could avoid it.

But I would still bear Christianity no real ill will if I could just put it behind me and forget about it, like math class and Top 40 music and TV. I would tolerate Christians with the same patronizing indulgence that I do toddlers and street schizophrenics if they weren't constantly trying to make their delusions mandatory for the rest of us. I'm not the sort to go around spitefully disillusioning people and proselytizing for atheism—it would feel as gratuitously mean as telling children that Santa isn't real or they're going to die someday. I'm happy to humor the childish. But when they start trying to ban contraception or push around homosexuals or force educated people to keep straight faces when they talk about "intelligent design," it's like: sorry, the grownups are trying to talk here. Go play with your imaginary friend a while.

Christianity

WHOLESOME TV PROGRAMMING

A THOUSAND FUCKING YEARS OF ANNUNCIATIONS, CRUCIFIXIONS, PIÉTAS AND ASCENSIONS.

WITCH ELIMINATION

MAKING SEX DIRTY

Contributions of the World's Religions

"Part II: Islam," October 11th, 2006

In the last month Berlin's Deutsche Oper cancelled a production of *Idomeneo*, which was to have featured the decapitated heads of Christ, Mohammed, and the Buddha, for fear of violent reprisals (one assumes from the notoriously savage and vengeful Buddhists) and Muslims around the world once again observed their most sacred rite, angry chanting in the streets, in response to the Pope's citation of a medieval scholar's condemnation of Islam. I have as much respect for the Pope's opinions as I do for Britney Spears' husband's, but I am also getting a little tired of the angry chanting in response to every perceived symbolic slight from the West. I don't like seeing free societies censoring themselves because they're so skittish about the threat of violence from touchy Muslims. What a bunch of bullies and crybabies. Let me extend to the Muslim world a belated welcome to modern society, where we all get offended every day and we've just had to toughen up about it. Are any of you familiar with the Western saying about "sticks and stones?" Not to be confused with the traditional Islamic nursery rhyme:

Sticks and stones
May both be thrown
At the victim of a rapist

But guns and bombs
Are the only balm
For the insults of a Papist.

Five years ago I was thinking of doing a cartoon trashing Islam, but my saner friend Megan restrained me. But now I've reconsidered, reasoning: screw it. Islam did drag the warring, barbaric Arab world into the comparative enlightenment of the eleventh century, but it's also kept it there ever since. The last time Islamic culture really had anything going was in the middle ages, when they built some beautiful mosques, invented zero, named the stars and kept the work of Aristotle in print while Europeans were pretty much just plowing.

These days, though, it's become even more moronic and thuggish than Christianity. Its adherents have made the praise of God, *Allahu Akbar,* as familiar and beloved the world round as that comforting homily *Arbeit Macht Frei.* It's a faith that thrives in impoverished nations with authoritarian governments and crappy-to-nonexistent educational systems, like a rot flourishing in darkness, whereas Christianity, which was once just as lethal a religion, is largely contained within democracies that have institutionalized the separation of church and state. Which separation turns out to have been instituted for good reason; our founding fathers had noticed that when the absolutist dogmatism of the church was allied with the armed force of the state, the first order of business was invariably to start killin' folks.

If this is a war between cultures, and we have to pick sides, obviously I'm on ours—"ours" meaning the side of secular, pluralistic democracy. But I have as much invested in the battle between the apocalyptic Christians and the fanatic Muslims as I do in the ancient and tedious conflict between Sunnis and Shiites.

Islam

ANGRY CHANTING

JIHAD

FATWAHS

THOSE EXCELLENT BEAN PIES

Contributions of the World's Religions

"Part III: Judaism," October 18th 2006

Soon after filing this cartoon I had the opportunity to view an astonishing private collection of political cartoons, among them rare pamphlets of anti-Semitic cartoons published in Nazi-occupied Holland and Vichy France. These included caricatures of the Big Four: Stalin, Churchill, FDR, and The Jew—a thick-lipped, hook-nosed businessman—licking their chops as they divvied up Europe. This same leering figure of The Jew was depicted pulling strings behind the scenes to set the war in motion. (After all, think about it: who were the chief beneficiaries of the Second World War? That's right: *The Jews.*) I have no wish to join in this ancient and execrable tradition, and I hope it's clear that I'm going comparatively easy on Judaism, a tiny and marginal religion that's suffered enough what with the Holocaust and being shut out of country clubs without being further insulted by cartoonists. I was much harder on both the Christians, who, for all their martyrish whining, enjoy cultural dominance in this country, and the Muslims, who are batshit.

Still, there's no letting anyone off the hook in this cartoon series. The Jews have their own silly rules (any belief system that proscribes bacon is self-evidently discredited) and delusional claims (like their divinely appointed historical centrality, a belief shared by 100% of human societies). But at least they don't have any hooey about an afterlife. And they are generally a sane and peaceable people, except when the question of the Middle East arises, on which subject many of them suddenly reveal themselves to be homicidally insane. Otherwise intelligent and reasonable people will explain that the Palestinians aren't really civilized human beings like we are and complain bitterly about the blatant pro-Palestinian bias in the U.S. media, so that all you can do is nod and say thoughtful, sympathetic things like "Mm" while thinking up ways to change the topic or reasons why you have to leave. (My friend Ben, who has traveled frequently in China, tells me that mainland Chinese have a similar pocket of rabid irrationality regarding the issue of Taiwan; even the most intelligent, liberal, gentle, and humorous of them all agree that if the Taiwanese ever try to formally break away, they will nuke their asses without hesitation.) Why the people who built New York City and Hollywood are willing to fight to the death to keep a parched strip of land whose top tourist attractions include The Dead Sea is one of many things that I Would Not Understand because I am without faith.

Shortly after drawing this I had a pastrami sandwich at Katz's deli. For me, the pastrami sandwich at Katz's rivals the cathedral at Chartres and the Blue Mosque among the finest contributions of the world's religions.

Judaism

SUPERMAN

UNSURPASSED FASHION SENSE

HATS, →
100% OF THE TIME.
(NEVER SHOULD'VE
GONE OUT OF STYLE.)

THE HAIR,
NOT SO MUCH. ←

BUT I DO NOT KID
WHEN I SAY I COVET
THESE SMOKING
JACKETS. →

PASTRAMI

DISCOVERED BASIC SCIENTIFIC PRINCIPLES OF MONOTHEISM, UNIQUE IMPORTANCE OF JEWS

Contributions of the World's Religions

"Part IV: Hinduism," November 1st 2006

I have an old childhood affection for the Hindu pantheon, inculcated by a copy of the *Bahagavad-Gita* given to our family by airport Hare Krishnas when I was a child. It was heavily annotated by the guru who was then head of the International Society for Krsna Consciousness, who resembled a bullfrog. Every one of his annotations, regardless of the verse to which it was appended, explicated that verse as a command to chant the name of Krsna all day long. Even at age ten I could see that his interpretation was monomaniacally narrow, slanted to support his own literal-minded practice, and had little to do with the text. What blew my young mind were the color plate illustrations. These exerted the same kind of absorbing fascination on me as did some of the trippier Jack Kirby *Fantastic Four* comics and certain psychedelically inspired album covers. The Hindu pantheon was like a kind of superhero team—men with blue or gold or green skin, multiple faces and arms, and animals' heads, men wielding maces and tridents and axes and conch shells, breathing fire, blowing bubbles containing galaxies.

I particularly remember an allegorical illustration of a man on the stairway leading up to salvation and down to perdition. As is always the case in such illustrations (and in real life), the path to eternal bliss looks as bland as a 'Fifties ad, but the road to damnation is dramatic and fascinating, full of intriguing characters. Personifications of anger, lust, and envy were trying to lure or tug the guy downward to spiritual destruction. Anger is the one who really caught my imagination: like Charles Manson with blue skin and a flaming mane of red hair and a villainous red moustache, blazing red eyes, and a pair of big red pirate pants. I unabashedly loved, and still love, Garuda, the messenger of the gods, half-man and half-eagle, who is basically Hawkman. The story about Garuda commanding the ocean to give a sparrow her eggs back chokes me up as reliably as the *The Selfish Giant* or *Blade Runner*.

But then you also get the caste system and suttee. Why does it always seem to be such a short step from belief in a divine creator to setting women on fire?

Hinduism

MOST FUCKED-UP PANTHEON SINCE THE LEGION OF DOOM

"TAKING IT WITH YOU"

CONCEPT OF REINCARNATION

Contributions of the World's Religions

"Part V: Buddhism," November 8th 2006

I admit it: I took it easy on the Buddhists. It's the only religion that seems to be based on reason and insight rather than faith. It at least goes to the trouble of making some sense. It's the one that was beginning to appeal to me in my late teens, after I'd lost interest in Christianity but before I got distracted for a couple of decades by girls and drink. They seem to be the only religion that can seem to resolve a theological dispute without resorting to torture, pogroms, or massacre. The Dalai Lama explains that if they were to find that their metaphysical beliefs were to be contradicted by modern physics, why, they would simply have to alter their beliefs. Contrast this to the undignified behavior of fundamentalist Christians, who invent convoluted explanations to explain that the Devil planted fossils to confuse us or demonstrate that the six "days" of Creation in Genesis, if you throw in the Doppler shift divided by quantum something-or-other, actually correspond to our Earth days times one trillion.

And my personal experience with Buddhists has been impressive: a Buddhist friend of mine, having had occasion to feel wronged by me, was neither reproachful nor vindictive; instead he felt sorry for me. One of my favorite jokes by the late comedian Bill Hicks was about some thuggish good old boys in Alabama who waited for him outside the stage door after one of his stand-up routines. "Hey, buddy, c'mere!" They yelled at him. "We didn't like that joke you told about Christians in there. We're Christians!" "So," he said, in laconic challenge: "Forgive me."

A reader wrote in to the *City Paper* after I ran Part I of this series to complain that I ought not to have depicted the crucifixion. In fact I hadn't; what she mistook for a crucifixion was my pastiche of a stained-glass representation of the Annunciation. Later I hesitated before running Part III, Islam, and asked my editor whether he had any concerns about potential angry chanting, firebombing of the paper's offices, or internet beheadings of editorial staff. He said that as long as I stayed away from any depictions of You-Know-Who (blessed be his name) we should be all right. I was pleased that this week's cartoon provided occasion to depict both the crucifixion and Mohammed. The race is on: lynch mob vs. Fatwah! I await the winner.

Buddhism

ONLY DEITY WHOSE BELLY CAN BE RUBBED FOR LUCK

NO   **NO**   **YES**

BEST HATS, NO CONTEST   "NOT KILLING PEOPLE" AS RELIGIOUS OBSERVANCE

The Democrats' great electoral sweep may have come too late to revive my hope in democracy or faith in humanity. I gave up on my fellow Americans as irredeemable troglodytes two years ago, and now that it finally seem to have penetrated the dim national consciousness, like light arriving from a long-dead star, that the war in Iraq isn't going so well, and that the Republicans aren't as responsible and virtuous as they say they are, I find I just can't care anymore. It's like your ex-girlfriend wanting to get back together with you after she dumped you for someone else. The swing voters didn't turn against the war because it was trumped up on lies, or because it's killed half a million people for no reason, but because we're not winning.

Ultimately, I think, it was not Iraq but Katrina that destroyed most Americans' faith in this administration's ability to conduct the war. They lost a war right here on American soil, in plain, unspinnable view of the national media, leaving thousands of our fellow citizens looking like refugees from Darfur. It was only then that most people suddenly realized what had been obvious to liberals for years: these guys have no fucking idea what they're doing.

Many pundits in the national media are imagining that the Bush administration must be cowed by the election results, and that the new realities of the political landscape are going to dictate a more conciliatory attitude. What country have these people been living in for the last six years? Do they remember how Bush was going to be "a uniter, not a divider," or how his administration was going to have to "tack to the center" after they lost the popular vote in 2000? Why is anyone still attributing conventional political motives or strategy to this administration? They're less like a governing body than a cult holed up in a desert compound waiting for the apocalypse. They don't care about consensus or compromise, about "reaching out to the other side," or about the will of the electorate. The new realities of the political landscape don't dictate shit to them; they have never been, nor are they now, members of "the reality-based community." Reality is for perfessors to study on. The Bush administration creates its own reality, one casualty at a time. They are digging a mass grave called History.

Still, there's no denying it was a relief to wake up the day after an election and not be a loser for the first time in recent memory, and a cruel pleasure to savor the sight of the weeping Santora.[1] The dependable thing about Republicans is that, skilled though they are at seizing power, they inevitably destroy themselves as soon as they're allowed to wield it. They just can't help it; they can't bear pretending to be decent or civilized one second longer than they have to, and they tear off the pleasant smiling human masks and start devouring the handicapped live on national TV. After only six years in power they've succeeded in making the name "Republican" synonymous with venality, warmongering, and sexual molestation. Lincoln Chaffee, a relatively progressive Republican, said again and again in this campaign that his constituents told him that they liked and supported him, they knew how much he'd done for their state, but they just couldn't vote for him this year. That "(R)" appended to his name might as well have been a swastika. The party's reputation has been more irredeemably sullied than at any time since Watergate—except that by the end of Watergate even congressional Republicans had enough integrity to refuse to support a president who'd been clearly exposed as a bungling criminal. This Republican congress remained obedient lapdogs until they realized, too late, that their leader had become a political liability.

I only hope the Democrats won't squander their mandate and waste the taxpayers' time and money with a lot of pointless, vindictive investigations. Ha, ha! Just kidding. I hope they launch investigations and hold hearings and appoint special prosecutors, relentlessly probing into the buildup to the war and Cheney's closed energy hearings and Halliburton and the NSA spying program and Abu Ghraib and Guantanamo, until every last member of Bush's administration has resigned, gone to jail, or hanged himself. The Democrats have been treated with unbelievable contempt for the last six years—pushed around, shoved aside, mocked, and vilified as weaklings and traitors. To quote noted political strategist The Thing: "It's clobberin' time."

---

1 A reference to the family of Rick Santorum, a truly dislikable Pennsylvania Republican who'd made a crusade out of anti-homosexual bigotry.

Notice how Creationism is only ever treated seriously in news stories about the political controversy surrounding evolution, never in actual science stories. When this week's science articles about astronomers' precisely measuring the rate of acceleration of the universe's expansion through observations of supernovæ mentioned that the universe began its acceleration about 6.3 billion years ago, none bothered to include the disclaimer, "unless, as Creationists argue, the universe is only six thousand years old, in which case the acceleration is recalculated to have begun in 1956." In the story about the sequencing of the Neanderthal genome it was mentioned that the evolutionary lineages of Neanderthals split from that of humans about half a million years ago, and that they share between 99.5 and 99.9% of their DNA with us, with no mention of the hypothesis that they were instead the descendants of Cain. This is because science reporters, displaying the blatant secular bias endemic to the liberal media, only ever talk to scientists, and not glossolaliac dingbats or busybodies on small-town school boards. Science stories are just for grownups, so they don't need to make obligatory reference to Santa Claus and his eight prancing reindeer.

The poor Neanderthals had a nice thing going in Europe for hundreds of thousands of years until invading hordes of hateful hairless little *homo sapiens* showed up and overran the place, like a relentless wave of gentrifying yuppies buying up a blue-collar neighborhood, turning South Baltimore into Federal Hill, driving up real estate prices and property taxes, bringing with them pestilence and coffee houses, hunting off all the game and eliminating pitchers at the local bars. Gradually the Neanderthal were driven westward across Europe until they were holed up in western Spain and Portugal, where they died out about 28,000 years ago. Nobody knows exactly what happened to them; some scientists speculate that they may have interbred with human

beings, and looking around the supermarket in C____ County I can see evidence to support this. We won't know for certain until the genomic analysis is complete. But I do have my own theory, based on what little I know of more recent human history. I think the same thing happened to them that happened to the American Indians and Tasmanians when Europeans showed up: we exterminated them. We're a killer species, like sharks or ebola. Hard to know how much we'd owe them in reparations at this point. Maybe the Riviera. On the other hand I probably shouldn't get all maudlin and P.C. about the plight of the noble oppressed Neanderthal, since if my ancestors hadn't wiped them out I'd be living in Africa now, where there are leopards.

"Dark energy makes us nervous," one physicist admitted this week. I would go so far as to say it creeps me out. We know it exists, but nobody has any idea what it is, except that it exerts a repulsive force that's causing the universe's expansion to accelerate, and it accounts for *73 percent of the mass in the universe.* Anytime you hear some expert or commentator on TV or the radio acting confidently as though he knew what he was talking about, bear in mind: we live in a universe where *nobody knows what 73 percent of it is.* My own theory: *ha'ants!*

On the subject of people pretending to know what they're talking about, "health news" has always seemed fluffy and dubious to me, each new study seeming to contradict the last, most of them announcing some amazing new finding that will Let You Live Longer! We're so terrified of death in this country we'll buy any bullshit claim to extend longevity. No wonder it was so easy for one terrorist attack to turn us all into blubbering fascists, eager to forfeit our rights, clamoring for the blood of innocents in revenge, begging the Daddy party to get those bad men and keep us safe. One of science's most solidly reliable findings, consistently corroborated by 100% of the available data, is that you are going to die. My advice is: drink up.

Recent Scientific Discoveries

GENETICISTS ARE ANALYZING THE ENTIRE GENOME OF THE NEANDERTHAL!

ASTRONOMERS HAVE CONFIRMED THE EXISTENCE OF DARK ENERGY AND EINSTEIN'S DISCARDED "COSMOLOGICAL CONSTANT."

BIOLOGISTS HAVE FOUND THAT RESVERATROL, A COMPONENT IN RED WINE, INCREASES LONGEVITY AND ENDURANCE.

...AND CREATIONISTS SPECULATE THAT THE "SERPENT" IN THE GARDEN OF EDEN MAY ACTUALLY HAVE BEEN AN ALLOSAUR!

"Secret Vices of the Liberals," November 29th 2006

Every time another Social Conservative is exposed as a hypocrite and a fraud, which lately seems to be semiweekly, I pose the same question: must every last social conservative in America be publicly revealed as a closet homosexual, compulsive gambler, alcoholic or drug addict before the whole rotten, posturing, sanctimonious movement is finally discredited? I asked this when the televangelists of the Eighties all turned out to be trailer-park whoremongers; when William Bennett was revealed to have blown millions of dollars in Vegas casinos; when Bill O'Reilly had to pay millions of dollars in hush money to cover up the crude bullying come-ons he made to an employee; when Rush Limbaugh went to rehab for painkillers, and again when he was arrested at an airport bound for a sex tour of the Dominican Republic with a suitcase full of Viagra. I wearily posed it again most recently when Mark Foley was caught writing dirty e-mails to sixteen-year-olds and Ted Haggard confessed to buying crank from his regular male prostitute.

The answer to this question is: evidently so. Each time, the same tedious, predictable drama of Condemnation and Expulsion has to be acted out, the body politic purged of yet another impurity. The latest player in this tired scenario, Ted Haggard, moved within only a few days from Act I, Flat Denial, through Act II, Partial Admission—feeble Clintonian evasions even more embarrassing than the whole sordid truth would have been—to Act III, Unconditional Confession. In a few years he may be able to jump back on the evangelical gravy train by being Born Again Again, a redeemed sinner ministering to those who share the same problems. In the meantime, the rest of the pious mob shake their heads, pick up their stones, and resume throwing.

I do not join in the universal condemnation of these men and their timid little crimes. Mark Foley seemed creepy and pathetic, but hardly the inhuman monster his former colleagues fell all over each other to recoil from and abominate. My first reaction to the Haggard scandal was that Michael Jones, Haggard's hired escort, had exercised execrable professional ethics and bad business sense by ratting out one of his clients to the national media. The public destruction of these men delights me not because they were degenerates, but because they were hypocrites.

Social conservatives are inevitably undone not by their perversion, but by their repression. Foley, a bachelor in his fifties still afraid his parents might realize he is gay, made furtive, drunken, clumsy advances toward the most inappropriate possible targets. If he had been a little braver—or a Democrat—he could've comfortably cruised the bars of DuPont Circle looking for young men who'd be impressed by his power and status. Which would still be sleazy, but would, as they say in Washington, be going through accepted channels. And poor Haggard's mistake was to hire the only hustler in Denver with a social conscience.

These men are not exceptions or betrayals to the cause of social conservatism; they epitomize it. It is not by some ironic coincidence that Foley chaired the Missing and Exploited Children's Caucus, or that Haggard was one of the leaders of the crusade to ban gay marriage. It's called "projection." What social conservatives loathe most passionately in others are the weaknesses they're trying most desperately to repress in themselves. A 1996 University of Georgia study indicated a clear correlation between homophobia and repressed homoerotic arousal. Suzy Spencer, an author who's conducting a survey on sex in America, has found that a lot of good old boys who like to think of themselves as 100% straight are secretly meeting at truck stops to suck each other's cocks. I've noticed, on road trips

Secret Vices of the Liberals

NOAM CHOMSKY
LINGUIST, INTELLECTUAL

IN THE END, ANCHAL'S LACK OF SELF-CONFIDENCE IS WHAT GOT HER SENT HOME.

HOW TYPICAL OF TYRA: PROJECTING RESPONSIBILITY FOR OPPRESSION ONTO THE VICTIM.

HUGE FAN OF "AMERICA'S NEXT TOP MODEL"

RICHARD DAWKINS
BIOLOGIST, ATHEIST

O MY GOD I AM HEARTILY SORRY FOR HAVING OFFENDED THEE AND I DETEST ALL MY SINS BECAUSE I DREAD THE LOSS OF HEAVEN AND THE PAINS OF HELL BUT MOST OF ALL BECAUSE THEY OFFEND THEE MY GOD WH

SPLAKK

SELF-FLAGELLATION

HOWARD ZINN
HISTORIAN

REMEMBER THE RAISIN! HOZZAH!

WAR OF 1812 REËNACTOR

BILL CLINTON
FORMER PRESIDENT

YES — BETTER TO FACE IMPEACHMENT THAN TO ADMIT THAT THAT SEMEN COULD NOT HAVE BEEN MINE.

IMPOTENT FOR THE LAST 15 YEARS

"Secret Vices of the Liberals," cont.

through the Red States, that billboards admonishing **"REAL MEN DON'T USE PORN"** and spittle-flecked radio sermons in support of **"righteous hate"** are most densely concentrated in the same areas as advertisements for porn emporia and massage parlors. Hysterical, militant virtue seems to flourish in direct proportion to the preponderance of temptation and the weakness of the local will. It's not the godless degenerates of the coastal cities that evangelicals are really screaming at in reproach; it's themselves.

How many more stern, immaculate preachers of Moral Values have to be exposed as chickenhawks and crankheads before it becomes axiomatic that anyone who's obsessed with the looming menace of the Homosexual Agenda is a closeted homosexual, that anyone publicly preoccupied with sexual predators and the safety of our children is a child molester, just as we can fairly assume that anyone driving a Hummer is also anxiously answering spam for penis enlargement? Why, after all, would someone imagine that homosexuality represented a threat

to the institution of marriage unless it posed an immediate and personal threat to his own?

Conservatism claims to hold a realistic, unsentimental view of human nature, advocating a form of government that accommodates people as they really are, as opposed to those idealistic liberals who think that well-intentioned social engineering can legislate them into a better shape. And yet conservatives only ever seem to apply this political philosophy to aspects of human nature like selfishness, greed, and callousness toward the suffering of our fellows–what is called "the free market"—and not morally abhorrent aberrations like sexuality. Why can't conservatives accept the implications of their own ideology? Human beings are weak-willed and lecherous. We want what is bad for us. We adore our vices. No human institution in five thousand years has been able to eradicate them. Which is really the more implausible utopian scheme— reducing greenhouse emissions or Just Saying No to Drugs? Socialized medicine or teen abstinence?

Republican Sex Toys

THE INVADER*

$44.00

THE BISHOP

$32.00

"THE SUPREME"

$475.00

THERE'S NO RIGHT TO PRIVACY ON *THIS BABY!*
AS THE BENCH TILTS FARTHER AND FARTHER
TO THE RIGHT, THE *SLIPPERY SLOPE®* GETS
STEEPER AND THE WOMAN'S BODY IS VIOLATED.
NINE ATTACHMENTS, RANGING IN SIZE
FROM THE SOUTER TO THE THOMAS.

THE DOWNSIZER
PENILE REDUCTION SYSTEM

$42.00

THE PRIVATIZER

$35.00

THE CHASTIZER

$27.00

THE KISSINGER

NO LONGER AVAILABLE

*FULL STRAP-ON CAPABILITY

INFLATIBLE WELFARE MOTHER
"SHE *BEGS* FOR *MORE!*"

I'LL GIVE YOU SOMETHIN' FOR NOTHIN'!

$57.99

OUR EXCLUSIVE Rumsfeld® COLLECTION

SAY, "UNCLE SAM," BABY!

O HELP! INFAMY! YOU CAN'T DO THIS! I HAVE RIGHTS!

A VARIETY OF "UNIQUE" AND "INNOVATIVE"
METHODS OF MAKING YOUR FAVORITE
DETAINEE BEG FOR CLEMENCY.
IT'S ONLY TORTURE IF YOU DO IT RIGHT!

November 30th, 2005

We have arrived at an historic moment here at *The Pain*: sitting down to write this week's artist's statement, the artist finds he has nothing to say. I have no new policy initiatives to present on Iraq. Panel 1 summarizes what has been my official position on Iraq for the last three years. I am uncomfortably aware that I am, as they say, not contributing anything constructive to the debate.

On the other hand, I tried contributing to the debate back before the invasion. "What the fuck?" I argued. "Invade Iraq? *Why* exactly would we do that? That's a terrible idea." Hundreds of thousands of my compatriots and I flooded the streets of Manhattan, and completely encircled the White House in DC, to protest the invasion. (You may not have seen this on TV; it only happened in real life.) We silly knee-jerk peaceniks trotted out our usual defeatist, conspiratorial rhetoric: the war had nothing to do with 9/11, it was based on lies for suspect motives, it would turn into a quagmire, it would confirm the Arab world's most paranoid fears about America and only make them hate us more, mew mew mew. We got called a bunch of America-hating hippies and accused of giving aid and comfort to the enemy.

We antiwar demonstrators didn't *know* that there were no Weapons of Mass Destruction in Iraq, at least not with the same degree of absolute certainty that our opponents knew that there were. Of course we were at a disadvantage, not having access to the highly classified false intelligence on which our elected leaders based their decisions. Yet the fact that we were right and the Bush administration was wrong suggests, at the very least, that any Democrat who voted to "authorize the use of force"—the current euphemism for "having people killed"—was even more credulous than the kinds of people who believe that drum circles and giant puppets are feared in the corridors of power. This is the most generous interpretation of their motives. A less charitable one would be that they were so cowed by political pressure that they signed off on the deaths of thousands of Americans, and hundreds of thousands of Iraqis, out of fear of looking weak or unpatriotic.

This is not just to say, "Told you so," although that is one of the few joyless consolations available to the left under Bush. After an historical fiasco of this enormity, it's worth looking back to take note of who actually knew what they were talking about and who turns out, in retrospect, to have been completely full of shit. So let's just say this once, in print, and then we can all quit pointing fingers and playing the blame game, move on and look forward: we far-left antiwar liberals were right about everything. Invading Iraq was a mistake. The war is a quagmire. Our own intelligence agencies warn that it's recruited more terrorists and made us less safe. And now we're stuck there. We told you so.

A few months ago I did a cartoon semiseriously proposing the revolutionary new policy of Trying to Win, which would involve, among other things, increasing troop levels. Of course doing this would involve the unspeakable thing that no politician even wants to think about, much less mention in public—reinstating a draft. Sending *rich* people's kids over there? But if we really want to achieve anything resembling "victory" in Iraq this may be our only option. I'm an old guy now and no longer know anybody of draft age, so this is easy for me to say. Could I accept even one person I know being killed or maimed in the cause of trying to salvage George Bush's pointless war?

This Thanksgiving I met a young man in the army who's being shipped first to Hawaii for six months but then to Afghanistan. He was a smart, interesting guy; we talked about cartooning, gunnery, movies, and military history, about which I know a fair amount just because I am a boy. He likes studying the big classical battles of antiquity that play out like chess games; I am a sucker for the stories of Thermopylæ and Cannæ. The idea of people like him being sent to Iraq makes me want to wait for Paul Wolfowitz in a dark alley with a jar of Vaseline and a very large American flag on a pole—the kind with the carved brass eagle on top, its wings spread.

I read some anxious speculation this morning that this war may define Bush's presidency in the same way that Vietnam

What's Your Iraq Strategy?

"STAYING THE COURSE"

TRYING VERY HARD NEVER TO THINK ABOUT IT AT ALL

REINSTALL SADDAM AND GET OUT

GET CRACKING ON THIRTY-YEAR CAMPAIGN OF BLAMING DEFEAT ON LIBERAL MEDIA

defined Lyndon Johnson's. My own analysis is: d'ya think? Except that LBJ is also remembered, by those dwindling few dweebs who remember anything that happened in the dim years before the internet, as a master politician who rammed through civil rights legislation and the Great Society social programs, while George Bush will also be remembered as the idiot boss's son who cut taxes for his campaign donors and let the poor wade through their own sewage for a week after a hurricane. Perhaps his presidential library should be located in Fallujah.

Already we're hearing the first grumblings about how the liberals and the media are the ones subverting American efforts in Iraq. I'm afraid we're going to have to listen to exactly the same dumb gullible assholes who supported this war angrily explain to us why it's our fault we lost it for the next fifty years. We'll read it in labored, stentorian newspaper columns by blowhards transcribing Republican talking points like kids copying their reports out of the World Book; in ponderous, vapid tomes written by impressively credentialed dim bulbs at right-wing think thanks; and, most of all, we'll hear it from every Fox-watching redneck who still doesn't understand how his country turned into just another bankrupt has-been empire.

The most infamous use of this scapegoating tactic was the "stabbed in the back" slogan repeated throughout Germany after their defeat in World War I. The German armies hadn't been defeated on the battlefield, no—they'd been Stabbed in the Back by certain subversive political elements on the home front (You Know Who). We've had to listen to a tired variation on this story about Vietnam for the last thirty years. There are still guys in dive bars across America telling anyone who'll listen, which isn't me, that it was the liberal media who lost that war.

An alternative explanation is that it was the Vietnamese who won it. In the Errol Morris documentary *The Fog of War*, the former Foreign Minister of Vietnam explains to the former Secretary of Defense Robert McNamara:

> "Mr. McNamara, you must never have read a history book. If you had, you'd know we weren't pawns of the Chinese or the Russians. McNamara, didn't you know that? Don't you understand that we have been fighting the Chinese for a thousand years? We were fighting for our independence. And we would fight to the last man. And we were determined to do so. And no amount of bombing, no amount of U.S. pressure would ever have stopped us."

Iraq is not Vietnam, but the pertinent similarity is that the American troops are mercenaries (albeit well-trained and highly motivated ones), whereas our enemies are motivated by ideals (albeit depraved ones). Therefore, we will give up before they do. In the meantime: car bombings, IEDs, kidnappings, beheadings, death squads disguised as police, mass graves, armless children, civil war. Fucking George Bush, man.

This is what my friends and I are always reduced to whenever the subject of Iraq comes up—shaking our heads and clutching our brows and cursing, rendered speechless by the evil and incompetence of it all. But despite the bitter fantasies of conservatives, not even the most avid Bush haters are able take any satisfaction in seeing our most pessimistic predictions vindicated. It's just too awful. The only thing that still sporadically rouses me to livid outrage, that seizes me with the impulse to drive down to the White House and clutch the iron bars of the fence and scream obscenities 'til my throat is raw, is the fact that none of it ever needed to happen at all.

December 20th, 2007

Seeing Saddam Hussein strung up by a shouting lynch mob last week achieved what one might have thought was impossible: sympathy for Saddam. Which is ridiculous, obscene—like feeling sorry for Pinochet or Idi Amin. That dirty back-alley execution epitomized the fiasco we've made of every single aspect of Iraqi occupation. Saddam's trial was a farce, he was convicted on what was, for him, a relatively minor massacre, and he was executed in bloodthirsty haste before he could be held to account for any of his more infamous crimes, like the gassing of the Kurds. The execution was handled with the efficiency and decorum that distinguish all such occasions throughout the Arab world. I still fondly recall the ghastly, emaciated corpse of the Ayatollah Khomeini being tumbled naked out of its coffin and flopping among the raving mobs of mourners like a punk surfing a mosh pit.

I can't help but feel almost sorry for the neoconservatives who masterminded this invasion. They finally got everything they ever wished for, and it all turned into a nightmare. It's a big grisly Monkey's Paw for Red America. And, unlike the horrified parents in "The Monkey's Paw," who can hear their son's mangled corpse shambling toward the door, coming home, they're shit out of wishes.

Things did not go unexpectedly, inexplicably wrong in Iraq; they went predictably, inevitably wrong. Although many of the hacks and apparatchiks who advocated this war were academics, none of them seems to have learned the lesson that utopians and revolutionaries and would-be conquerors have learned over and over throughout the centuries, mostly at the cost of other people's lives; that history never turns out like it's supposed to. It's always stranger and messier, and it never, ever ends.

I find I miss Saddam, in the same way I miss Donald Rumsfeld, or like I missed Luca Brasi after he was killed off in *The Godfather*; he was just too good a character to lose. That Saddam!—remember "the mother of all battles," that creepy photo-op with the terrified hostage boy, the softporn science-fiction-novel-cover paintings that adorned his sleazy bachelor-pad palaces? That freeze-frame of Donald Rumsfeld shaking hands with Saddam back in the Reagan years seems more and more the iconic equal of that photo of Nixon shaking hands with Elvis. I'm starting to realize that someday, after this terrible time is over, we're actually going to miss these guys. We'll be like those aging hippies who long for the golden age when they had Strangelovean villains like Nixon and Kissinger in the White House to hate. We'll shake our heads as we reminisce about the Dick-Tracy rogues' gallery who filled our daily headlines: the macho tinpot megalomania of Saddam, the bureaucratic word salad of Rumsfeld. What cartoonist could have invented the insane hair of Kim Jong Il or the graven sneer of Dick Cheney? Most of all, we'll look back with something like wonder at the routinely jaw-dropping, unparodyable imbecility of the smirking boy-king George W. Bush. As Crazy Earl says in *Full Metal Jacket*: "When we rotate back to the world, we're gonna miss not havin' anybody around who's worth shootin'."

I just couldn't let Saddam die. I know the man was a brutal dictator and a butcher of men, and I ought not to celebrate him as a figure of fun. Partly this is just that perverse impulse in me that refuses to take seriously what everyone else regards as unassailably sacrosanct or taboo. I am inexplicably cheered by the idea of his surviving, like Elvis, in our imaginations. Perhaps he lives on as a symbol of ineradicable authoritarianism and brutality in the world, a reminder that as long as human beings are cringing hierarchical animals that defer to authority, the sociopaths among us will inevitably rise to the top. Wherever there is a country held together by fear, wherever people are raped and tortured in secret prisons and buried in mass graves, Saddam is there. Wherever we bankroll dictators and look the other way from atrocities and genocides, whenever we shake hands with devils for the sake of political expediency, Saddam is there. Wherever there is misguided and hubristic American bungling, wherever we use our military might to turn brutal dictatorships into chaotic bloodbaths, Saddam is there. Saddam will be with us always.

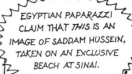

I've often said that the main challenge facing political humorists these days is to keep ahead of the absurdity curve as each day's news outstrips the previous day's attempts at parody. I've learned that on the day Saddam Hussein was executed, some Iraqis claimed to see his face in the moon. Also, Saddam Hussein's sister is rumored to have hired *a sorceress* to render Saddam *invisible*. So now there is an *invisible Saddam Hussein* at large. Once again reality shames me with the paucity of my imagination.

My colleague Tom Hart and I agreed over Belgian Ales this week that we both feel we've already drawn all the best cartoons there are to be done about the current political situation. He'd suggested I draw something about the proposed "surge" in troop level—a reinstatement of the draft, maybe the conscription of all the frat guys and bridge-and-tunnelers we see drinking in Manhattan every Friday and Saturday night, me cashing in on the sudden surplus of single women—but then we remembered that I'd already drawn this exact cartoon months ago. My own most elegant statement about Iraq was "The Iraq Monument," drawn back in February 2005, when the more respectable press was still gamely trying to pretend that the war might yet turn out to have been a good idea.

This is symptomatic of the terminal burnout afflicting anybody who's followed politics with passionate interest for the last six years. The political situation feels like it's remained stagnant for a long time, leavened only by the occasional absurdist atrocity. It's hard to believe this war has gone on for three years. America's involvement in World War II only lasted four years, and every day the papers were screaming with news: *Patton's tanks race across Africa! We've crossed the Rhine! VICTORY!* Unfortunately our solution to every international conflict is to try to win World War II again, which really only works once. Now, in Iraq, we're already occupying Berlin and Hitler's dead, but we still haven't won. The war just drags on and on without advances, without goals, each day's headline only another depressing new

confirmation that it's an irredeemable historic clusterfuck. This morning's: "Double Bomb Kills Scores in Baghdad."

And it doesn't look like things are going to get better any time soon. George Bush has unveiled his secret master plan for victory in Iraq: (Slightly) More of the Same. The Democrats, finally in a position to exert some control, are boldly drafting a Symbolic Nonbinding Resolution. Whenever the Democrats win an election it's always a little like when the Sea Monkeys you ordered finally arrive and turn out not to be the frolicsome homunculi illustrated in the ad but semimicroscopic brine shrimp who live about two weeks.

If George Bush were a Roman emperor he would've been put to the death of the Little Cuts a year or two ago. Unfortunately we are a civilized nation, so we have to let him condemn another thousand or so of our soldiers to pointless deaths before he can be driven into exile in the most desolate and backward of our conquered barbarian lands, Texas. (Though if he tries to drag us all into another war in Iran, as seems to be his wish, I would not be shocked if a Troubled Loner with no proven ties to the military or intelligence community were to get off a lucky shot.) Once the Democrats take the White House, *then* we'll see some changes. Just like when Nixon took over from LBJ and got us out of Vietnam as promised.

Sorry, everybody—things are bleak enough without me being such a bringdown. Let's look up from our artist's statement and around at this Lower East Side coffee shop on a chilly gray Monday morning and try to think of things to cheer us. Here's one: a girl's body never looks so lovely as when she's sitting on a backless stool, her bottom thrust out and her back arched forward, her shirt pulled up to expose the indrawn curve of her spine and those gentle sacral dimples, and, if you're very lucky, the faintest downy indentation of the gluteal cleft—the ogler's equivalent of the elusive green flash.

IN IRAQ IT IS RUMORED THAT SADDAM HUSSEIN'S DAUGHTER HIRED A SORCERER TO RENDER HIM INVISIBLE.[1] JOIN US FOR THE ADVENTURES OF

Invisible Saddam

IN IRAQ!

IN WOMEN'S LOCKER ROOMS!

IN AMERICA!

WHAT'S THAT BEHIND YOU?

[1] "IN DEATH, SADDAM FASCINATES SUPPORTERS," ALL THINGS CONSIDERED, 8 JANUARY 2007.

I'm afraid the math in panel 2 really does add up, more or less. According to nationalpriorities.org (which also provides you with a list of more earthbound spending equivalents than my own, for bleeding-heart liberal pipe dreams like education and health care), we've spent 362 billion dollars on the war in Iraq. (This figure is based only on congressional appropriations and doesn't come anywhere close to the real total, which would include private contracts.) The United States population just recently hit the 300 million mark. There are a thousand millions in a billion, so the cost of Iraq works out to over a thousand dollars per person. Which comes out to one high-end flatscreen HDTV (anywhere between $400 and $1800, depending) per person, or one hot tub (currently retailing at well over $3000) per family.

I'd really wanted to use lap dances as a unit of measure, but with lap dances still going for a mere twenty bucks a pop it'd just be too many. I mean, really: who needs twenty lap dances? As long as you're willing to debase yourself, for that price you might as well spring for a call girl. Plus I can't see this dour, prim administration springing for even one lap dance for anyone— not with the President surrounding himself with a sexless retinue of spindly lady lawyers and preaching abstinence in Africa. Now Big Bill, on the other hand... maybe that could be his pet project as First Dude in the Hillary administration, just like literacy is for Laura Bush. Lap Dances for all New Orleaneans!

I really only drew this cartoon because it afforded me an excuse to draw George Bush as a cross between Captain Nemo and Aquaman and Mr. Cheney as Saddam. It seems to me almost obscene even to mention the financial cost of the war, since that's the most paltry and unimportant of the costs we're paying

for Bush's hubris and incompetence. Do I actually care how much imaginary money of the future we're spending on Iraq? Not really—unless we consider, as here, what we could have done with it if we'd known we were going to blow it on nothing anyway. (The same way I didn't really care much the year I lost an appalling amount of virtual money on the stock market, until it occurred to me that, had I known it was just going to vanish as though it had never existed, I might as well have taken it all out in cash and used it to fuck someone like Claudia Schiffer. Only then did the true grief of acceptance set in.) But this is the concern that finally seems to have penetrated even the tough, tendony, desiccated little hearts of Republican bean-counters. Well, that and losing the elections.

It always cracks me up ("cracks me up" in the sense of infuriates and depresses me) to watch Republicans act like hardheaded, down-to-earth fiscal realists when the Democrats propose one of their pie-in-the-sky social programs—health care for children or some such shit—demanding, "How are we going to pay for this? Where's the money going to come from?" Notice they never, ever pose such questions if the money's going to go toward killing tens of thousands of foreigners. Because this would be tantamount to treason. Conservatives don't go in for social engineering when it involves giving money to poor people here—only if it means demolishing existing countries on the other side of the planet and building completely different ones in their place. Why the hell not? What's stopping us? We create our own reality! We'll be greeted as liberators. It's a New American Century! A lap dance for every Iraqi!

JUST THINK...
What We Could Have Done With the Money We Spent On Iraq

MOVED ALL AMERICANS UNDER THE SEA!

1 FLATSCREEN HDTV FOR EVERY INDIVIDUAL AMERICAN *OR* 1 HOT TUB FOR EVERY FAMILY.

GIVEN IT ALL TO SADDAM HUSSEIN IN EXCHANGE FOR STEPPING DOWN.

The dates cited in this cartoon have been double-checked. I drew Gerald Ford for the first time on December 20ᵗʰ. He died six days later. Okay, funny coincidence, but not exactly uncanny—Ford was ninety-three years old, after all, which is old even in President years. But then, on January 31ˢᵗ, I drew a generic blond bimbo sitting on Saddam Hussein's lap, toyed with the idea of making her Pamela Anderson, but then I remembered that no, Pam Anderson's already been a punchline in *Borat*, and instead decided to make her Anna Nicole Smith. Eight days later she drops dead at age thirty-nine.

Close call for Pam Anderson! It was only on a whim that I'd made that character Ana Nicole Smith, mostly because I sort of secretly liked her Trimspa ads on the New York subways. I have a very hard time telling most celebrities apart from one another (I only recently learned that Bret Farve plays baseball and Hannah Montana is fictitious), so my arbitrarily naming the character in this cartoon, unaware of the terrible power I was wielding, was like firing a shotgun blindfolded at the Golden Globes.

My cartoons are killing people. This is just like that *Twilight Zone* episode where Burgess Meredith plays the Satanic cheroot-chewing typesetter with the printing press that makes calamitous headlines come true. Obviously the next step is to test this theory, to see if it's just a crazy fluke or true cartoon voodoo. Which brings us to this cartoon's titular question.

Several candidates suggested themselves by foolishly appearing in the news: Vladimir Putin reproached the U.S. for destabilizing the world with unilateral violence, and Joe Lieberman chastised antiwar critics for demoralizing our troops. Vlad "The Impaler" Putin's one to talk about unilateral violence. He's been killing off his rivals and critics like a fucking Borgia—with *radiation*, no less. It seemed fitting that his only hope of survival

should lie in being consigned to the iron mask of Dr. Doom.

Joe Lieberman stopped being human long ago. You can still smell what's left of his soul when he gets too close. Only donations from corporate lobbyists keep him propped up and walking the halls of power, twitching and grimacing and giving the thumbs up, galvanized like a dead frog's leg into a grotesque travesty of life.

Dinesh D'Souza, for those happily ignorant of such things, is paid by conservative think tanks to be a minority and an immigrant who argues that racism no longer exists in America, and that affirmative action hurts African-Americans. He is the equivalent of the happy cartoon pig in the chef's hat who invites drivers to pull over and fill up on bar-B-Q pork.

William Wegman is my personal standard for artistic cowardice and failure. Any time I take any kind of artistic risk—drawing a cartoon I worry might be too weird or offensive or just not funny, beginning an essay without any idea of what my thesis will turn out to be, or contracting to write a screenplay, which I don't know how to do—I remind myself that the alternative is to be William Wegman. There is no uncertainty in William Wegman's life. William Wegman does not experience doubt. Every day when he wakes up, William Wegman knows exactly what he's going to do: take another photo of his motherfucking dogs. The fact that he has not yet put a bullet through his own brain and keeps breathing air and eating food and taking photos of his motherfucking dogs is some sort of testament to William Wegman's mineral insensitivity, invincible shamelessness, or just a pure mulish will to live.

If any of these people dies in the next week or so, it can mean only one thing: that I now wield the power of life and death. And then men shall fear me.

ON DECEMBER 20TH, 2006, The Pain DEPICTED PRESIDENT GERALD FORD.
ON DECEMBER 26TH HE DIED.

ON JANUARY 31ST, 2007, The Pain DEPICTED ANNA NICOLE SMITH.
ON FEBRUARY 8TH, SHE FUCKING DIED.

IT IS NOW CLEAR THAT TIM KREIDER'S PEN WEILDS THE POWER OF DEATH.
THE OBVIOUS QUESTION IS:

Who Shall I Kill Next?

VLADIMIR PUTIN

DINESH D'SOUZA

WILLIAM WEGMAN

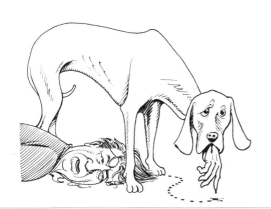

JOE LIEBERMAN

"What's Your Non-Binding Resolution?" February 28th 2007

I arrived at this week's cartoon concept by the traditional method: by sitting around drinking beers with friends. At Baltimore's Cross Street Market Big Jim announced his non-binding resolution To Never Drink Again over his first beer in two years. A chorus of bold and admirable Non-Binding Resolutions followed.

Our lives are full of non-binding resolutions, but most of us, unlike the Democrats, have too much dignity—or maybe it's just a capacity for embarrassment—to make a solemn, pompous media event out of them. You knew you could count on the Democrats to take an unequivocal purely rhetorical stand against the pointless slaughter in Iraq as soon as they were in power. At last, real leaders with the political will to put a stop to this madness, in theory! As long as we're making such ambitious non-binding resolutions, why not also resolve to give free health care to all Americans and cut greenhouse emissions and ban handguns and distribute public school funding equally among districts and provide public housing for the homeless and limit the legal rights of corporations? This could be the greatest imaginary country on earth.

What's Your Non-Binding Resolution?

TO QUIT DRINKING!

TO READ ALL THE BOOKS ON MY SHELF.

TO BREAK UP FOR GOOD THIS TIME.

TO NEVER LAUNCH ANOTHER UNILATERAL, PREEMPTIVE WAR AGAIN.

The Republican God is based on Edward Steichen's photographic portrait of J.P. Morgan, who believe it or not looks far more imperious and anthracite-eyed than my cartoon, like an anarchist's caricature of the Heartless Capitalist Bastard. The Democratic God, obviously Jerry Garcia. I'm not a deadhead—that's just how the Democratic God unavoidably comes out looking. It's a choice between the stern patriarch who enforces your nine o'clock curfew with the threat of physical punishment and watches you with an inappropriate gleam out of the corner of his eye vs. the cuddly ineffectual dude you call by his first name who wants to smoke pot with your friends.

I've always been bemused by that hardassed conservative Dad aphorism, "Money doesn't grow on trees!" Because if you think about it, that may be true, but food, clothing and shelter do. The same kinds of people who say that also like to say, "You think the world owes you a living?" Of course it doesn't; it just gives you one anyway. Or at least it used to, before some canny genius circa 10,000 B.C. came up with the idea to lock up all the food and make people pay to get it. My least favorite of these standbys is the one they like to yell out of passing car windows at the kinds of shiftless hippies who've nothing better to do than protest perfectly legitimate wars: *"Get a job!"* I always shake my fist after them and shout,*"Never!"*

I suspect that most of us have a hardassed Conservative Dad/Dick Cheney voice in our heads, constantly reproaching us for being so lazy and weak and indulgent, telling us to grow up, get a job, settle down, quit our whining, nose to the grindstone, nothing's free. It's important to keep in mind that that guy's an asshole. Arthur C. Clarke said that man's true purpose in the universe is to enjoy himself. "The goal of the future is full unemployment, so we can play," he wrote. "That's why we have to destroy the present politico-economic system." Who are you going to believe: the guy who invented communications satellites, or the kinds of people who gave us Compassionate Conservatism and the war in Iraq?

I wonder sometimes whether Muslims assume that God is punishing them for their sins with monsoons and tsunamis the way some Christians proclaimed that God was smiting us with 9/11 for our wickedness. Although we always hear this prim told-you-so talk from the dingbat Christians about everything from AIDS to the Challenger disaster being divine retribution for our social sanction of sodomy, or of Katrina as a deluge sent to destroy that Babylon on the Gulf of shameless tit-showing and daiquiri-drinking, we never seem to hear it applied to the Bible Belt itself, even though that's the region God keeps hammering relentlessly with tornadoes and floods. You'd think they'd get the message already.

"The religious right will not acknowledge what a merciful person Jesus was," despairs Kurt Vonnegut. "They enjoy punishment." Christianity has historically provided a useful text for criminals, bigots and fools. Ann Coulter notoriously summarized her reading of the book of Genesis: "God gave us the earth. We have dominion over the plants, the animals, the trees. God said, 'Earth is yours. Take it. Rape it. It's yours.'" This is what you might call a rough paraphrase, somewhat influenced by Coulter's own creepy misogyny. Some Christians would argue that this sort of thuggish interpretation ignores God's implicit charge to stewardship. Others, however, warn that environmentalism is perilously close to pantheism. In retrospect, God maybe would have been wiser to assign the job of taking care of the planet to the penguins or lemurs.

I think the twenty-first century is going to be what optimists like to call a challenge or learning experience or a time of opportunity—what the rest of us call a catastrophe. And so far Christianity seems to have nothing of any use to say about the unprecedented and overwhelming problems we face. In Africa, where businesses are losing a lot of weekly work hours to funerals, the Catholic Church is still preaching abstinence and opposing condoms. New Orleans was recently destroyed and the polar icecaps are melting, while most evangelicals in America think the most urgent issue facing the country is gay marriage.

Christianity will continue to thrive in terms of sheer numbers, since its popularity seems to correlate, along with high birthrates, to poor education. But as for contributing anything helpful to the human debate, it's now less like the stern authority figure depicted here than the senile patriarch of the family, still angrily banging his cane on the floor and demanding attention even though he's just gabbling about something that didn't even happen back in 1947. I'm afraid it's time to wheel Dad off to the home.

God:
Republican *or* Democrat?

Time is money.

... and I looked, and I was like: "it's all good."

Republican	Democrat
· DIDN'T MAKE ENOUGH MONEY FOR EVERYONE	· MADE AIR, WATER FREE (SOCIALIST?)
· THOUGHT UP WHOLE 'LIVING BY EATING OTHERS' SYSTEM (SOCIAL DARWINIST?)	· CREATED "ENVIRONMENT," (SPOTTED OWL, SNAIL DARTER, ALASKAN WILDLIFE, ETC.)
· LEVITICUS, DEUTERONOMY	· BEATITUDES
· PAIN, HANGOVERS, FAT, BABIES	· SEX, DRUGS
· WOMEN PREFER DUDES WITH MONEY, POWER	· PLANTED ALL THAT EVIDENCE TO TRY TO DISCREDIT CREATIONISM
· CONSISTENT, INEXPLICABLE SUPPORT OF ISRAEL	· SON TURNED OUT ALL RIGHT, GOT INVOLVED IN SOCIAL CAUSES
· SMOTE INDONESIA WITH EARTHQUAKES, SLAYING 70	· SMOTE ALABAMA WITH TORNADOES, SLAYING 20

This week's unifying theme: things that were incredibly fun to draw.

At first I assumed the Slobodan Milosevic story must be a news parody, *a la The Onion*. (It's harder and harder to tell these days.) It is a joy to know that such things can happen in the real world. Alas, they did not actually drive the stake through Milosevic's heart; it was a three-foot-long stake driven into his grave about where his heart would be. In other words, a politically symbolic desecration rather than a serious attempt to keep the undead down. All real vampire hunters know that staking with ash plus decapitation is the only way to be sure. (Yes that is Hitler as the Wolfman and Stalin as Frankenstein's monster, and Abbot and Costello as the vampire killers.)

I first learned of the Putin story from a former editor of mine now living in Moscow:

> Putin keeps repositioning his likely successors, and journalists keep dying mysteriously. You may have heard about the latest reporter death. He was about to publish some stories about Russian arms sales to Iran and had already pissed off the Kremlin by reporting on a failed missile test. The official version is that he jumped five stories to his death in his apartment building while still holding his groceries.

As Vladimir Putin has more and more dissidents and critics murdered I intend to gird him in more of the armor, cloaks, and accoutrements of Victor von Doom until finally he disappears into the guise of the feared Lord of Latveria. Speaking as a spectator/satirist of the world, rather than an inhabitant of it, I can't help but enjoy how Putin is morphing into a real-life supervillain out of Marvel comics or James Bond films before our eyes. After meeting Vladimir Putin for the first time, George Bush reported: "I looked the man in the eye. I found him to be very straightforward and trustworthy and we had a very good dialogue. I was able to get a sense of his soul." It seems that Bush is just as keen a judge of character as are his own supporters. You have to wonder, now that that Putin proved to be a ruthless Mafioso and a Stalinist sociopath, whether Bush has had cause to second-guess his Presidential superpower of soul-perception.

Perhaps it is unsporting of me to pick on the Japanese military, which has admirably left everybody alone since their cheeky attempt to conquer the Pacific hemisphere sixty years ago, but then again, since they keep refusing to acknowledge, let alone apologize for, the rape of Nanking or any of their other war crimes, I guess they can stand a little good-natured ribbing. Plus the opportunity to draw cute big-eyed Mangafied characters bombing Pearl Harbor, raping and beheading civilians, and blinking dazed and blackened like Wile E. Coyote in the ruins of Hiroshima proved irresistible.

The last panel is a pastiche of the famous cover of *Captain America* #1, which showed Cap slugging that clown Hitler. What I wouldn't give to see Cap sock George Bush right in his lying mouth. But then, Cap's greatest power has always been to inspire. As long as we keep fighting the criminals who have hijacked our government, refusing to sanction the traitors who disgrace the name of America with their wars of conquest and their kidnapping, torture, and spying, Captain America is not dead. This week, Dick Cheney's errand boy, Scooter, was convicted of perjury; Chuck Schumer called for Alberto "The Torturer" Gonzales' resignation; and Republican Senator Chuck Hagel mentioned the possibility of impeachment. Long live Captain America!

You Think I Make This Shit Up?

SOMEONE HAS *DRIVEN A STAKE THROUGH SLOBODAN MILOSEVIC'S HEART.*

YET ANOTHER RUSSIAN JOURNALIST DIES IN FREAKISH CIRCUMSTANCES

THE JAPANESE DEFENSE FORCES HAVE ADOPTED A CUTE CARTOON MASCOT NAMED "PRINCE PICKLES"

...AND CAPTAIN AMERICA IS DEAD.

I take it as a foregone conclusion that the war is lost, as does, apparently, almost everybody in the military or the government who knows what he's talking about. Only George Bush and his most faithful henchmen down in the bunker are still issuing official promises of victory. However, I knew Iraq was going to be a disaster back before we ever invaded it. How can this be? How am I such a prescient visionary? How come I am so much smarter than Paul Wolfowitz? Wolfowitz was professor of international relations and dean of the School of Advanced International Studies at Johns Hopkins University; I, as an undergraduate at the same institution, drank too much, read almost nothing assigned, and doodled inattentively through the stupefying History of Occidental Civilization, 1650 - Present. So but how come he was wrong about Iraq and I was right?

For one thing, I've noticed that in real life, nothing ever goes according to plan. Think about how you've gone out to run a few easy errands, like pick up a library book and buy some razors and cat litter, and how unexpected little inconveniences inevitably conspire to thwart even those not-exactly-hubristic goals: the library's cut back their hours, they're out of the razors you use, you run into your neighbor who's got a flat tire. I figure occupying a foreign country and fighting an insurgency and rebuilding its infrastructure is probably even more complicated than my usual afternoon errands. One thing (maybe the only thing) we can learn from history is that it *never* goes according to plan—not even the plans of grand champion planners like Napoleon. Although I didn't pay close attention in Occ Civ in college I did watch a lot of Stanley Kubrick films, and I internalized the lesson that even meticulously laid plans inevitably go to pieces due to random, messy unforeseeable factors—passion or madness, fate, bad luck. Always remember the Fool's Motto: *Nothing is Foolproof.*

But nobody listened to me, and now look. Just look. The Democrats have voted for a March 2008 deadline for withdrawal, apparently assuming we'll have everything pretty much tidied up over there by then. But our Commander-in-Chief is going to veto that bullshit; he's going to get the situation under control with this "surge" of 20,000 more troops. The current situation, and our political leaders' response to it, is best epitomized not by any cartoon of mine but by the famous Shel Silverstein cartoon of two guys shackled by their wrists to a dungeon wall, hanging about fourteen feet off the ground, with one tiny barred slit of a window high overhead. One of them whispers to the other: "Now here's my plan..."

One thing nobody's said out loud, because no one wants to hear it, and it's such a fundamentally un-American sentiment, is that maybe there is no solution. Maybe Iraq is a Kobyashi Maru, a no-win scenario, a test of character that we are all failing. It was not just a strategic mistake but an international crime and, if you believe in this sort of thing, an irredeemable mortal sin. It's difficult even to discuss the situation realistically in the mainstream media because you're not allowed to use words like *shitstorm* or *clusterfuck*. But the main reason it's impossible for politicians of either party to say these things is that to do so would imply two horrific, unfaceable admissions: that all those lives were wasted for nothing, and that no one has any idea what to do now.

Another reason the Democrats aren't going to yank the troops out of there anytime soon is that we can't. The whole point of the invasion was to get the oil. The whole world runs on oil, see. And the problem is, the oil is running out. World leaders understand this—I'm sure Mr. Cheney has explained it to George—and the major players are now scrambling to position themselves for what promises to be a nasty every-man-

Why We Lost In Iraq

THE TREACHEROUS FRENCH/LIBERAL MEDIA ALLIANCE.

THE ENEMY'S SECRET SUPER-WEAPONS!

OLD KALASHNIKOVS

"FOUND" ARTILLERY

HOMEMADE BOMBS

ROCKS

"NOT GIVING UP"

BECAUSE **ISLAM** WAS THE RIGHT RELIGION!

BECAUSE CAP SAT THIS ONE OUT.

for-himself-type brawl over the dwindling energy resources as industrial civilization implodes. The Russians have enough oil and natural gas to maintain their current stylish standard of living for another thousand years. Don't you worry about the Russians. The wily Chinese are forging better alliances in Asia and Africa than we've ever had, and are also whistling and looking innocent while building a modern army that is probably not exclusively for rescuing stranded hikers.

Our own main national product these days, America's equivalent of Belgian ale or Peruvian wool or those foot-and-a-half-long cigars they make in Andorra, is the most terrible military machine in the history of the planet. So our best play seemed like using that to try to take over the Middle East, where, conveniently, there's lots of oil, but, inconveniently, everybody hates our guts. We and the British have secured the contracts to Iraq's oil (previously held by the Russians and French—sorry, suckers!), but if the flimsy little government we've propped up there collapses later on in the same afternoon we pull out only to be replaced by some fervid-eyed mullah crying Death to the Great Satan, then it's like it was all for nothing.

And the thing is, we kind of have to have the oil. We really need it. Seriously, we wouldn't even have invaded if we didn't need it so bad. There are library books to return, razors to pick up. That's like three gallons right there, and that shit is not free. So I mean come on, you see how it is. Kitty needs her litter! Just let us keep the oil and we'll go home, okay? What do you say? Deal?

Support Our Troops by Buying Shit Today!!

ITEM #114

ITEM #115
Support Our Troops

ITEM #116
Half My Ass is in Iraq

OIL ISN'T FREE

April 27th, 2006

Although I have not personally owned a television for the better part of a decade, I will admit to a brief addiction to "The Amazing Race" when I lived in Seattle two winters ago, which I blame on the bad influence of my friends Aaron and Carolyn. This happened to be the season featuring the hideously engrossing abusive relationship between former *Playboy* model Victoria and her cruel, shrieking boyfriend Jonathan. (I am even more loath to confess that we also watched the follow-up interview with this awful couple on Dr. Phil.) I regard this backsliding into TV viewership with the same fondness and caution that I do the occasional dalliance with oral narcotics: as a cautionary reminder of how unhealthily fun they are.

Last week it was "news" that John McCain gave a speech in which he said exactly what he's been saying all along about Iraq in slightly less equivocal terms. It occurred to me that this is likely to compose 97% of our "news" about the presidential campaign for the next two years—market-tested speeches that everyone understands will have no bearing on reality after the election, non-issues made much of, invented scandals, trivial "gaffes," photo-ops and sound bites, weak jokes and slander— in other words, a constant, heavy, inexorable deluge of bullshit. Candidates should have to *do* something in a campaign—prove themselves worthy through feats and contests and heroic deeds,

like the Twelve Labors of Hercules. Talk is cheap, prettyboys: let's see you *slay* something.

This cartoon afforded me an early crash course in drawing all the major Presidential candidates. Interestingly, although I've known I couldn't vote for Hillary Clinton ever since she voted to "authorize the use of force" in 2002, while drawing her face for the first time I discovered within myself hitherto-unsuspected depths of loathing for her. Insofar as it's possible to discern these things about politicians, who are by definition essentially dishonest creatures, she appears to give a shit about nothing other than her own ambitions. I don't believe that she is likely to be the Democratic nominee for the Presidency, not only because the big donors are already jumping ship to the less personally repellent Barack Obama, but because I suspect that, deep down, Americans still hate black men less than they hate women. Nevertheless, if she does end up running against McCain or Giuliani, I suppose I will just have to gulp back the bile, think of Big Bill back in the White House, and touch the screen beside her name. One of the few dubious consolations of having the Clintons back in the White House will be seeing Bill and Hillary's unwholesome relationship back in the pornographic glare of the public spotlight. They are the Jonathan and Victoria of American politics.

THE AMAZING *Presidential* RACE

NO MORE BORING SPEECHES AND PHOTO-OPS! INSTEAD, CANDIDATES FACE A SERIES OF DECISIONS AND CHALLENGES TO DETERMINE WHO WILL WIN THE **ULTIMATE** PRIZE!

ROAD BLOCK:

PERSONALLY TRACK DOWN AND KILL OSAMA BIN LADEN

DETOUR: "I.E.D. OR I.U.D."

SERVE ONE TOUR OF DUTY IN IRAQ
* OR *
ANSWER ONE UNSCREENED QUESTION ABOUT CONTRACEPTION/ABORTION

ROAD BLOCK:

WORK AT MINIMUM WAGE FOR ONE FULL YEAR

DETOUR: "CRY OR FRY"

PRODUCE CONVINCING TEARS OVER ONE UNINTERESTING PLIGHT
* OR *
EXECUTE ONE PRISONER

We condemn our ancestors of only a few generations ago for their ignorance and prejudices, for their opposition to women's suffrage and civil rights, for owning slaves. These all look like glaring, inarguable evils in historical hindsight. But we're pretending to a moral superiority that we haven't done much to deserve. Human nature hasn't undergone any radical improvement in the last century.

I fear that history will judge us unforgivingly for our heartless treatment of animals as commodities, and for the mass extinctions we're heedlessly causing. The world's frogs and bees are inexplicably dying off, and we've driven the elephants insane with grief. Animals may not be worthy of the same legal rights as human beings, but they do have a capacity for suffering—they certainly experience pain and fear, and I would also argue, as someone who has to jam his cat into a box to move twice a year, dread. As beings with some capacity for empathy and compassion, we should maybe take pause for thought before imprisoning and torturing them. Although our prehistoric ancestors would probably look on our sentimental remorse over vanishing species like the Bengal Tiger with incomprehension. Their reaction would be: *You've finally killed off the tigers? O, what a strong and noble people you must be! You must have made a paradise on earth!*

It may be that all the crimes of humanity throughout its entire history—its savage wars, the slavery and rapine and torture, the extermination of races and eradication of cultures—will pale in comparison to the ruination of the planet now being perpetrated by us. We're squandering the world's resources on trips to the mall for more junk food and toys, wantonly wrecking the place like frat boys trashing a hotel room. Our economic model is predicated on infinite expansion, but we live in a finite world; it's what the writer Kim Stanley Robinson calls "an imaginary relationship to a real situation." My friend Nell, a science reporter, tells me that someone recently did a rough accounting of the sum total of copper on the planet, and calculated that approximately one third of the copper is still in the ground, another third is currently in use in construction, computers, etc., and the last third is in landfills. That is to say, a third of the extant copper on this planet has been *thrown out.*

Lately I've started feeling anxious and guilty every time I toss out a wooden coffee stirrer or plastic shopping bag I was given twentty seconds earlier. Waste as a lifestyle is starting to seem not just stupid and irresponsible but something more like sinful. My friend Megan told me about a trip she and her husband made to a computer recycling facility here in New York; they were aghast at the towering heaps of obsolete computers, keyboards, monitors, printers, and scanners. The creepy feeling I keep getting about not only my own life but about Our Way of Life is: *this can't last.* My friend Ken is uprooting his whole life and moving to Missouri to join an energy-independent community, believing that after all the oil runs out industrial civilization will just plain collapse. Even I am giving some thought to putting solar panels on my cabin. The great challenge of our generation and the ones to come after us is not to defeat Islamic terrorism (I mean come on—if those clowns actually *won* the War of Civilizations and didn't have the Great Satan to hurl themselves futilely against any more they'd kill each other off inside of fourteen months); it's figuring out how to build a sustainable way of life that we can pass on to our descendants.

We used to know how to do this—we did it for millions of years. The trick is how to do it with six billion people on the planet without all of them living in squalid poverty. One thing we know is that we're not all going to get to live the way we Americans have been living for the last fifty years, each man an Elvis, with his own mansion, three TVs, and a fleet of cars. Which is why it's hard to picture Americans being the pioneers in this societal project. At some point in the last hundred years we went from being a nation to a market, from a race of fearless dreamers, inventors and explorers to fat-assed infantile consumers. No generation in human history has ever been more ill-equipped to take care of itself. If my friend Ken's darkest predictions come true, we will all eat our pets and then die about two weeks after the supermarkets are looted.

Why Will They Hate Us in the Future?

OUR TREATMENT OF ANIMALS

BURNING UP ALL THE FOSSIL FUELS, SQUANDERING NATURAL RESOURCES, OZONE DEPLETION/GLOBAL WARMING

FAILING TO EXTERMINATE REPUBLICANS WHEN WE HAD THE CHANCE

NOT MAKING *BUCKAROO BANZAI VS. THE WORLD CRIME LEAGUE*

Having been raised by Mennonites who mildly disapproved of the doctors on *M*A*S*H* because they were abetting a war effort, my encounter with Dick Tracy comics at age nine was not unlike the experience of the child of militant Vegans discovering Snickers bars or bacon. A gentle childhood of Tigger, Snoopy, and, at worst, Bugs Bunny cartoons, and then, suddenly, without warning: deformed guys getting *shot through the throat*. My panels in this cartoon are in fact reproductions, drawn from vivid memory, of the gruesome tableaux in which these infamous hit men, gangsters, and spies met their ends. A comparison to the originals will only demonstrate to the reader how unnecessarily fussy and cluttered my own drawing is compared to the inimitable style of Chester Gould, starkly legible as a chalk outline.

It's been strangely unsatisfying to watch the Bush administration unravel—it's certainly lacking in the sick vicious thrill of seeing Flattop's corpse pulled from the water or 88 Keys tommy-gunned in a railroad shed or the Brow *impaled on a flagpole,* with Tracy making some grim pronouncement about justice over their corpses. For one thing, it's just taken too long; it's like your first girlfriend apologizing for cheating on you ten years after the fact. And there's never any real moment of reckoning; the criminals are always caught on some technicality instead of being held to account for their true crimes, like Al Capone going to jail for tax evasion instead of for gunning down dozens of his business competitors. Alberto Gonzales is taken sternly to task in a nonbinding resolution over a scandal that only true wonks can bear to follow in any detail instead of for flouting the Geneva Conventions and the Constitution, legitimizing torture and spying on U.S. citizens, and generally dragging the United States of America down to the moral stature of a seventeen-year-old Congolese warlord. Paul Wolfowitz is forced to resign over a non-issue that's it's hard for even his enemies to fake indignation over instead of his instrumental advocacy for a pointless war that's now cost over three thousand Americans and at least ten times as many Iraqis their lives. And in the end, instead of the electric chair, everybody gets a public pat on the back from the President and goes on to makes even more money as fellows at right-wing propaganda mills.

And public enemy #1? He'll never get his just desserts, or even confess. George doesn't seem to have the capacity for even the repressed, stunted sort of self-castigation that tomented Nixon. I've read that he intends to spend his ex-Presidency not, like certain other ex-Presidents, building houses for the destitute or preventing the spread of AIDS in Africa, but defending the same disastrous policies he's pursued in office, setting up a think tank to continue fighting the global threat of Islamofascism and encouraging the spread of Democracy in the Middle East. Of all the sentences ever to dribble out of George W. Bush's mouth, the creepiest and most frightening, the one that reminds me of a true sociopath, is his boast that he sleeps better than you'd think. As my colleague Tom Hart says, George has already had his conversion experience, back when he quit drinking and accepted Christ. He's not about to have another one. There'll be no blinding on the road to Damascus or eye-gouging anagnorisis for him, no matter how many bodies he piles up around himself.

You can't help but wish, sometimes, that earthly justice took a more immediate and unambiguous form—e.g., that of a relentless, hawk-faced detective growling, "Come on, you mugs—eat a little of this!" while spraying them all with leaden death from a Thompson.

"How Willl Bush/Cheney Stay in Power After 2008?" June 6th 2007

Another good-natured jibe at my friend and betting adversary Myla. Although Myla's psychological insights are uncannily astute, in our political wagers she consistently succumbs to the common fallacy of believing that Things Couldn't Get That Bad. So far, she has lost the following bets: 1.) that Chief Justice John Roberts would prove to be the moderate he presented himself as during his confirmation hearings and 2.) that there was no such person as Marvin Bush. To decide the former bet, we chose the next major abortion case to come before the court as the litmus test, and, per my prediction, Roberts voted along with the majority to uphold the so-called "partial birth abortion ban," even when the health of the mother was at risk. The latter bet was resolved with a simple google search. To be fair, it's easy to understand her incredulity; I mean, *Marvin*? (Marvin is the youngest and, if such a thing is measurable, least impressive of the brothers Bush.) For all her formidable intellect it seems Myla has yet to learn one of the oldest rules in the book: never bet against a pessimist.[1]

Our next unresolved bet is that the Bush administration will somehow try to cling to power beyond the 2008 election; Myla says, No way, it's a sucker's bet, I'm ashamed to take it; I say, Let's just wait and see. It's true that I felt this was more of a sure thing back when we originally made the bet, when the Bush administration's hubris was unchallenged. These days Karl Rove's dream of a permanent Republican majority has gone the way of the Third Reich and New Coke, and I get the feeling even George doesn't want to be President any more. Only Dick Cheney continues to thrive unnaturally, bloated and ruddy from the blood of innocents. But I still suspect that when they won power they had no intention of relinquishing it, any more than they ever intended for American troops to withdraw from Iraq when they invaded it.

In 2004 some Republican party apparatchik floated the idea of developing contingencies for postponing the election in the event of a disruptive terrorist attack, an idea that got shot down before it was airborne. (As I told Myla: "No, but that's just the kind of low-level flack They *would* get to broach the idea, in case it caused an uproar!") Now that I've learned about these ominous-sounding new provisions, the National Security and Homeland Security Presidential Directives NSPD 51 and HSPD-20, my old suspicions are revived. The implications of these directives are not exactly clear, as the *SF Gate* column where I read about them elides some crucial points, so this may just be standard ...so this may just be standard left-wing paranoia. But recent history has shown, for those who needed reminding, that any expansion of governmental power will always be abused. It's encouraging to know, strictly from a handicapping standpoint, that American democracy might yet be overthrown in a fascist coup.

---

1   I forgot the proviso: unless he is spazzing. Please see footnote to "The Pain Predicts," October 12th, 2005.

How *Will* Bush/Cheney Stay in Power After 2008?

JUST RUN SOME OTHER DAMN BUSH WITH RUNNING MATE DICK CHENEY

*AN ACTUAL BUSH

OH, A LITTLE SOMETHING CALLED THE NATIONAL SECURITY PRESIDENTAL DIRECTIVE/NSPD 51

LOOK 'ER UP!

SIMPLY TRANSFER THE PARASITE-MIND FROM CHENEY TO THE FRONT-RUNNER

OLD-SCHOOL!

Surely even the chronically cynical readers of *The Pain* are not immune to a little unironic, sentimental nostalgia. Recent world events—the Iranians taking hostages and threatening the stability of the Middle East, the Russians threatening to aim their nuclear missiles at European capitals—have reminded me wistfully of my own youth, the days of the Carter administration. Does anyone remember the novelty songs, "Bomb Iran" (to the tune of "Barbara Ann") and "Ayatollah" (to the tune of "My Shirona")? "*Come to America and DIE-atollah! Hit you in the face with a PIE-atollah!*" And let's pause a moment to think of all the great art and pop culture about Cold War espionage and apocalypse: John Le Carré! James Bond! *Dr. Strangelove*! Military nuts and novelists used to fantasize about the totally excellent Third World War we could have with our new generation of kick-ass conventional weapons if only the Soviets would invade Western Europe. But the treacherous commies never did, leaving our military/industrial complex with a fifty-year case of atomic blueballs. America still approaches every conflict as though it were the long-imagined Big One, W.W. Three, "nucular combat toe-to-toe with the Russkies," sending in aircraft carriers and bringing on the heavy tanks and cruise missiles and radar-invisible bombers by the thousands, even if it's against a guerilla insurgency holed up in caves.

On a recent flight I sat next to a girl who was reading *The 9/11 Report,* which I could not help but observe was a funny thing to be reading on an airplane. Yeah, she said, she had to read it for a class on postwar American history. It was the first thing they'd read that wasn't about the Cold War, she griped. I ventured to ask: "So, do you remember the Cold War?" Of course she didn't; she was three years old when they tore down the Berlin Wall. (I don't remember the fall of the Berlin Wall, either, but this was for other reasons.)

Kids a generation older than me, the Boomers, still remember having to do "duck and cover" drills in school, since in those days the only known protection against the blast, heat and radiation of a thermonuclear explosion was the material out of which public school desktops were composed. By the time I was a kid, they'd pretty much given up on offering us any pretense of protection (unless you, like Congress, were scientifically illiterate enough to believe that Reagan's "Star Wars" scheme could work) and this sort of shrill panic had been numbed to a more matter-of-fact, back-of-the-mind awareness that, yeah, the world could always blow up any time, but what are you gonna do? Answer: Party like it's 1999! Which was, in a way, sadder.

Young people today, who do not even recall the Soviet menace, may have a hard time believing that these drunken bumbling oafs who assassinate each other like Medicis or Klingons, resolve hostage situations by gassing to death everybody involved, and can't even rescue a fucking submarine, were once considered the single most sinister and implacable threat to freedom on this planet. (Although not as hard a time as they'll have explaining to their own children why we were so terrified of a few thousand scrawny brainwashed religious freaks with box cutters and bombs made out of shoes that we eagerly agreed to forfeit all civilized conduct and abandon our birthright as a free people.) Do not underestimate them. You can't take your eye off the Russians, man. Everybody from Napoleon to Hitler found out the hard way: they are absolutely not to be fucked with, especially not in the winter. Their president is essentially a supervillain: a former KGB agent and a judo expert who has his rivals and critics shot in the head, pushed off roofs, and poisoned with radiation, and he once kissed a little boy on the belly in public and nobody at all could stop him.

It's almost a relief to find ourselves back in a conflict we can understand, with enemies whose motives at least make a crude, Machiavellian sort of sense. The Soviets were a worthy nemesis, our equals and opposites, a shadowy rival superpower lurking on the other side of the pole, with their own space program, even, and armed with enough nuclear weapons to blow up the world six times over. Like us, they were an expansionist empire

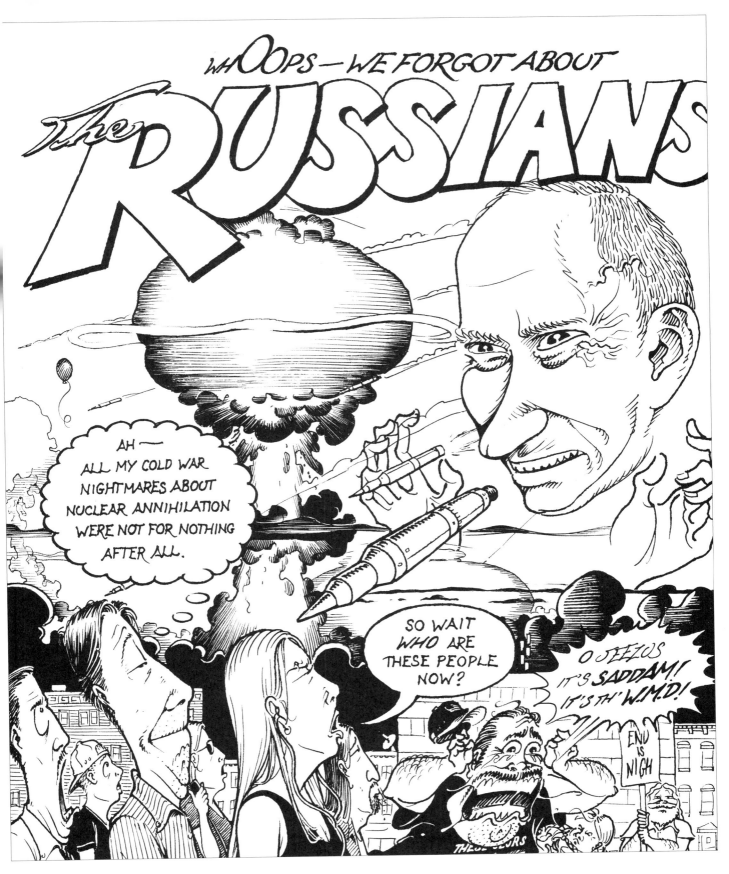

with dangerous delusions of a unique historical destiny. It was a great historical clash between two Western ideologies, Rousseau vs. Marx, Jefferson vs. Lenin—well, actually more like Henry Ford vs. Josef Stalin, as it worked out in real life, but you get the idea. Their leaders were half-dead gray-faced bureaucrats in bad suits, not dewey-eyed, bearded fanatics hiding out in caves. The Russians were like Braniac or Galactus, one of the big guns; Osama bin Laden is more like Mr. Mxyzptlk, or Mysterio— just a nuisance, some jerk who got off a lucky shot. Even the whole world-blowing-up scenario is too big and abstract to feel like a real possibility any more; it's almost clean and fun and comforting, like the cool destruction of Alderaan, compared to the grisly horrors of 9/11.

Believe it or not I drew the first draft of this cartoon years ago, back even before the Bush administration. This was during what looks, in retrospect, like a brief idyll between the end of the Cold War and 9/11, the Clinton years, when the most important issue confronting the nation was an act of fellatio. I felt like we were getting too complacent. Everybody acted as though, now

that the Cold War was over, we could finally quit worrying about nuclear weapons. Whew! That's a load off our minds. We still seem to believe this, except for a little prudent worry reserved for the threat of a "rogue nation" or terrorist group smuggling a couple-few-kiloton device into New York's harbor someday. But nuclear weapons aren't going away (and even if we dismantled every last one of the things on the planet we still couldn't do a collective memory wipe on the whole human race) and human nature isn't changing, either. As long as those two things are constant, the existence of the species remains provisional, at least until we get ourselves safely set up on some other planet. I'm relieved and thankful that the Americans and the Russians somehow managed not to drop the nuclear football for fifty years, but is that supposed to mean we can sound the all-clear now? For how long? For the next hundred years? The next thousand? Just another late-night meditation for those of you who aren't already planning to poison your kids over terrorism, Peak Oil, and global warming.

Jesus — Can't We Just Nuke Our Way Outta This?

IRAQ

GLOBAL WARMING

DOMESTIC SCANDALS

PERSONAL ISSUES

If I overstate my case, please bear in mind that all opinions are offered merely to render my recent trip tax-deductible. I do think we are a better country than China, although not as much better as we like to think. One thing that makes us maybe not as good as we like to think is our continuing insistence on doing business with China, despite their uncool authoritarianism. The sheer size of the potential consumer market has made us drunk with greed, like a man blinded to a girl's dangerous craziness by her huge breasts. The Chinese seem to have abandoned the centralized economy of Communism and embraced a Darwinian form of free-for-all capitalism, but prudently decided they definitely want to keep the authoritarianism. No reason to throw the baby out with the bathwater!

China is, in effect, the Republican utopia: the complete deregulation of business combined with a draconian government unaccountable to any fickle and ignorant electorate and able to exercise control over people's personal lives. In effect, the deal the Chinese government made with its people after Tiananmen Square was: *okay, we'll let you make money but you still can't vote.* And The People spoke with one voice, saying: *How much money?* So now if you want to give taxi rides in a wobbly ice cream cart mounted on the back of a motorcycle or charge parents to let their children frolic on a lake floating in plastic bubbles without any air holes, good luck to you. But you still can't have more than one child or move wherever you want or practice any weird religions.

I would much rather live here than there, if only for the modern plumbing, good coffee, and the bottomless font of internet porn. But I found that my least favorite things about the Chinese were pretty much the same as my least favorite things about the Americans: a tunnel-vision fixation on money; an unexamined faith in their inherent national superiority; and a disregard for other cultures not so much contemptuous as utterly

incurious. In other words, they act about like every other empire in history.

Beijing right now is what I imagine America was like circa 1910: the wild years of capitalism, a country drunk with industrial brawn and deregulation, blindly tearing down anything that's not currently making money and racing to build as many 700 ft. x 700 ft. buildings in as short a time as possible. Construction cranes stand among the buildings like Martian war machines. It's not unlike a science-fictional urban dystopia of the Seventies, a cautionary tale about sprawl and pollution: chunky, graceless apartment buildings blistering with air conditioner units and generators and thickly veined with ugly snaking ducts and cables; gleaming featureless department stores that stretch for blocks; the air is semi-opaque with dust and smog, the sun a weak bright spot in the grayish-white haze. The American city it reminds me of most is Atlantic City, except that instead of a single line of gargantuan hideous buildings receding in one-point perspective into the distance the gargantuan hideous buildings extend infinitely in every direction. You can drive forty-five minutes and still be, to all appearances, downtown.

Conservationists in America think of the demolition of Penn Station as the pivotal What-Have-We-Done moment in our history that gave us pause and caused us to reconsider the wholesale trashing of the past. Maybe the Chinese will experience the same belated epiphany after they bulldoze the Temple of Heaven to build more condos. Right now they're still busily demolishing the last of the ancient hu tong, the low, walled, labyrinthine neighborhoods that for centuries were the heart of Beijing, to make way for new improved gargantuan hideous apartment buildings.

Not that we Americans are any great æsthetes. I came home furious from a visit to France years ago because I realized that a modern industrialized nation did not have to be ugly; it could

Why We Are Better Than The Chinese

OUR REVERENCE FOR OUR PAST AND LOVE OF BEAUTY

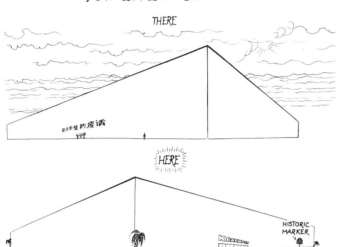

WE WOULD ONLY EVER INVADE A COUNTRY WHERE WE KNEW WE WOULD BE WELCOMED.

WE KNOW THERE'S NO NEED TO CRUSH DISSENT WHEN YOU CAN IGNORE IT.

SHEER PHYSICAL ATTRACTIVENESS

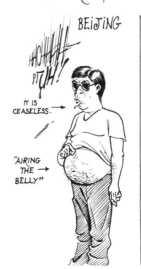

take pains to preserve what was traditional and lovely if the culture valued those things. Apparently we Americans actually chose strip malls and lightboxes, either out of ignorance or indifference to any value other than the bottom line. Or maybe it was something more willful and perverse, what Mencken called "the libido for the ugly."

"...the love of ugliness for its own sake, the lust to make the world intolerable. Its habitat is the United States. Out of the melting pot emerges a race which hates beauty as it hates truth."

Truth, too, is in scarce supply in China. I was disappointed to find that even the educated and comparatively cosmopolitan Chinese I've talked to—even political cartoonists—parrot the Party line on Tibet: it was a very backward country before we arrived, we've improved life for the people there, they're grateful to have us there. There's an ethnocentric condescension, if not blatant bigotry, in evidence toward the Tibetan people. One friend of mine had a Chinese girlfriend who said of them, "They don't have food—they have *cheese*" (this last spoken with an especial disdain as the Chinese do not comprehend cheese and fear and despise it). It's an innocent arrogance reminiscent of the British attitude toward their colonies in the nineteenth century—a distinctively Imperial perspective.

It is as malevolently naive, in its way, as our own obtuse optimism about Iraq: we'll be greeted as liberators, with dancing and flowers, it's just a minority causing the violence, ordinary people don't want us to leave. Look at all the schools we've painted! The Chinese like to talk about the schools they've built in Tibet, too. To be fair, even the Dalai Lama says we should be grateful for the educational advances the Chinese have brought. But meanwhile they're moving thousands and thousands of Han Chinese into Tibet, overwhelming the native population and effectively eradicating their culture, demolishing the few remaining authentic Tibetan buildings in Lhasa and converting it into a generic Chinese city—chintzy gleaming department stores scrawled with da-glo ads, concrete-block government buildings, a dismal sprawl you can see filling the valley from the roof of the Potala. The unintentionally chilling Chinese term for their Tibet policy is "grasping with both hands." Here we used to call it Mainfest Destiny—or, as a Schoolhouse Rock cartoon had it, "Elbow Room."

Sometimes I'd walk around watching women play badminton in the streets and remember, *I'm in a fascist country.* I remember the old men who used to gather early every morning by the lake near my apartment to practice calligraphy, dipping their long bamboo brushes in the lake and painting in dark lakewater on the flagstones. The characters shrank and vanished as they dried, like flowers withering. It's easy to forget that authoritarianism isn't all jackbooted thugs and re-education camps; it's not like Mordor, where the landscape is blasted and the skies ever dark with ash. Most people are left alone to live their lives, no more or less happy than ours, as long as they don't cause any trouble for the government. It's only the fringe-oes, the political cranks and religious freaks and do-gooders, the activists and bloggers and cartoonists, who get the discreet cautionary talking-to from the government. One expat told me an astonishing story about someone being *taken out for ice cream* by the secret police.

A more apt (though less funny) drawing for panel 3 would've been the Tiannamen Square Tank Guy standing alone in an empty street, looking irrelevant and silly, with no tank to face off against and no TV cameras to record him. It's not entirely true that we don't crush dissent in this country; we've just learned that's no longer necessary to go to all the trouble of a massacre, which looks bad on TV. All you have to do is corral the dissidents, arrest them on some bullshit excuse, and hold them without charges for a few days until whatever they're protesting is over, then worry about the lawyers later. But even this is mostly cosmetic, to keep any unsightly hippies away from the Republican/G11/IMF delegates. The real democratic insight is that you can allow all the dissent you want and it will have no effect whatsoever as long as the media doesn't report it, or reports it with the same patronizing chuckle as they do the annual dip of the Polar Bear Club.

Don't get me wrong; I'm glad to live in a country where I can protest in the streets without being ground under the treads of a tank, and draw these cartoons without being sent to a Political Reeducation Camp. My friend Mike's second deepest fear, after not having enough pasta to go with his sauce, is of forced collectivization, all us cartoonists and computer programmers being conscripted into building dams or baling hay. If that ever happens here, Mike and I will both seek quick and painless deaths.

On returning I find myself hoping that, *contra* the dire predictions of every would-be economic futurist in this country, the Chinese will not be the next world superpower. When I was in school they were telling us it was going to be Brazil—"the sleeping giant," as it was then called. These days the Brazilians seem too preoccupied with soccer, kidnappings, and the most magnificent asses on the planet to bother with the dull work of empire building, but I am still rooting for them over the Chinese. Like us, they are a violent and sex-obsessed democratic people, to whom I would be pleased to pass the torch of world leadership. *Thongs, not Wongs!*

"You ain't from around here, are you?"
I get that question a lot in C_____ County, Maryland. It's not necessarily hostile (though it definitely isn't friendly); just the same kind of provincial suspicion of Outsiders that you see in the less frequently visited parts of China, where it's still a novelty to get your photo taken with a white person. The thing that kind of rankles is, I am from Around There; I watched Nixon's resignation speech in the same cabin where I'm living now. But my geographic background isn't what they're really asking about. What they mean is, I didn't go to their high school; I appear to have gone to college; I don't talk or look like them.

There really is a certain distinctive look Around Here, which must be due at least in part to a small and somewhat stagnant gene pool. "Natives in Traditional Dress" is the first time I've ever been able to capture the distinctive C_____ County features; the mean, squinting eyes, lower lip and jaw pushed forward in a sort of pugnacious sulk. It's a type as distinctive to its area as the Gallic nose. (You see the same face in ungentrified South Baltimore bars.) This drawing was copied directly from a photo in a local publication called "The Barhopper," in a two-page spread of shots taken at the Southern Rock Wood Stock [sic], each of which is like a Diane Arbus portrait.

Moving back to C_____ County from New York City always gives me a nasty culture shock. I live in a county where the best-selling beer is the Silver Bullet, Fox news or NASCAR is on in every bar, pop country is ubiquitous on the muzak in stores. Evolution is still being debunked and members of the Green party are called "watermelon Marxists" (green on the outside...) in the editorial pages of the *C_____ Whig*. And blow-dried dudes are blasting Starship's "We Built This City on Rock and Roll" from their convertibles.

But none of these shocks is as profound as going from the company of Manhattanites, the most depressingly beautiful and well-dressed people in America, back to the grotesques who inhabit C_____ County. Mullets and sunburn, tank tops and ballcaps, mirrored wraparound shades, beer bellies, goiters, sagging leathery skin, tattoos that look like the paintings people used to get airbrushed on the sides of their vans. Jesus—they're *trolls*, I'm surrounded by trolls!

This is all unconscionably classist of me, I know, and I'm probably torpedoing my chances of ever winning a seat on the town council. But you do not live here; you can't imagine it. It's like deepest Appalachia oozing into the junkiest, run-down, outermost rim of suburbia. Tracing this region on a road atlas over the weekend, I christened it the Scum Belt. Nestled between the Rust Belt and the Bible Belt, the Scum Belt roughly follows the contour of Route 40 across the country, twisting through the cruddy rusting outskirts of Indianapolis, St. Louis, Kansas City, and Salt Lake City, and lined the whole way with cheap motels, liquor stores, used car lots, fast food franchises, and junkyards.

A few hundred yards offshore from my cabin is a sandbar where dozens of powerboaters and jetskiers congregate every weekend to do nothing—they just park out there and drink Coors Light all day in the sun, like bored teens in an inland town cruising Main Street on Saturday night. Occasionally a jetski makes a noisy foray into my cove to do the aquatic equivalent of a few donuts before roaring out again. Often I fantasize about trying to knock the riders off by hitting them in the heads with a potato cannon, or perhaps some more conventional firearm.

And yes I have often seen not only motorized wheelchairs but mothers pushing strollers, whole families, and single men, all on foot and carrying drooping plastic bags full of groceries

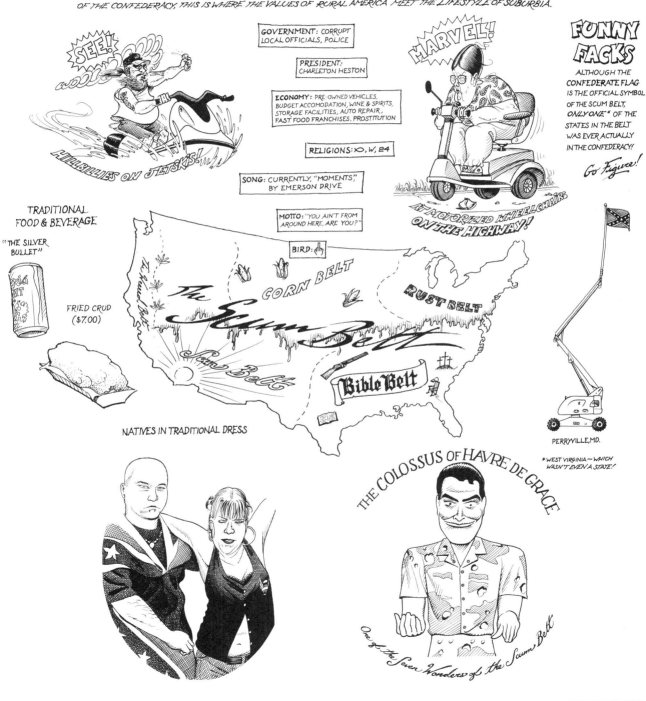

or booze, on the shoulder of Route 40. It has always seemed to me like the lowest point of degradation to which a human being could sink to find himself walking along the shoulder of Route 40. I speak as one who has himself been such a man.

Other things I have seen on the shoulder of Route 40: an old Polish man bicycling around the world in sagging jockey shorts who asked me for souvenir quarter; a black man retracing the route of the Underground railroad on foot, who wondered whether there was a foot bridge over the Susquehannah (there isn't); and a man dressed as Jesus Christ, dressed in shining white robes and lugging a big wooden cross over His shoulder. When you see Jesus Christ on the shoulder of Route 40, you double back to ask Him if you can do anything to help him. He asked me where He could find a Laundromat.

I have to admit to an involuntary admiration for the man whose Confederate flag display is depicted here. He lives beside I-95, just north of the Millard Tydings Bridge over the Susquehannah and south of the Perryville exit. For a while he flew the Confederate Flag from a pole in his lawn, proclaiming to all travelers on the Eastern Seaboard that we, the people of C____ County, remain proud supporters of the wrong and losing side in the Civil War. This is not the part I admired. What impressed

me against my will was when, presumably in response to some neighborly request, municipal order, or petition to remove the flag, he either rented or purchased a cherry picker in order to elevate the flag to an even more defiantly conspicuous height. All politics aside, there is something you've got to respect about that kind of deeply committed cussedness.

The Muffler Man depicted is located at a garage on Route 40 in Havre de Grace. The Muffler Man used to be a plain old cowboy when I was a kid, with a white shirt and brown pants, but in 1991 he was repainted in desert camos to Support Our Troops in the first Gulf War (remember that one, the shorter one where we won?). His giant cowboy hat kept blowing off in heavy winds, threatening life and property, but it's still stored in the garage. It was almost as difficult to accurately draw his demented and frightening expression as to capture the unwholesome mix of recessive traits that comprise the C____ County phenotype. For the record, the owner of the garage is a friendly guy and a good mechanic and no slur upon him or his business is implied by the inclusion of this image. It's just a weird and scary idol that looms, leering menacingly, over the ruin of Route 40—our own shoddy local T.J. Eckleburg.

Hello:

Making blanket statements about all Southerners being racists Christians who want to maintain a stranglehold on the culture of the country at large is a bit dishonest. The Midwest is also quite full of the same sort of idiot you caricature. People are working very hard in the south to change how screwed up it is—but we are working against a cultural momentum that even the Civil War didn't break. Some appreciation from New Englanders and people from the West Coast would be nice, for once, instead of being lumped in with the crazy Republicrat/libertarian religious fundamentalists. Isn't the inability to draw distinctions and treat people as individuals essentially what you lambaste in your comic?

Have a good day.

APC

APC,

No offense to you and your right-minded Southern brothers-in-arms intended. (I myself grew up and lived for many years in Maryland, which, as far as anyone north of the Mason-Dixon line is concerned, is Dixieland.) I'm afraid broad, unfair generalizations are to some extent the tools of the trade. But I no more mean to condemn all Southerners as bigots or evangelical dingbats than I mean to call all Americans warmongering rednecks, or all Muslims scimitar-waving maniacs. As far as I am concerned all the decent, gentle, humorous people of the earth are all on the same side in an age-old, endless war against ignorance, bigotry, and cruelty. What with all the noise and rancor of the culture wars in America, it's sometimes easy to forget about our allies behind enemy lines, fighting the good fight like the Resistance in Vichy France. My apologies for undercutting morale.

Vive la Resistance!
Tim

The news is full of speculation about the 2008 Presidential campaign—now in its third year, with the election itself still as unimaginably distant as Resurrection Day—and about the various PR stalling tactics being deployed by the Bush administration to try to placate the public on Iraq. The media has to try to turn all this propaganda into a suspenseful narrative with some significance, because in between news segments they run commercials for cars and Viagra that they want us to watch. All this effort to get us excited about speeches and straw polls and surges and reports barely disguises the fact that most of it is theater, the end result a foregone conclusion. Maybe this is just the same kind of psychic numbing you experience as you get older and notice that the Middle East is still on the brink of Armageddon for the 21,900ᵗʰ consecutive day.

In modern elections, the smart money is almost always on the guy who looks more like a game show host. But people are so bitterly disillusioned right now that they might be ready for at least a dramatic cosmetic change, like changing our national hair color rather than our personality. So I suppose Hillary or Obama might win the Presidency. But I'm having a hard time caring. It would certainly be a disappointment if the Democrats figured out a way to lose this election, but I already lost whatever was left of my provisional respect for this country after the 2004 election. That's when my fellow Americans stood up and proudly showed the world what they really are.

There's been some fuss and clucking inside the beltway over Alan Greenspan's recent book because he criticized the Republicans' fiscal recklessness, but of rather more interest to me is something else he wrote: "I am saddened that it is politically inconvenient to acknowledge what everyone knows: the Iraq war is largely about oil." I think it's a little let's call it sheltered of Greenspan to imagine that "everyone" knows this—it would sound like the most treasonous pinko faggotry to the "FREEDOM ISN'T FREE" T-shirt-wearing patriots of the Scum Belt—but it's still a refreshing shock to see it said in print by someone you'd pretty much have to call an Insider. Hillary Clinton understands this, Obama knows it, Edwards knows it, and none of these people, if elected, is going to withdraw our army from Iraq until we've established a puppet government that'll hold together long enough to sign the oil revenue-sharing agreement and guarantee us our supply for the next fifty years.

Perhaps in this cartoon I am affecting a more fatalistic view of our capacity for change than I really hold for the sake of a gag. An occupational hazard. Pessimism's just funnier than optimism, is all. Humor is the invention of despair. Humor's what you use when you're out of hope, the way you'll go to Taco Bell if you can't afford food. But I've learned the hard way that it's possible to affect a cynical attitude for the sake of humor for so long that it becomes your default worldview, and it can be hard to find your way back out of it again.

Last year around the holidays, traditionally a bleak time, I told my friend Boyd, "I really think things are about to turn around for you and me." He responded: "You realize you say this same thing every year around the holidays." I had not. It was disheartening. Things never do turn around for us, but I keep saying it, as reliable as Charlie Brown kicking the football.

But in order for both individuals and nations to change, things first have to get as bad as they can get. No one goes to rehab because they're worried they've been drinking too much lately and some of their friends are telling them they might have a problem; they go because they come out of a blackout to discover they've bankrupted their country and gotten it stuck in a military quagmire on the other side of the world for reasons that seemed to make sense last night but which they can't quite remember now. Perhaps in our collective catastrophe there is hope for us yet. Maybe George Bush is our American Bottom.

Spoiler Alert!

WE WILL ELECT A RICH WHITE GUY PRESIDENT.

WE'RE NEVER LEAVING IRAQ.

I WILL LOVE THE *IRON MAN* MOVIE NO MATTER HOW MUCH IT SUCKS.

YOUR LIFE WILL NEVER CHANGE.

I've found myself thinking about the next terrorist attack a lot lately, partly because I am now living full-time in New York City, terrorist attack capital of the country, and because here in the northeast it's what I've come to think of as terrorist weather—the clear light and crisp air of early autumn. A couple of weeks ago I asked my friends Alex and Kristen, both New York lifers, whether they ever worried about it. They both hesitated and conferred via eye contact before admitting that, yeah, they kinda did. "Do you?" they asked. "I think about it pretty much every day," I said. We all relaxed, at ease in our shared terror.

The inevitability of another attack, our helplessness and ignorance of its time, place, and nature, all combine to form a constant, low-level drone of anxiety in the nerve endings, just a few degrees warmer than the normal background radiation of the fear of death that suffuses everyone's internal universe. You try to figure out how you'd get out of the subway between stations; you imagine all your friends anxiously calling and emailing to find out whether you're okay; you look up and wonder whether that plane isn't flying awfully low over the city. Kristen happened to be a block away from a water main explosion at 40th and 2nd Avenue this summer, which everyone in the vicinity at first assumed must be a terrorist attack. She reported that in addition to the other, more intense and immediate emotions that seized the crowd, like panic and mortal terror, there was an unmistakable strain of relief—at least the waiting was over, it was finally here, this was it, the next attack. Like letting out your breath after holding it a long time, or of being startled after prolonged suspense, or at finally being struck after waiting, crouched and flinching, for a blow.

I've noticed that I spend a lot less time worrying about my own safety when I'm in New York than I do worrying about my New Yorker friends when I'm away from the city. This seems somehow related to the fact that most of the people who went berserk with gung-ho bloodlust after 9/11, aching for some nuclear payback (among whom I must regretfully include myself), were not people who'd actually experienced the attacks in New York or DC or Pennsylvania, but people who'd seen them on TV. Alex and Kristen once related a telling anecdote about watching some "50 Greatest Moments in TV History" special together. As the countdown neared #1 and all the most obvious choices were checked off the list—the Kennedy assassination, the moon landing, the *Challenger* disaster—they became more and more stumped as to what the top TV Moment could possibly be. It turned out, of course, to be 9/11. Alex and Kristen just looked at each other, nonplussed, like: *Oh, right—for most people that was on TV.* They had seen it through their living room window.

I think that on some level most Americans who saw the attacks on TV experienced them as a spectatorial event, as unreal, and so their reaction was also unreal—it was the reaction you'd expect to see in an action movie. (The montage of lots of guns being loaded and locked, with tough-guy dialogue like "You ready?" "Let's go!") None of the New Yorkers I know were angry after 9/11; what they were was sad. Maybe this is why the craven, bellicose hysteria that followed the terrorist attacks in America contrasts so unfavorably to the stoic reaction of Londoners during the Blitz. When something horrible happens to you it's not that it automatically ennobles you so much as it forces you to endure it whether you like it or not. Whereas when you see or imagine something terrible happening to someone else, your empathetic imagination runs hideously amok, and you can indulge all kinds of inane fantasies about heroically avenging them. Which fantasies we have, unfortunately, turned into foreign policy.

This cartoon hardly exhausts all the reasons to look forward to the next terrorist attack, and I've already started work on Part II. I am hoping there will not be another terrorist attack before next Friday since if that happens my editors in Baltimore are sure to ixnay it and I'll have to come up with another idea quick.

Reasons to Look Forward to the Next Terrorist Attack

EVERYONE'LL CALL.

MAYBE RENTS WILL FINALLY COME DOWN.

MAYBE I WILL BE KILLED AND THEY WILL BE SORRY.

ANOTHER DECADE'S WORTH OF POLITICAL CARTOONS.

It's impossible to predict what the political reaction to another terrorist attack will be. Given the ugly turn public opinion's taken against the Bush administration since Katrina, my guess is that they'll get savaged for failing to prevent it, the way you might've thought they would've been the first time around. But who knows?—maybe everyone will rally around the President again and support an attack on Iran. Let us not underestimate people's cowardice, gullibility and bloodlust.

We do know that the Bush administration will protest that "nobody could have predicted this," that they'll discourage us from indulging in unconstructive criticism and second-guessing—"playing the Blame Game," they call it—and that they will blame the Democrats. They'll blame us for opposing wiretapping and waterboarding and generally being big terrorist-appeasing sissies. And we know that the dingbat Christians will blame the fags.

I still remember, about a week after 9/11, the first time I heard some government official explain, "These people hate freedom," and thought to myself: "Didn't Commander Adama say that about the Cylons on the old *Battlestar Galactica*?" It was at this moment that I realized how stupid the official response and how low the level of public understanding was going to be. After a twenty-four-hour cæsura during which the entire ceaselessly chattering media machine was stunned into welcome silence, everyone in the country from Falwell to Chomsky who could get in front of a camera or onto an op-ed page started telling us that This Only Went to Prove What They'd Been Saying All Along, and that it would never have happened If Only We Had Listened to Them. I'm afraid we'll probably have to hear a lot more of that sort of thing next time around.

I have heard that there was a lot of desperate cathartic life-affirming sex (it would be the opposite of the truth to call it "casual") in New York in the weeks after 9/11. I rue that I missed out on it. This time I am dug in here for the duration and, assuming I am not killed in the next attack, I intend to catch some of the erotic blowback.

My friend Jim, in whose plush vibrating TV-room recliner I drew this entire cartoon, wondered idly how such a giant Muslim robot would be powered, and immediately answered his own question: "oil." Jim believes that this panel is likely to earn me some hate mail, or maybe even get one of them fatwas slapped on my infidel ass. I, who have over a decade's experience drawing grotesquely offensive things for publication, can predict exactly what is likely to come of it: nothing at all. However, in the unlikely event that I do get fatwaed and am caught in the media spotlight, I already have my sound bite ready: "Which would you say is a saner response to the possibility of another terrorist attack—trying to find some way to laugh at our fear, or being so frightened we're willing to give up our rights and invade countries that weren't involved?" Yeah—*that'll* make 'em stop and think in Wichita!

All kidding aside, if I am killed in the next terrorist attack, please do not say, "Tim Kreider wouldn't have condoned any violence in his name. He opposed the war, and he wouldn't have wanted his death to be used as an excuse for more pointless military action." No. Please forget about all the silly nonsense I wrote about not giving in to bellicose hysteria. If I am killed by terrorists I want the entire Middle East blasted flat by high-megatonnage thermonuclear weapons in retribution for my personal death. Tell them, "This is what happens, Larry. This is what happens when you fuck a stranger in the ass."

More Reasons to Look Forward to the Next Terrorist Attack

MAYBE BUSH WILL FINALLY GET BLAMED.

DESPERATE CATHARTIC LIFE-AFFIRMING CASUAL SEX

MAYBE THIS TIME THEY'LL HIT SOMEPLACE THAT VOTED FOR BUSH

MAYBE IT'LL BE REALLY COOL!

Ms. C.-H., being born into old aristocracy, has exquisite continental manners at her disposal but can also be hilariously voluble on the subject of American culture after a couple of Pernods. I hope none of my readers will hold this cartoon against her; it was I who urged her to draw her least favorite things about America, despite her misgivings. Her perspective on this country as an outsider is invaluable to me; for example, I'd never noticed how scarily ubiquitous the American flag is here until Ms. C.-H. pointed it out to me (she invariably refers to it as "the bloody Republican banner of the U.S."). It was because of this that I realized that the violent nationalism so rampant here is not a feature common to most countries. You tend to see jingoist fervor, and the corollary fear and hatred of foreign enemies, fostered as distractions by despotic governments in countries with crappy economies and low national self-esteem, places like North Korea, Iran, and Pakistan—and here.

As for Ms. C.-H.'s last panel, I will say only that it disappoints me to see her violate the sacred trust between mentor and intern by betraying confidences gleaned in a professional environment in such an indiscreet manner. But it would be beneath me to censor her.

It was at the insistence of M. Kreider that I drew it. Personally, I would not be ungracious to my host country. Except for my stay in New York, I did not see it at its best, merely M. Kreider's not-to-be-disclosed location in the most rural area of the East, known as "The Stick."

It is to my horror that I observed for the first time the young people of America drinking to the point of futility. I have often seen them to behave in this way abroad, in Europe, but I give them "the advantage of doubt" on the assumption that such shameful conduct is an overabundance of enthusiasm caused by the spirit of holiday. But I saw that this hasty and terrifying drinking, which I previously have associate only with late alcoholism, is the normal Friday night between them. They drink to the point of vomiting, and they suffer from amnesia, they can not walk without overturning, and still get back to drink more. The girls excitedly expose their breasts to the delighted hoots as if

all breasts, like alcohol, are a thrilling and unprecedented novelty in this country. All cry Woo! repeatedly and at length. It is to be pitied by those better than me, but for me it is just disgusting, and to depress.

The obsequiousness of the clerks is particularly grating. Here they host in a manner informal and familiar, and sometimes share a surname with you, but I learned that there were no plans for that. Often they are investigating the health or welfare, a survey that does not make sense as the only acceptable response is, "fine." On one occasion, I am greeted by a French saleswoman in a clothing store who asked me how I am and when I reply "Fine" in American English, she turns to the time involved and said in French, "As if I care how it is." Thus the obvious lie is exposed.

The "balloon of thought" contains a vulgarity in my mother tongue. It must be excused.

In the third panel, I depict myself besieged by the flags as axes. I was shocked to see so many flags when I came here. Not in Hungary, neither in Italy nor in France, is it so much — there it is only on municipal buildings. But here they are flying everywhere, on the libraries and the museums and the schools and the stadiums and the places of business and the private residences, as they are sold as stickers for cars and refrigerators and decorations and on "T-shirts" and caps and jackets and for the tattoos. I do not know how they can look to Americans, but abroad, they are frightening, gestures of hostility, like the angry boasts of the drunken. If I can be forgiven for observation, it is only a weak man who needs to boast of his prowess.

Unfortunately for Mr. Kreider and his cat, he is only the most humorous example of this trend, seen everywhere in the country. In particular among people without children, the love of animals is like a mental illness. They address them in cooing voices of parents with many endearments cloying. They greedily purchase clothing and accessories for the animals, traveling with them in the car, they bring them uninvited to social events. I am amazed to see women in New York, carrying small tremulous dogs in the purse. It is a symptom of excessive wealth and profound loneliness, perhaps the definition of the syndrome of America, that fat and unhappy land.

THiNGS NOT TO MiSS iN AMERiCA

DRAWN BY MR. KREIDER'S INTERN, MS. PHELAETIA CZOCHOLA-HAOTANZ

THE ARTIFICIAL FRIENDSHIP OF THE CLERKS.

THE TERRIFYING BELLICOSITY OF THE PEOPLES.

THE ALCOHOLISM OF THE YOUNG.

TO DOTE UPON THE ANIMALS AS ON THE CHILDREN.

"What Else They're Calling Mohammed," December 5th 2007

As of the morning of this writing (Monday May the 3rd) Gillian Gibbons, the British teacher who allegedly insulted Islam by letting her students name a teddy bear Mohammed, is being sent home from Sudan rather than imprisoned or flogged. As punishments go, being sent home from Sudan is pretty light. So unless some devout go-getter back in England murders her for afterlife extra credit, the story on which this cartoon was based is already over. It was, in any event, only ever borderline news, the sort of lurid, sensational item that gets perfunctory notice in the *New York Times* but makes the front page of the *New York Post* for a week, with outraged punning headlines and photos of a teddy bear in a turban. But the vein of comedic potential there was too rich for me to pass up.

And frankly I've had it with this guy Mohammed, and all the violence and oppression his name's inspired. His adherents have turned the praise of his name—*Allahu Akbar*—into a universally recognized signal to take cover. You'd've thought the massacre of thousands of innocents on 9/11 might've been the tipping point, but this teddy bear business is truly over the line. Sometimes absurdity outrages us when atrocity cannot.

We in the West are performing the experiment, for the first time in human history, of living without faith. And we're a mess. We're heavily medicated and in therapy, addicted to anything we can get our hands on, fucking everything that moves, buying tons of shit no one could possibly need, and making up wonky, overhauled, jerry-rigged religions that make even less sense than the old ones, all in a desperate effort to stop feeling so empty and afraid. I love us. I think we're heroic, even if we are doomed. We are under attack by enemies who suffer no such spiritual malaise: they are flush with clear-eyed certainty, they think they know the mind and will of God, and they are wrong about everything. *The best lack all conviction, while the worst/ Are full of passionate intensity.*

Doubt is no day at the beach, but certitude is more like a day at Dachau. What certitude gets you is the Final Solution, Manifest Destiny, the Great Leap Forward—evils so enormous it's hard to believe mere human beings were their agents. We Godless infidels may be a bunch of fuckups and addicts and flakes, but we are, at least, better than that. If our only alternatives are existential confusion or Assholism, I know which side I'm on. I await the fatwa.

What Else They're Calling "Mohammed"

STUFFED EMU(?) WON AT SKEE-BALL, 1992

MIXED DRINKS

"BLOOD OF THE PROPHET"

- CAMPARI FOR THE BLOOD OF THE MARTYRS
- DASH OF BITTERS FOR OUR HUMILIATION AT THE HANDS OF THE ACCURSED ZIONISTS AND THEIR INFIDEL PUPPETS
- GARNISH W/ CHERRY FOR THE VIRGINS PROMISED US IN PARADISE

ALL KINDSA THINGS

HURRICANES

THAT-WHICH-CANNOT-BE-NAMED

"What To Do When the Fatwa Comes."

I received a long and intelligent letter this week taking me to task for my rather reductive reactionary screed last week. It was a letter so well-informed and thoughtfully reasoned that I had a hard time following it and was inclined to respond: "Hm, yeah, sounds like you've got a point there."

My letter-writer was right: I succumbed to exactly the kind of pointless outrage that seems to be the intended effect of most of the articles in the *New York Post*, which made the maligned plush toy Mohammed a *cause célébre* for the better part of a week. Just this week I saw another squib in the *Post* about Muslims stoning women for the crime of getting raped, or cutting off their clitorises—I don't even remember, I've repressed it already, it was yet another Islamo-fascist atrocity to rile up our self-righteous red-blooded loathing of the swarthy mustachioed Other and sell a few more papers. The likelihood that it is well-deserved loathing doesn't mean one ought to lower one's guard against manipulation by the yellow press.

My reader's irrefutable points notwithstanding, I'm still going to maintain that in a world that offers very few alternatives that a person can get excited about, there is nonetheless a qualitative difference between ignorant faith and secular rationalism, between totalitarian theocracies and nations with an institutionalized separation of church and state. And despite our imperialistic shitheadedness and heedless greedy wreck of the planet I would much rather live here in the latter than there in the former, if only for the vices.

I'm afraid this week's cartoon is more of the same puerile and xenophobic silliness. So far, no fatwa. At least not as far as I know, although admittedly I haven't been paying close attention to the news. But I figure being issued a fatwa is like winning the Nobel Prize; someone probably gives you a heads-up. At the very least some reporter probably calls first thing in the morning to hit you with the news and ask you how it feels. I already have a number of safe houses lined up to flee to in friendly nations.

IMPORTANT DISCLAIMER: DO NOT KILL THE CLERIC MOQTADA AL-SADR OR BRING ME THE HEAD OF WILLIAM WEGMAN. THIS IS A JOKE ONLY. YOU WILL NOT RECEIVE THE THOUSAND DOLLARS.

WHAT TO DO
When the Fatwa Comes

FIGHT FATWA WITH FATWA!

ATTENTION, FANS OF THE PAIN: I OFFER A REWARD OF ONE THOUSAND U.S. DOLLARS TO THE ONE WHO KILLS THE CLERIC MUQTADA AL-SADR!

AN ADDITIONAL THOUSAND IS OFFERED TO THE ONE WHO BRINGS ME THE HEAD OF WILLIAM WEGMAN!

LIE LOW A WHILE.

?

IMMEDIATELY AND UNCONDITIONALLY WUSS OUT.

I SINCERELY REGRET ANY UNINTENTIONAL OFFENSE MY IGNORANCE MAY HAVE GIVEN TO FOLLOWERS OF THE PROPHET (BLESSED BE HIS NAME) AND A RELIGION FOR WHICH I HAVE ONLY THE DEEPEST RESPECT.

THERE IS NO GOD BUT ALLAH, AND MOHAMMED IS HIS PROPHET.

A LITTLE YANKEE KNOW-HOW!!

ALLAHU AKB

YEAH Y'KNOW WHAT EAT SHIT AND DIE, ALLAHFUCKER!

WOMWOMWOMWOM

"They Hate the Hot," January 2nd 2008

I hope it shows no disrespect to the late Benazir Bhutto to mention that, as world leaders go, she was a looker. Check out some old photos of her in her youth. Dreamy! Now she's gone, another victim of those sworn enemies of sex, al Qaeda. Her assassination is a tragedy for Pakistan but did give me the opportunity to use a dumb cartoon idea that's been in my head for some time.

This premise first occurred to me when I learned, after the Valerie Plame scandal had already been in the headlines for a year or more, that Valerie Plame was *hot*. I was shocked. Most of my usual news sources—newspapers, radio—are non-visual, and I'd had no idea that she is a *very* *attractive* *lady*. "Oh yeah," one of my friends told me. "Joe Wilson left his wife for her." Jeez *Louise*—if I were in possession of some top-secret information she wanted, I'm afraid I'd blurt it out right away just to impress her, inadvertently forfeiting any incentive for her to contrive circumstances for some unguarded post-coital chitchat. I'd like to see her in one of those tight black leather Emma Peel bodysuits that are standard CIA-issue for lady spies.

Apologies for not drawing Anna Politkovskaya, the Russian journalist whom Putin actually had killed. I firmly believe her to have been hot in her youth, based on photos of her and of her hot daughter, but could not find any old photographs of her suspected hot young self to use as a reference. So instead I chose Yelena Tregubova, whom Putin merely tried to have killed. She, also, as you can see, is a major babe. Her book "Tales of a Kremlin Digger" was critical of the Russian government's suppression of free speech, so they detonated a bomb outside her apartment.

She reportedly missed being killed because she decided to stay an extra few minutes curling her hair—*saved by her hotness!*

I'm not sure whether this cartoon touches on some subtle truth or is just stupid. The world's tendency toward misogyny has only been roiled up in the last century since women have begun assuming more reproductive and economic autonomy and asserting their political power. Women are well known to be the only thing Muslim terrorists fear, their Kryptonite. Religions that worship a father-god have historically been down on women, and it's the countries where those are still the official state religions—not naming any names here—where you hear about the stoning of rape victims and ritual clitorectomies.

It's not just the barbarian lands where the hatred of females has yet to be eradicated. A lot of the weird unreasoning vilification of Hilary Clinton is hard to explain as anything other than misogyny; it's not just because she's a Democrat that the most rabid loathing of her comes from the Right, traditionally your manliest political orientation.

Beauty is something we desire, and nine hundred and ninety-seven times out of a thousand we can't have it, and what we desire and cannot have we come to resent. On sultry summer days in Baltimore, when the local girls—some of them troublingly young—would break out the tube tops and Daisy Dukes, webmaster Dave invariably ended up "screamin' for burqas." My evil friend Ben used to mutter, every time we'd walk past another hair-raisingly gorgeous woman on the streets of the East Village: "I hate them all."

THE ASSHOLES OF THIS WORLD HAVE ONE THING IN COMMON—

They Hate the Hot

VALERIE PLAME — HOT.

(PLUS, A SECRET AGENT. WHAT IS HOTTER?)

DICK CHENEY: NOT.

IF I CANNOT EXTORT LOVE, THEN BY CUNNING CAN I ATTAIN PLEASURE?

...FOR HEAR ME, WAVES: THUS I CURSE LOVE!*

*DAS RHEINGOLD, SCENE I.

DISSIDENT JOURNALIST YELENA TREGUBOVA, FUCKING HOT.

VLADIMIR PUTIN: : NOT SO HOT.

IF I CANNOT INSPIRE LOVE, I WILL CAUSE FEAR.*

* FRANKENSTEIN, CHAPTER 17.

BENAZIR BHUTTO — HOT!

MUSHARRAF — UM, NOT?

I FEEL PRETTY/ OH SO PRETTY/ I FEEL PRETTY AND WITTY AND GAY—

AND I PITY ANY GIRL WHO ISN'T ME TO-DAY!*

*WEST SIDE STORY

WILL NO ONE STOP THESE FIENDS? WHO WILL BE NEXT?

ME, IN MY NEW RACCOON COAT!

BOYD, JEALOUS OF MY SPLENDID APPEARANCE!

IT WILL BE MINE.

I have to admit I really do feel sorry for Hillary, who, as of this writing (the evening of Tuesday the 8th) looks likely to lose her second primary.[1] I wouldn't vote for her—I just have this helpless gut-level empathy for the bitter disappointment she must be experiencing. I almost feel like she should be allowed to be President just because she wants it so much. I feel the same way about John McCain, who won't get another chance (and, cheeringly, looks like he'll win New Hampshire) and I felt the same about Bob Dole back in '96. She probably is better prepared to be President than Obama is. And he's not any less beholden to corporate interests than she is. But Obama's appeal, as everyone but his campaign staff admits, is based more on what he is, or seems to be, than on anything he's done. It's about his race, his youth, his oratorical magic. It just isn't fair.

But Presidential politics are not like local or even senatorial elections, which are decided on the basis of mundane factors like voting records, issues, and name recognition. They're mythic rituals. And even curmudgeonly cartoonists have to admit that it would be an inspiring vindication of the myth of America we all like to believe in to see a black man become the president of the United States. Especially after eight years of the worst, most smug and undeserving, arrogant and entitled white man of all, the *whitest* white man, the very embodiment of Whitey, The Man: George W. Bush.

It's an irony and a shame that the most interesting election campaign in my lifetime comes just after I became incapable of caring about it. I remember how, toward the end of his career, when David Brinkley would reappear during elections as an elder commentator, he no longer even bothered to conceal his boredom and contempt for the whole dull charade. He'd seen it all too many times: the campaign promises, the attack ads, the "gaffes," the "bounces," all the fake horse-race excitement. And a lot of the current excitement is just advertising hype—the same artificial excitement they have to generate every four years just to keep up the ratings, no matter how foregone a conclusion the election is. Reading a recent article about the imminent New Hampshire primary, I was reminded that Bill Clinton's celebrated "comeback" in '92 was coming in second to Paul Tsongas. I haven't thought of Paul Tsongas in fifteen years. And I think I may have voted for him. So let's bear in mind that the current epidemic of Obamamania may be no more significant or enduring a phenomenon than the ascendancy of Paul Tsongas.[2]

But there's more to my indifference than a healthy resistance to media noise. The last eight years have taken a lot out of anyone who cares about this country, much less the kind of sap who squanders a lot of intellectual energy and passion on politics. The 2000 election, stolen in a bloodless coup, was an unbelievable affront to democracy that ought to have had angry mobs firebombing the Supreme Court building, but the 2004 election was, in a way, even more profoundly demoralizing, in that it appears to have been fairly won by appealing to the good old honest stupidity, bigotry, and cowardice of the American electorate. We'd already had four years of George Bush by then, Iraq was clearly a disaster, and a majority of voters said: yes, more of this guy.

It wasn't just the elections that ground me down but the Bush administration's daily assaults on intellectual honesty, common sense, and basic fairness and decency. It was seeing people like Karl Rove acting publicly proud of things than any normal, well-brought-up person would be ashamed of. I remember a few years ago people went around sputtering with speechless outrage all the time; you'd overhear respectable, taxpaying, homeowning citizens wishing aloud that someone would just shoot the President already. But after seven years of it we've all gone morally numb, limp, and apathetic, like condemned men in the last hour, until even the war in Iraq has become sort of like *The Simpsons*, something I'm aware is still on but never bother to watch anymore. Babies who are abandoned at first scream their lungs out for a while, but after that doesn't work, they lapse

---

1   As testament to the ephemerality of conventional wisdoms, today, the morning of Wednesday the 9th, it turns out she's won it. I find I am relieved for her but also horrified, since I don't actually want her to win. I'm an idiot.

2   Another imperfect prediction, as it turned out.

Looks like a No-Win Election for Me

IF OBAMA WINS I'LL SECRETLY FEEL SORT OF SORRY FOR HILLARY.

IF HILLARY WINS, IT'S MORE OF THE SAME FOREVER.

IF EDWARDS WINS, IT'S AT LEAST FOUR YEARS OF

...AND, OF COURSE, A REPUBLICAN COULD STILL WIN IT.

into silence and passivity. It's not just the barroom warriors who supported the war who are trying to forget about it; so are those of us who passionately opposed it. It's just too awful to bear thinking about any more—except for the guys coming home maimed and traumatized, and the families of the dead, who don't get to choose.

Maybe even more damaging than these specific outrages has been the gradual erosion of optimism that comes from having lived through forty years of elections. I used to get excited about campaigns, and got my hopes up that things might actually change for the better. I voted for the few candidates who actually said anything that sounded sane or reasonable in the primaries, watched them lose to candidates who told people what they wanted to hear, and then dutifully voted for whichever stuffed shirt the Democratic Party foisted off on us in the general election, from Mondale to Dukakis to Kerry, and glumly watched them lose to fake Jesus freaks, fag-bashers and warmongers.

Almost as bad as seeing your candidate lose is seeing him win. Even the best of men and intentions are contaminated when they come into contact with the corruption of the real world. Washington, D.C. is where the world at its most venal oozes through the skin of civilization like a boil. And the best of men are seldom the ones who run for office. Jimmy Carter may well have been one of the few authentic Christians to sit in the Oval Office,

but his ineffectual presidency ended in the dragging humiliation of the hostage crisis. And for all my fondness for Big Bill as a cartoon character, the Clinton administration, from "don't ask, don't tell" to the Starr Report, was one long, embarrassing exercise in compromise, concession, and defeat. The single best moment of the Clinton presidency was election night 1992. I took big bites out of a raw onion with some friends in Baltimore that night, for reasons that would be difficult to explain in this context.

At this point in my life I no longer believe that one individual is going to change things. It's much, much easier for one man to make things catastrophically worse—George Bush single-handedly dismantling the Constitution and Geneva Conventions, like some asshole going on a shooting spree at a playground—than to make things better. But perhaps this just means that I no longer have any right to draw political cartoons and write screeds that'll discourage idealistic, hopeful, excited young people. It's just pointlessly mean, like telling high school kids that their current friends are probably not really going to be their best friends 4-ever. Don't mind me, kids. It's your generation, and maybe this will even be your year. I hope you all have a blast and get laid doing campaign work. I hope your guy wins it. Eat the onion. And savor the taste of it, because it may have to last you a while.

I stumbled upon your cartoons and I think they put America in a bad light.

I love these United States.

It would be a better place if your cartoons were less likely to tear it down or try to make people feel bad about important events.

Can you think of things you like about AMERICA???

Think on what you can do for this nation, not in the ways you want to slam it around.

please, it is time to grow up.

Roofer

Roofer:

I think the things I love about America are not things you would appreciate or understand. Such as the fact that I am free to draw my cartoons, and that you are free to think I am an asshole. As one American to another, I agree: it's a great country.

Tim Kreider

Hi Tim,

Thanks for your reply.

OK, I too love that you are free to draw cartoons and I do think you are one of those assholes. I do appreciate and understand these things.

Lets help others learn to love.

Enjoy,

Andy

Throughout all the Quixotic marches and rallies my friend Megan and I attended during the buildup to the Iraq war, we often spoke of George with a certain fond, exasperated familiarity, like a very difficult friend: "Oh, *George*." Back then he seemed like that kid in *The Twilight Zone* who ruled his small town because he could turn anyone who questioned or contradicted him into a jack-in-the-box—a surly, petulant child despot, omnipotent and invincible. These days the pugnacious reverence he inspired in his supporters has guttered out into embarrassment. Even the tabloids have turned on him, printing stories about his relapses into drinking and his imminent divorce. It's almost as hard to remember that he's still the President now as it was to believe he was the President in that interlude between his inauguration and 9/11, when he was still just a joke.

Except every once in a while you hear something that reminds you that he's still there, and he doesn't know he's not relevant any more. Like his line about the possibility of securing a Middle Eastern peace treaty by the end of the year: "Actually I am on a timetable," he joked. "I've got twelve months." George is loath to admit to caring about such things, but he must secretly long to secure some sort of legacy beyond a whole new section of Arlington National Cemetery. Hoping that peace in the Middle East, a goal that has eluded world leaders since 3000 B.C., will somehow happen within the year for his own personal benefit is vintage George. It's like he just tuned into this whole Middle East thing and wonders what's the big holdup, can't they move things along any faster? You tell yourself you can't possibly be shocked by his ignorance, provincialism, and presumption any more, and yet the guy still manages to leave you speechless one more time.

More ominous was his recent speech at the stupendously tacky Emirates Palace hotel in Abu Dhabi, asserting that Iran is a grave threat to world peace and urging all our dear friends in the Middle East to stand united to oppose them. Do not make the mistake of imagining that there are certain things George and his administration would not dare to do any more now that his popularity rating is in the high single digits. They don't behave like politicians, with half an eye on public opinion or practicality, but more like a decadent, inbred royalty or a third-world military junta. Their political philosophy might be best synopsized as: Who's Gonna Stop Us? If they want to attack Iran—and they do—I assure you they will. I am aware that it would be politically suicidal, logistically impossible, and might well result in the final collapse of the United States as a world power. They will do it anyway. One thing we ought to have learned from the last eight years is that just because it's unimaginable doesn't mean it can't happen.[1]

---

1 In the end, good old cause and effect did catch up to Bush/Cheney after all, albeit too late to affect the outcome of the 2004 election or save the thousands dead in Afghanistan or Iraq. Again, please see my footnote to "The Pain Predicts" (October 12th, 2005) for a defense of what now looks like a let's call it alarmist attitude.

Remember George?

What's *That* Guy Up To?

NEGOTIATING A PEACE TREATY
IN THE MIDDLE EAST.

HE SPENDS A LOT OF TIME ONLINE.

HE'S ON THE ROAD, MAN, GETTIN'
BACK IN TOUCH WITH THE PEOPLE.

AND — WHAT'S *THAT*, GEORGE?

Space is to me what God is to religious people, with the drawback that it doesn't care about me but the advantage that it does exist. I was a front-line soldier in the heroic but doomed defense of Pluto back in aught-six; I once addressed the Forum on Outer Planetary Exploration 2000-2020 at the Lunar and Planetary Institute; I even applied for a job (!) as a writer at the Hubble Space Telescope Institute. I remember I drove down to Baltimore the night before my interview in a rainstorm without working windshield wipers and got up so early the morning that I accidentally brushed my teeth with Deep Heat. It was an ill omen. At the interview I successfully name-dropped Charon and the Drake equation off the top of my head but blew the whole deal when they asked if I had any web experience and I thoughtlessly mentioned my website, thepaincomics.com. As fate would have it, the first cartoon that the horrifyingly beautiful woman interviewing me happened to click on was one called "Another Day, Another Dollar," which depicts a miserable wretch at his office job, a job that apparently consists of hammering nails through his own hand. "No no, don't worry," she told me. "Honesty is the best policy." They didn't hire me.

I also spent more than a few hours as a kid out in dark fields watching the skies for U.F.O.s, hoping to be abducted, so I take more than a passing interest in the latest mass sighting. The O. in question is described as cigar-shaped, 400 yards long and covered with lights that changed color, and having zigzagged through the sky. Bear in mind this was in Texas, where, as one witness says, "everyone is afraid it's the end of times." My friend Jim, who alerted me to this story, is just relieved that prominent figures in the media (by which he means the hosts of the *Today* show) are coming clean about their own U.F.O. sightings, since it makes him feel comfortable finally discussing our own sighting some years ago. I myself would still prefer not to speak of this incident in print, since the circumstances do not make us sound like unimpeachable witnesses. Still, mason jars of Yuengling porter aren't exactly hallucinogenic, *Dumbo* notwithstanding, and Jim and the other dude in the parking lot and I all agreed on what we saw.

Last week my colleague Tom Hart wished aloud that the aliens would finally come, just to mix up the news for once. He's right; the news has been getting old lately. The war in Iraq seems like it isn't ever going to end, the economy's not getting any better, and the Presidential campaign, now in its 374ᵗʰ week and which feels like getting your faith in democracy pulled out through your nose with a long skinny hook, is only halfway through. Like Tom, I'm sick from all the junk that makes up the bulk of our informational diet—meaningless speeches and unintelligible violence, so much sound and fury. Enough of this dismal earthbound bullshit.

What do you think the big headlines were in 1666, the year Newton posited gravitation as a universal force, discovered that white light was composed of the spectrum, and invented differential calculus, or in 1905, the "*annus mirabilis*" when Einstein confirmed quantum theory by analyzing the photoelectric effect, introduced special relativity, and proposed the formulation that matter and energy are equivalent? The Great Fire of London and the The Anglo-Dutch War; the Russian Revolution and the Russo-Japanese War. Essentially, the same as any local six o'clock newcast: Who Got Shot and What Burned Down.

The discoveries and insights of the Newtons and Einsteins are the real history of our species, the slow, painstaking climb from ignorance to understanding. It's the work of those few cloistered freaks in every generation who take a frivolous interest in understanding the universe instead of the important business of Getting More Things or just killin' folks. Sometime this year the Large Hadron Collider will commence operation in Europe, which might confirm certain extradimensional theories of gravitation. (Our own congress cancelled funding for a similar supercollider in the nineties because we had more important things to spend the Peace Dividend on, like war). Will we hear about any of its profound new insights into the structure of the universe on CNN? Maybe—unless Hillary commits a "gaffe" that day, or the Israelis launch a rocket attack on Hamas, or another dirtbag blows himself up in Fallujah.

Enough Local News

ASTRONOMERS HAVE DISCOVERED THAT GALAXIES WITHOUT CENTRAL BULGES HAVE BLACK HOLES.

A "DEATH STAR" GALAXY IS BLASTING A NEIGHBORING GALAXY WITH A JET.

ASTRONOMERS HAVE MAPPED POOLS OF DARK MATTER.

...AND THERE'S BEEN A RASH OF U.F.O SIGHTINGS.

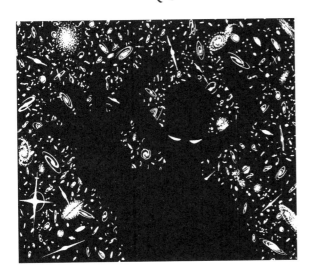

Last week my friend Jim sent me a message saying, "Hey man all the money in the world is going away." This was the first I had heard of the popping of the housing bubble and subsequent implosion of the stock market. I guess if the end of the housing bubble means fewer hideous chintzy McMansions blighting the countryside or lower rents in Manhattan I am for it. But more likely it means me living in the little lodge behind my friend Megan's house, like the Fonz. The truth is, I don't really understand what the stock market or the economy even are. I've never really known what "The Fed" is. When people start talking about things like interest rates I usually just nod judiciously and think about sex or replay scenes from *Star Wars* in my head.

However, I am pretty sure that people who purport to understand these things for a living don't actually know a lot more about them than I do, since things like last week occur with some regularity. I am of course happy to see George get blamed for this, and anything else bad that happens, but I'm not sure it makes any more sense than it does to blame the tribe's shaman for a plague. Though his administration's official policy of looking the other way and whistling while corporate America does whatever it wants seems like it might've been a contributing factor. And it is noteworthy that in all the discussion of the economic downturn I haven't heard anyone mention the Bush administration's reckless and nonsensical fiscal policy of deregulating business and giving huge tax breaks to the richest taxpayers while simultaneously launching two major military invasions and indefinite foreign occupations—the equivalent of quitting your day job to pursue your ambition to write the great American novel while at the same time finally buying that ranch in Montana you've always dreamed of.

On the one hand, there's something childishly exhilarating about financial catastrophe, a vindication of my private theory that our whole economy is founded on bullshit. I've never quite believed that things like "service" and "information" are commodities in the quite same way that, say, steel is. It seems somehow ignominious to me that more Americans are now casino dealers than tool and die makers. And it makes me nervous that nobody knows how to make anything any more. Look at those McMansions: why do they cost a million dollars and yet look so cheap and flimsy while older, smaller, more modest houses look well-made and substantial? Part of me rejoices at the puncturing of the illusion of the New Economy, wrongly imagining a return to some saner, reality-based system, instead of what's more likely to happen, which is me learning to eat Fancy Feast.

Because unfortunately I am one of the prime beneficiaries of the bullshit economy—a happy bit of flotsam on a frothy sea of graphic design and advertising and publishing and marketing. It's not as if *I* know how to do anything useful. I draw a cartoon. I have some money invested and I have yet to ask my financial advisor whether it still exists. I figure, what good will it do me to find out? Might as well live it up while I can. Once the money runs out it's down to the mall to make sandwiches all day for Mr. Fuckerman (rhymes with *Zuckerman*). Long have my friend Ben and I dreaded the day when we would at last be reduced to Making Sandwiches at the Mall. This is the final humiliation, the *ne plus ultra* of failure. Of Mister Fuckerman I can say nothing. He appeared unexpectedly at the eleventh hour, early on Monday morning, when my cartoon is due. He is the embodiment of our fate.

After All the Money's Gone

A RETURN TO THE BARTER SYSTEM.

TIME TO GET REAL JOBS.

WE'LL HAVE TO LEARN TO MAKE STUFF AGAIN.

MAYBE WE COULD ATTACK SOME COUNTRY THAT STILL <u>HAS</u> MONEY AND TAKE THEIRS!

Lately I've been having these thoughts about the election that I don't see reflected anywhere in public—not in print, at least.

This weekend I was talking politics with a couple of female friends in Baltimore, and found myself kind of troubled by their motives for supporting/not supporting Hillary Clinton. One felt like she ought to vote for her out of gender solidarity, as a protest against the kind of prejudice that women in positions of power are routinely subjected to in our society. The other detests the fact that she came to power through marriage, and that she's stood by her philandering husband. Both of them worried about her fitness as a role model for young women. What creeped me out was that neither of them seemed to base their opinions on Hillary's voting record, or her stand (such as it is) on the issues—it was all about personal identity politics and reactions based on their own life experience. And these are smart, university-educated, thoughtful and well-read people. It made me feel uncomfortably like some chauvinistic patriarch circa 1912 having a cigar and brandy in a men's club, chuckling off the notion that fickle, emotional females could be trusted with the solemn responsibility of the vote.

But this sort of haruspication at election time is hardly an exclusively female fallacy. Who knows?—maybe on some level I'm only opposing Hillary because she seems like a mean old lady and supporting Obama because he's a skinny loquacious guy like me. (After all, my original choice was John Edwards, who looks *uncannily* like me.) Most people cast their votes for visceral, not rational, reasons. The fact that Hilary's tearing-up gambit actually paid off in the polls seemed to me like a convincing argument for the repeal of not only the nineteenth amendment but of universal suffrage. Maybe it's as good a time as any to admit, after two thousand years, that democracy was a nice idea that just didn't pan out, people have proved themselves morons after all, it turns out Plato had it right all along: what we really need is an oligarchy of philosopher-kings. The only problem would be finding any philosopher-kings in this country. Carl Sagan and Johnny Cash are dead.

If it comes down to a dismal Hillary-vs.-McCain choice in November, I suppose I will have to pull the lever for Hillary, if only because I would vote for the N.A.M.B.L.A or American Nazi party candidate or a lycanthrope before I'd vote for anyone still willing, after the last eight years, to call himself a Republican. The only thing that gives me any reason to look forward to eight years of a Hillary Clinton Presidency is the prospect of Big Bill back in the White House, getting' sucked off, eatin' gravy fires, smilin' and wavin' at all his enemies. Everybody I hate in this country will die of apoplexy, blood vessels bursting in the brains of conservatives like fireworks across the land.

Let us not consider this election a foregone conclusion, though, especially if it does come down to Hillary and McCain. Although I can't think of one issue on which I agree with John McCain—except that we're both anti-torture, which some of you may still recall did not used to be an issue—I still find him more trustworthy and likeable and deserving of my respect than Hillary Clinton, and since I'm way off the visible political spectrum I suspect quite a lot of more moderate swing voters do, too. And there are a sizable number of voters in this country who just feel a deep unreasoning gut hatred of Hillary Clinton for reasons probably having a lot to do with their mothers. The Democrats are geniuses of defeat. As recent history has demonstrated, they can lose to absolutely anyone.

Let's not lose perspective: Americans are not turning back toward the Democratic party because they've realized the war in Iraq was wrong or that their birthright as American citizens is being taken from them. It's because the economy's falling apart and their jobs look uncertain, and they're frightened. Rudy Giuliani and Mitt Romney didn't miscalculate by appealing to fear again; it's just that this year Americans are more afraid of joblessness than they are of terrorists. Heedless of Darryl Worley's admonitions, they've forgotten all about 9/11; al Qaeda is already so 2001. But if there's another attack before November they will panic and stampede, in landslide numbers, back to the safety of the tough old warmongering white guy.

A Hillary victory over Obama would be demoralizing enough, extinguishing this freak generational flareup of political optimisim and marching us back to drab, cynical, compromised business as usual—like when a dog gets loose in school and everyone briefly goes apeshit but then it's *Okay, fun's over, kids— everyone back to your desks*. But it would be unimaginably worse if

My Horrible, Horrible Thoughts

IF SOMEBODY SHOOTS OBAMA THE WHOLE COUNTRY WILL HAVE TO FEEL LIKE SHIT FOR A LONG, LONG TIME.

THE BEST THING THAT COULD HAPPEN TO THE REPUBLICANS WOULD BE ANOTHER TERRORIST ATTACK.

EIGHT MORE YEARS OF CLINTONS.

THE REPUBLICANS COULD STILL WIN.

Hillary won the nomination by default because somebody'd shot Obama. If that happens, she may yet get her wish to be another LBJ—a capable, unglamorous bureaucrat thrust into thankless power by the death of a far more charismatic and beloved leader, hobbled by a hopeless war she supported against her better judgment, unloved and reviled.

I know you've thought about this. We all have. I'm sure it's the first thing Obama and his family thought about when he considered making a run. (In the Chris Rock comedy *Head of State*, about the nation's first major black Presidential candidate, when Rock's character is first approached with the idea of making a serious run for the office he lapses into a brief reverie in which we see him standing behind a podium while a brass band plays and balloons and confetti fall around him, grinning and waving for 1.7 seconds before somebody shoots him.) And yet it remains taboo to speak of the possibility, and not just for the same superstitious reason that even atheists still add "God forbid" when alluding to some dreadful possibility. It's taboo because of what the possibility would seem to suggest about us as a people. There's a whole constellation of motives surrounding the support for Barack Obama, some of them pure and noble. But one of the more complicated ones is an assuaging of collective guilt, a need to prove to ourselves that we're past the days of blatant discrimination.[1]

But there are four centuries' history of institutional racism on this continent, millions of angry ghosts, a curse to haunt generations. There are still vast, savage swaths of up-front, unapologetic bigotry in this country. I spent fifteen years living in a county where guys in diners or bars would casually drop the old N-bomb early on in a conversation just to test you out, to see if you were one of them or some hippie liberal nigger-lover. This wasn't in darkest Alabama or anything—it's technically within the East Coast megalopolis, between Baltimore and Philadelphia, just off I-95. There are millions of people out there in America who chuckle over the wit of the nickname "Obama-Osama." And thanks to our Second Amendment, they can all have top-of-the-line, high-powered rifles with telescopic sights.

Recently I looked through a book of lynching photos. Being a squeamish person, I couldn't bear to do more than glance at the burnt and dangling corpses and instead spent my time looking at the faces in the crowds. I am horribly fascinated by these faces. What can these people have been thinking? These aren't candid photos, taken surreptitiously—they're posed group portraits, trophy shots, like hunters grouped around a twelve-point buck. The people in the crowds look directly into the camera; their eyes are bright, their expressions tough and smug, humorous and defiant, as if they're all in on the same dirty joke and you're some prim schoolmarm who just walked in on the punchline. I could only find one little girl who looked uncomfortable, and as far as I could tell hers was more of a little-girl "ew" face of distaste than any kind of proto-moral horror. These people thought of themselves as restoring the social order, protecting Southern womanhood. The guy who shoots Obama will think of himself as a hero, a martyr to the Real America, and so will a lot of his redneck brethren.

If that happens—God forbid—it will be a tragedy not only for one man, those who love him, and those who had pinned their political hopes on him, but for the whole nation. It will threaten to persuade us that the worst among us somehow are representative of us all. Just when we were on the verge of a symbolic redemption in the eyes of the world, it'll confirm that we are a lawless, violent nation of racist killers. We'll have to try to resist that interpretation. Progress is always viciously opposed. Political leaders who threaten to disrupt the business of hatred by advocating irresponsible notions of peace and unity, from Anwar Sadat to Yitzhak Rabin to Melitus Mugabe Were and David Kimutai Too, are routinely shot. Shit, they killed Socrates and Jesus and Lincoln and Gandhi. The only thing to do is not let the bastards win. Someone else will have to step forward into the line of fire, and someone else after them.

One of my friends, who wishes very much to remain anonymous, voiced her worry that, if Obama is elected, any missteps or shortcomings that in any other President would just be subject to the usual second-guessing and derision will instead become fodder for bigots, reinforcing racist stereotypes. This inspired a panel of evil genius which I was too cowardly to run in the Baltimore *City Paper* but offer here as a bonus for the delectation of you connoisseurs. You may only look at it if you promise not to get mad. Okay? Remember: you promised. Very well then.

---

1 I've been told that this taboo existed mainly among white people; black media outlets were talking much more openly and matter-of-factly about fears for Obama's safety.

ONCE ELECTED, OBAMA PROVES LAZY AND SHIFTLESS.

This is turning out to be a very weird electoral year. In some ways it's been a surprising triumph of participatory democracy over our wonky, rigged electoral system—voters are turning out in record numbers with genuine enthusiasm, primaries like my own home state of Maryland's have actually mattered for the first time in my life, all the supergroomed big-haired millionaire white guy candidates have been defeated early, and the insurgency of the Obama campaign has wrecked the presumptive inevitability of a Clinton restoration. It's also shaping up to turn into another 2000-style historic mess without clear rules or precedent.

As of this writing, my own home state's primary has yet to be decided. For the first time in memory my vote is more than a formality. It's cheering to hear so many people saying: "This is the first time my vote has ever counted"—except if you think about it it's also kind of infuriating. Why should this be? Isn't this, you know, America? Aren't we all allegedly citizens of a democracy? Why, for decades, have people in Iowa and New Hampshire been allowed to choose which candidates the rest of us get to vote for? It's insulting even to have to think about such places as Iowa; never having to think about them is one of the benefits of not living there.

I've never quite understood by what shadowy process the initial group of uniformly conservative, hawkish, pro-corporate primary candidates emerges: do the Masons/Illuminati/Trilateral Commission vet them all before giving them permission to declare candidacy? Note that only Dennis Kucinich refuses to kowtow to the Guild Navigator. This is what dooms him to perpetual marginality. (By the way, in doing a google image search to get Dennis Kucinch's silhouette right, I learned something shocking: Dennis Kucinich's wife, Elizabeth, is a tall, leggy, redheaded dish twenty-nine years his junior. Why am I the last to learn about these matters of national importance?)

I never did come up with quite the right panel to express our very real trepidation at the unwelcome possibility that the party nomination might come to rest in the hands of "superdelegates," about whom we have never heard before and are suddenly learning rather a lot. Ideally this panel would've illustrated the threat of having all our votes rendered irrelevant by party insiders, but instead I got all distracted by superheroes. Which you could argue is the whole problem with our electoral process.

Understanding Our Electoral Process

UNKNOWN SHADOWY FORCES PRODUCE EIGHT TO TEN PARTY CANDIDATES

A SAMPLING OF IOWA DINGBATS AND NEW HAMPSHIRE CRANKS DETERMINES WHICH OF THESE CANDIDATES WE GET TO VOTE FOR:

THE PARTY NOMINEES ARE CHOSEN BY "SUPERDELEGATES" AT THE CONVENTION.

ULTIMATELY, THE PRESIDENT IS CHOSEN BY DIEBOLD® AND THE SUPREME COURT.

My childhood friend Michael and I used to play a little game called "Now We're Even," which involved punching, kicking, or otherwise physically assaulting each other and saying, "*Now* we're even!" "No, *now* we're even!" The game had no end; it could only escalate. The logic of this game was basically indistinguishable from that of most geopolitical revenge cycles. Unless the spiral of violence was interrupted by an injury or someone's mom, it could break out into the dreaded Grappling!, an all-out spazzy fracas in which no one could hope to emerge a true victor and the survivors envied the dead.

I drew this image simply because I couldn't bear not having seen it in print anywhere else. I kept not seeing what seemed like this pretty basic and germane information graphically represented in any U.S. media source. I had to draw it just to see it for myself, even though I feared it would turn out solemn and preachy, the sort of thing cartoonists do when they're gunning for a Pulitzer.

I finally broke down and drew it this week for a couple of reasons. Lately it seems the big complaint about Iraq has been how much it's cost. In terms of money, that is. One recent estimate, which includes private contracts, runs into the trillions. (That's twelve zeros.) I guess it's heartening to know that fiscal irresponsibility can still stir the American conscience to moral indignation.

Also, the news lately has all been electoral handicapping and gossip: *Hillary offers the number two spot to Obama! Eliot Spitzer got caught with a naked lady!* Meanwhile, somewhere on page 7, another five soldiers killed in Baghdad, another sixteen civilians dead in a bus explosion near Basra. It seemed like a reminder might be in order.

It's an indication of how tribal we still are as a society that it feels vaguely treasonous and lily-livered of me even to acknowledge, much less count up and make a big deal of, the casualties among our "enemies." Most Americans can probably tell you how many U.S. servicemen we've lost in Iraq (I myself lost count after 2000), but far fewer have any idea of the magnitude of the losses and suffering we've inflicted on the people of Iraq.

I regret to say that the proportions depicted here are more or less accurate. Estimates of civilian casualties differ widely, with the 30,000 President Bush reluctantly owned up to being at the low end of the range. Last month the leftie rag *The New England Journal of Medicine* published a paper placing the number of violent deaths in Iraq between March of 2003 and June of 2006 at 151,000. This would be roughly fifty times the number of people killed in the terrorist attacks of 9/11.

At first I'd envisioned drawing this as a bar graph (ingeniously using the twin towers as the bars) except then, on doing the calculations, I realized that this would be impossible unless the Baltimore *City Paper* were to print a special issue in which my cartoon would be a centerfold accordioning out to a length of about twenty-five feet. So then I decided to repeat the image of the twin towers as though they were a unit of measure, or those silhouettes stenciled on the sides of fighter planes to tally kills. I thought I had finished the cartoon, and the disproportion looked pretty grotesque and horrific, when I recounted and realized that, due to my remedial multiplication skills and perhaps a balking of my imagination in the face of the unbelievably grim figures, I had only reproduced twenty-five icons of the World Trade Centers— half the actual number. I still had to double it.

Jesus Christ we've killed a lot of people. I'm not even counting Afghanistan.

Perhaps it will sound naïve or paranoid of me to suggest that a massive, organized national project of killing tens of thousands of people in another country might be undertaken for anything other than wholly rational and well-intentioned reasons. It would be reductive of me to imply that we invaded Iraq solely out of revenge. All sorts of *casus belli* were run up the flagpole in the months preceding the invasion, most of them pretty obviously

specious. There were the ignoble reasons never mentioned, and, yes, there may even have been a few noble ones. But it does seem worth noting that soldiers *en route* to Iraq were shown grisly footage of 9/11 as part of their training, and a majority of them believed that their primary mission there was payback.

I won't say that we killed 150,000 people in Iraq in direct reprisal for 9/11, but I do think it's the reason we don't mind having killed them so much. This is why we aren't withholding our taxes or staging massive strikes or immolating ourselves in protest, why so many people who are otherwise at least passively decent, who spend a lot of money on their pets and hate to forget anyone on their Christmas card lists, can stomach the massacre of tens of thousands of innocent men and women and children. After what happened on 9/11, a lot of people somewhere in the Arab world—it didn't particularly matter where—were going to have to die.

I suppose it does make an Old-Testament kind of strategic sense: we've shown the world that any attack on the United States will be repaid fiftyfold, against some arbitrarily chosen country full of brown-skinned people. It definitely Sends a Message. It's really not so different from punishing a traitor by executing his entire family, razing his hometown, and seeding the ground there with salt, Saddam-style. Except that it's more like punishing him by executing some *other* guy's family, razing his hometown, and seeding the ground over there with salt. The Iraq war never had anything to do with sense or justice; it was more like a revenge killing, a mass human sacrifice. I hope we're starting to feel appeased.

The main difference between the two scales in your comic is that the casualties in 9/11 were direct and intentional. While the civilian casualties in Iraq are NOT intentional from us, and are ALSO at the result of the terrorists....you cannot possibly put all the blame on the US Soldiers. Wait...was I supposed to say the Bush Administration? Nope...I meant the US Soldiers. What you actually said was that the US Soldiers are responsible for all the deaths of Iraqi civilians. How do I know this? Well we both know that America isn't out to kill Iraqi innocent civilians. And President Bush cannot possibly be responsible for each and every solider. That is impossible. Good job at insulting the US Troops by calling them a bunch of blood-thirsty terrorists out to get Iraqi civilian blood.

Thank you very much for your time,
-An anonymous Stumbler.

Anonymous Stumbler:

Obviously I agree that planning the deaths of thousands of innocent civilians is more morally and viscerally repulsive than inadvertently causing deaths through stray missiles. But there's also something subtly monstrous about the psychology of killing thousands of people while feeling blameless because you don't admit to yourself that you're doing it. I know the U.S. military doesn't target civilians, but we also know very well that civilians are going to get killed in any war, so it's disingenuous to pretend that all those deaths are truly accidental. I guess intentions matter to some extent, but if someone I loved were killed by a bomb, I don't think I'd care whether he'd been killed on purpose by terrorists or were only the collateral damage of a foreign air force. I don't know, I only took one moral philosophy course in college and all I remember is the professor's Smoky Robinson imitation, so you tell me which is worse: killing 3,000 people on purpose, or killing 150,000 by accident?

Tim

You acknowledge the fact that the Bush administration and the soldiers do not directly target the civilians, but your comic implies otherwise. Your comic shows VP Cheney suggesting that the U.S should give them "five for flinching" (meaning the civilians, right?) Obviously, that implies a direct intention of targeting civilians... unless of course you are talking about the terrorists.

If you agree that the Bush Administration and the soldiers do not target the innocent, doesn't this mean you are against the war and NOT the Bush Administration? (Unless there are other issues that I am not aware about)

You ask which would be better: 3,000 intentional deaths, or 150,000 accidental deaths? I do see your point but you have to understand that war is war and people are going to die. It is tough to understand but while facing a threat and going to war, people will die.

A.S.,

I'm not saying our soldiers are no different from terrorists; I'm saying our dead are no different from Iraqi dead. Excerpt that they have a lot more of them. All I wanted was to convey, in stark visual terms, the rude mute fact of the disparity in casualties. We've killed fifty times more people in Iraq than terrorists have killed here. And it bothers me that about 1/500th as many people are aware of this as are currently experts on the opinions of Barack Obama's pastor or Hilary Clinton's precise whereabouts in Bosnia circa 1996.

My enthusiasm for extended back-and-forth debates with people I do not know is not inexhaustible. Let me suggest that we let the matter drop for now and resume exactly this same argument five years and a few tens of thousands more casualties from now.

Tim

A Little Follow-Up on That Whole Iraq Thing

I recently found an old thread on a comics message board about a "statement of conscience" my colleague Megan Kelso and I ran in the *Comics Journal* back in January of 2003, opposing the invasion of Iraq, to which hundreds of cartoonists appended their names. (We'd modeled this on the ads pro and con the Vietnam War signed by famous science-fiction writers and placed on facing pages in *Galaxy* magazine in 1968.) It read, simply:

> The undersigned cartoonists oppose the Bush administration's policies both abroad and at home in its response to the terrorist attacks of 9/11. The "War on Terror" is being used as an excuse to launch a unilateral and unprovoked invasion of Iraq for political motives, and to repeal the rights and freedoms for which this country first fought. The America we believe in doesn't attack first, or arrest its citizens without charges. If comic books have taught us anything, it is that Superpowers should only be used for good.

I hadn't read any responses to it at the time it was published, but there is a now certain bitter savor in looking back at the reactions of the dorkwad cognoscenti of the comics community.

One occasionally sees political leaders' lies replayed after they've been exposed and contradicted, but much more seldom do we get to reexamine some of the arguments, let's charitably call them, advanced by our fellow Americans in national debates later on, after the facts have come out and the consequences have followed. We should do this more often, because it is here that the real decision to go to war is made: not on the floor of the Senate or in the op-ed pages of newspapers or the studios of Sunday morning talk shows, but over dinner tables and in barrooms and on internet message boards. Often the participants in these discussions are unconsciously parroting the talking points of professional propagandists, which is why professional propagandists get paid so much. People need

logical-sounding rationales for their bloodlust; you can't win a water-cooler debate just by screaming, "Kill! Kill! Kill!" My old dance instructor used to tell us that "our thoughts are always only the shadows of our feelings," and I believe that all those cool, hardheaded arguments about WMD and UN resolutions and Saddam's tyranny and the threat he posed to the rest of the world and the plight of the Kurds were just so much respectable cover for berserk animal hatred and fear.

So in the spirit of pure malicious hindsight I am exhuming some of the highlights of that colloquy here and putting them on cruel display. I'll refrain from any editorial comment, as no rebuttal of mine could be more eloquently damning than the events of the last five years. I'm also not going to bother to correct grammar or spelling or even insert those aloofly devastating little [sic]s. (I realize that English spelling is pretty arbitrary and hardly a measure of intelligence, but sorry, snobby or not, I am unlikely to be swayed in my position on an issue as serious as whether or not to go to war by the opinion of someone who can't spell "masturbate.") I will even, with some reluctance, leave unspoken my theories on the implications of the curious frequency with which the words "real men" and "balls" seem to come up in pro-war arguments.

WE stood up for France and Germany and kept them from becoming a Communist Bloc. And what do we get? The cold shoulder when we need to stand up for ourselves. Contrary to Leftist propaganda Hussein is behind 9/11. The Axis of Evil is real, a loose alignment of Antiamerican states and that includes Iraq.

—masterman

so let me get this straight... megan kelso and joe zabel (who?) would have me beleive that they know what the United States government should be doing better than the president, dick cheney, colin powell and the joint chiefs of staff? i find that very hard to beleive, and pretty ballsy on their part to even think of. here's a thought... if your a liberal pink-o pascifist, just stay the hell out of war talks and leave it to men who actually know what the hell is going on!!!

—justapilgrim32

Masterman speaks the truth. Nuke Baghdad.

—Haddison

I love people who say there's no Smoking Gun, well in my mind what's next to a Smoking Gun ??? Usually a Dead body I don't want it to be me or mine.

—finar

What say we make the ad a double-page spread? On one side, list the creators in favor of, and on the other side list the creators opposed to? That way we can all sit back and have a good laugh at how silly all this crazy talk is and it won't seem to hurt so much when we're gagging on nukes and smallpox, courtesy of Saddam and his band of despots! Yeah, that's it. I'd much rather ponder the whys and hows of ethnic dischord while eating our nation's babies for breakfast, in the midst of some post-apocalyptic Jurassic.

—jeaoure

What a load of crap. 1. An invasion of Iraq is far from unprovoked. Iraq violated the terms of the cease fire. End of discussion. 2. An invasion of Iraq would be anything but unilateral. Ten European nations (Spain, Italy, Denmark, Poland, Britain, Portugal, Hungary, the Czech Republic, Slovakia and Albania) have voiced their support for an invasion. Australia and Israel are definitely on board. If another vote is taken in the UN next week, I'll bet many, many, more nations will follow suit (as they did with the last resolution). To call an invasion of Iraq unilateral and unprovoked is a lie.

—eric w

What a load of horse shit. I'm sorry for the language but that's what I believe. Name one civil liberty that is being taken from us? Just one

and give an example of when and how it was violated. [...]

Our government has not arrested any of our citizens either, all of the people arrested in the wake of 9/11 were here on visas or expired ones that have ties to terrorists. Provide proof that one, again just one, United States citizen was arrested and kept for no reason.

If we do go to war with Iraq we will be going to secure the freedom this nation was founded and fought for. If Saddam or any other maniacal person is allowed to hold over our heads the threat of nuclear or biological attacks then we don't have freedom we have fear. We are not going to war with Iraq to pick on other nations, we are going to war with Iraq to protect ours. And to be blunt if it comes down to our nation or thiers they can go to Hell.

—thomas C

I have ZERO problem with going in and taking this asshole out. As a nation we do stand to gain in strategic, political, and economic areas by moving forward with this war. If allowing Saddam to gain strength inspires other oil-producing nations to rise up and enter into contention with the U.S., use Saddam as an object lesson. If going to war with Iraq keeps me from having to pay $5 a gallon at the pump, I accept that.

If taking out Saddam and his regime gives North Korea enough of the willies to get out of their nuclear program, I'm all for it.

If taking out Saddam and his regime shows the rest of the world that we will not back down from a challenge, then I'm all for it.

War is, has been, and (despite the best wishes of liberals) always will be a part of the human condition. The only thing that is accomplished by refusing to go to war is that you allow those who don't refuse to go to war to get the better of you. Diplomacy is that language that nations speak to one another, when that language is no longer effective, war IS the only option. Embargoes have been meaningless, resolutions have been ignored, diplomacy has failed... the stick is what is left when it comes to this guy and we have to have the balls to use it.

While I understand the well-meaning intentions of the "doves"

A Little Follow-Up, cont.

I am thankful that pragmatic, serious, men and women are in the positions of power within this nation. Hopefully, Bush II can go the distance that his father didn't and wrap this idiot up once and for all, thereby reducing the need to do this again in the future.

—*nicholasw*

In conclusion, I guess we should all really be happy. Everyone forms a symbiotic circle. The Hawks get to rant and rave and drop half million dollar toys and blow shit up, as is their wont, and the liberals get to masterbate over the fact that the fascists in Washington are beating down the door and victimizing them and that Iraqi children are dying every day, and they might to relive the late sixties and listen to buffalo springfield and paint peace signs on their bellies, or be Rosa Luxemborg for a day, but at the very least, I get to watch the circus every day on TV. I look forward to watching gun camera footage interspersed with peace-sign painted hippie chicks. It's almost as good as a Jerry Bruckheimer film.

Now, i am getting back to my gamecube.

—*jsunlight*

That was five years ago. Those hundred and fifty thousand people were still alive then, the worth of their lives being debated by the likes of masterman, justapilgrim32 and nicholasw. It would be comforting to imagine, for the sake of the nation and my own peace of mind, that these posters were all fifteen-year-olds fed on an intellectual diet of Ayn Rand and *Punisher* comics. But I fear they may have been my fellow voters and taxpayers.

I will leave the last word this week to Khalid al-Ansary, an Iraqi employee of the *New York Times* who lost a friend in a suicide bombing this week. In yesterday's *Times* he wrote:

> At some moments, a thought comes to my mind, and I become at this moment a disbeliever, when I believe that God does not care for Iraqis any more. What is true are Oliver Goldsmith's famous words, that "one half of the world are ignorant how the other half lives."

TWILIGHT OF THE ASSHOLES

OKAY WE AMERICANS MAY BE DICKS BUT COME ON—

We Ain't So Bad

I MEAN, WHO'D YOU *RATHER* HAVE BE A SUPERPOWER:

THE *CHINESE?*

THE *RUSSIANS?*

MAYBE THE EUROPEANS?

OH RIIGHT... NEVER MIND.

MAYBE IF THE *WOMEN* RAN THINGS... YEAH— THEN THERE WOULDN'T *BE* "SUPERPOWERS"!

YEAH RIGHT. [See overleaf]

I was in Lhasa less than a year ago, and it is one of the places I love most on this earth. Watching the news footage this week of overturned cars burning in Barkhor Square in front of the Jokhang, the holiest temple of Tibetan Buddhism, was, for me, a little like seeing your childhood public library vandalized or your family farm turned into McMansions. It's hard to know what's happening over there because of the Chinese's crude (but effective) censorship tactics; *The New York Times* was relying for information on the Lonely Planet message board and phone calls placed at random to ten-year-olds in bread shops. But it's not hard to figure out who's more likely to be the aggressors in confrontations between the Chinese army and Buddist monks, or to decide whom to believe when it's the word of the Chinese government against, well, anybody else at all. The Chinese have released videos of Tibetans looting stores on Youtube (though note that they don't appear to be stealing merchandise but piling it in the streets and burning it in protest), but so far no video seems to have surfaced of the Chinese troops shooting into crowds.

For a sense of what Americans sound like when they're defending the Iraq war to the rest of the world, poke your head in on some online message boards and have a look at some of the comments on the riots in Tibet posted by Chinese: the Tibetans are barbarians, they should be grateful to the Chinese for being there, the Chinese put an end to all sorts of atrocities, offered them economic development, built schools. Again with the schools—you'd think that the great imperial powers of the world were just fanatics for education, like some sort of heavily armed truant board or PTA, invading icorrigible hooky-playing nations and forcibly building schools out of the stern, well-intentioned kindness of their hearts.

All of which rather sidesteps the issue that it's not their fucking country. I remember once talking to a Chinese political cartoonist—a bright, erudite, cosmopolitan woman—who nevertheless, on the subject of Tibet, innocently parroted the party line: well, they were invited there, Tibet was really very backward before the Chinese came, they were helping to develop the area, the Tibetans should be grateful to them. Replace *Chinese* with *Americans* and *Tibet* with *Iraq* and see whether this doesn't start to sound familiar.

In fairness to my conservative compatriots, even the most bigoted and bloodthirsty, God-guns-'n'-guts Red-staters cannot begin to compete with the kind of shockingly vile, xenophobic, racist rhetoric the Chinese can crank up: "the so called 'tibetans' r bunch of maggots and theives that have been spoiled by china's ethnic policy for over 60 yrs [sic]," "suck a big titi, you westren inferior white PIGS and Japanese asses, Tibet is part of China since 1271 A.D." Also worthy of note is that, as with most American pro-war messages online, the sentiments of the pro-Chinese writers tend to be thuggish, sputtering invective written in stunted sentences riddled with misspellings, seemingly typed with fists. (The above comments were culled from Youtube, which admittedly is not exactly the Athenian agora even when the subject is *Star Wars* fanfilms or fat kids falling off of things.) The Chinese at least have the excuse of writing in a second language. Still: "Suck a big titi"? Little do you know that we red-blooded Americans love nothing more than to suck a big tit*ty*, you Maoist chumps! Being forced to suck a big titty is as being thrown into the briar patch for us! Ha, ha!

It does seem as if many of the major powers—China, Russia, and America—are using "terrorism," a scary term you can apply to pretty much any armed group you don't like, as an excuse to move further in the direction of authoritarianism. I'm impressed that our own constitution—which is, after all, just a contract, a piece of paper—has so far actually succeeded in restraining us from becoming an out-and-out autocracy or conquering empire to the extent that it has.

We Americans undeniably have our little cultural foibles that make us a uniquely deranged and arrogant superpower (our pathological Puritan obsession with/phobia of sex, our totally unrelated fetish for guns, our lack of any meaningful value other than money, our inexperience with mass carnage on our soil and consequent disregard for foreign casualties, and, perhaps most dangerous, our innocent conviction that we know what's best for everyone), but we've acted no worse than any of the world's peoples have when they've had their chance to run things. Given such dominion, everyone behaves swinishly. Look at the British, the Germans, the French, the Spanish or the Portuguese—even the Beligans, for crying out loud—all of them have strutted their hour upon the stage. More tellingly, look at the obverse list of peoples whose names have become synecdoche for exploitation and atrocity: the Tasmanians, the Jews, the Algerians, the Aztecs, the Congolese.

Let's imagine for a moment that the Germans and Japanese had won World War II, or that the Soviets and Red Chinese had won the Cold War. It's always tricky to play "what ifs" with history, but it seems safe to say that Elvis and bikinis would not have ensued. We Americans may have acted like a ruthlessly exploitative mercantile empire since World War II, but at least we haven't literally tried to conquer the world or exterminated whole peoples (lately). All we wanted was to plunder enough resources to live like Space Age Pharaohs for a century or so.

And, really, if there has to be a superpower at all, who would you rather have running rampant across the globe: Russia, a gangster state? The fascist Chinese? You draw unflattering caricatures of Vladimir Putin, you get pushed off the roof of your apartment building by his personal hit men. You march in protest of the latest war in China, they don't load you in the paddy wagon and hold you without charges for a few days; they just shoot some of you and the rest of you run away screaming.

As a dissident and an artist, I'm grateful that I can call George Bush an idiot and a criminal without fear of any reprisal more severe than obscurity. One of the more oxymoronic arguments you hear made by hawkish conservatives is that we liberals ought to get down on our knees and thank God that we live in a free country where we can piss and moan all we want and not in an authoritarian state where (and you can almost hear them salivating over the details here) we'd be taken out and shot in the back of the head for criticizing the government—strongly implying that we should demonstrate this gratitude by shutting the fuck up.[1]

---

[1] A note on Panel 4: This panel is inspired by the naive feminist canard that if women ran the world there'd be no more wars and governments would finally invest in education and health care (witness the compassionate gynotopia ushered in by Margaret Thatcher).

This issue of breastfeeding vs. bottle-feeding seems to be to mothers what Israel is to the Arabs and Jews, what Taiwan is to the Chinese, or 9/11 to paranoid schizophrenics: everybody immediately abandons all civility and starts shrieking and whacking each over the head with poorly lettered signs. Something about motherhood brings out whatever's the female equivalent of machismo. I asked my friend Jenny, a member of the La Leche League, a breastfeeding advocacy group, whether there were any good epithets in that community for the opposing side, and she reported that although the formula feeders had some perjorative terms for breastfeeders ("militant lactivists" or the euphonious "titty gestsapo") there was nothing comparable to denigrate bottle-feeders. You'd think with years of ill will on both sides someone would've come up with something snappier. I guess leave invective to the professionals.

I don't mean to suggest that female concerns are any more trivial or marginal than men's. I think childrearing methods are at least as important to a society as, say, its economic system. I find the breastfeeding vs. formula debate about as compelling as the conflict over free markets vs. a centralized economy, over which millions of men have killed each other.

Hi Mr. Krieder,

I saw your angst about your lack of income, and I thought of a couple of things in response to your attitude toward making money off of your website. I don't understand why you'd feel a need to be apologetic about the prospect of doing so. More specifically: "that is not the sort of thing we do around here…"

Why the fuck not???? If people are enjoying what you do and finding value in it (as evidenced by the fact that they keep coming back for more), why not make them contribute to (or, as it sounds in your case, simply establish) your bottom line, especially if it enables you to keep on cranking out the 'toons? Why feel guilty about that in the least? Holy shit, bro, rake in as much as you can! If you eventually find yourself drowning in a sea of disposable income, you can assuage your guilt in the manner of Bill Gates, by starting scholarships for young artists, or buying clean underwear for your friend Boyd, or something like that. That's capitalism, and it's nothing to be ashamed of: you do something valuable for people, and people pay you so that you can keep on doing it.

Maybe it won't put your name in the billionaire's list next to Bill Gates, but it'll help pay the bills. So get over your guilt, and earn a living.

Best Wishes,
Mitch

Mitch,

My disdainful comment that "that is not the sort of thing we do around here" referred specifically to placing ads on the site. I'm not sure I can explain my reservations in any way that will make rational sense—it's very visceral and squishy, just a vague ethical/aesthetic squeamishness.

Did you know that *MAD Magazine* has started running ads? Well, they have. I don't know how old you are but if you're anywhere around my age (40ish) perhaps you can share in some of my sense of disappointment, almost betrayal, that they would run real ads side by side with their fake ads that expose the empty hype and blatant lies of advertising. Kids get duped and disillusioned by ads very early on in life. Maybe you still remember the first thing you ever bought that proved to bear no resemblance to the thing advertised (X-ray Specs? Sea Monkeys?). It was partly because *MAD* was ad-free that you felt you could trust *MAD*; you knew *MAD* had no agenda other than its vigilant and relentless mockery of all forms of bigotry, hypocrisy, and bullshit.

As an adult, it still depresses me when people advertising apartments on the "owners" section of craigslist turn out to be real estate brokers, or when bored horny teens turn out to be software programs. I don't remember the figures for how many thousands of advertisements the average American is subjected to per day, but they're ubiquitous, unrelenting, an unavoidable part of the fabric of our daily existence, worse even than Ray Bradbury imagined in *Fahrenheit 451*. There are ads on the highway, on the subway, in supermarket muzak, in movie theaters, over urinals, on hearses. There are ads for other TV shows in the corners of TV shows you're trying to watch. There are TVS in elevators, in the backs of cabs, in freaking gas pumps. I find it demeaning to be treated always only as a consumer, an audience, a target market, rather than as a citizen or a human being. Lie detectors work because they measure stress levels, and lying is (kind of hearteningly) inherently stressful for human beings; I think it must also have some unhealthy effect on the human psyche to be lied to thousands of times a day.

Well my rhetoric is getting all het up here. I don't mean to imply any judgment of your own decision to run thematically relevant ads on your site, which may well offer stuff your readers can use. For my own part, I feel like not running ads sets me apart from the false and clamorous world of commerce, where the agenda is always ultimately to get you to Buy More Shit You Do Not Need. The Pain is a sort of haven where the only agenda is the up-front one of my own crackpot opinions.

Here's hoping we can toast our material success with Krug on board one or the other of our Learjets in the near future.

Tim Kreider

THE ECONOMY'S IN THE CRAPPER — TIME FOR ONE OF THOSE
Get-Rich-Quick Schemes

MY GRAPHIC MEMOIR ABOUT GROWING UP BLIND AND LESBIAN IN THE SLUMS OF SÃO PAULO

MY SCREENPLAY ABOUT GANGSTAS AND REDNECKS TEAMING UP TO *FIGHT ZOMBIES*

A WHOLE GODDAM BOOK OF CAT CARTOONS

CUSTOM ASS TOURS OF THE MET

April 2nd, 2008

So desperate is the anticipation of never having to see George's mean, simpering face or hear his sniggering voice again that it's easy to forget that many of the problems he's created, exacerbated, or ignored in his two terms are likely to be long-lasting and all but insoluble. Though it'll be a relief just to have someone visibly in power who at least acknowledges that the*re* problems, after eight years of Neronian denial.

A European reader of mine recently asked me over beers, "So, Iraq: how long?" I was like: you're asking me? I figure either we'll maintain heavily fortified bases there until the oil runs out, around which the actual country can go to hell or not, or else it'll become so inconvenient and humiliating that we'll finally be forced to declare total victory and flee, and then pretend that the ensuing bloodbath was a completely unanticipated failure of whatever flimsy Iraqi government we've left propped up behind us. I don't know, don't pay any attention to me, I'm just a cowardly America-hating liberal. I know Freedom Is Not Free.

I understand less about the economy than I do about dark matter or my own car, but I notice that a lot of Europeans are currently visiting New York to shop, which is as hiariously cheap to them as Buenos Aires is to us. My friend Ken, who has retreated to an energy-independent community in Missouri where he's busily buying hand tools and cultivating a food-bearing forest, warns me that events are proceeding according to the Peak Oilers' darkest predictions about the coming economic crisis. He is strongly urging me to buy gold.

Then there's the wreck that's been made of the Constitution. Long, dense, heavily footnoted articles have appeared in places like *Harper's* detailing how power formerly distributed among the three branches of government has been consolidated in the executive or outsourced to private enterprise. These articles are too relentlessly, sadistically demoralizing for me to read, but their cumulative gist seems to be: we're fucked. The next President, like the first populist reformer taking over a banana republic after years of rule by a rapacious and nepotistic military junta, may find that the government's coffers and infrastructure have been too effectively gutted to begin to repair.

This is not to mention the ruin of America's name around the world. As the French foreign minister recently put it, "The magic is over."

I'm sorry to say it seems likely that America has gone over the hump. And when something as big as we are goes down, it tends to take a lot of other things with it. This week I am undertaking Edward *Gibbon's Decline and Fall of the Roman Empire*. I expect to find little in the way of cheering news in this work, but I hope it will provide some much-needed perspective.

Beyond the merely political problems lie the big apocalyptic 3 A.M. fears. The same reader who asked me about Iraq admitted that he could barely bring himself to contemplate the "Malthusian catastrophe" he fears is imminent. Our descendants might have to endure another thousand years of ignorance and squalor kneeling before black velvet altars to Elvis before some 30th-century Leonardo re-invents the futon and the toaster oven. But none of these worst-case scenarios—fossil fuel depletion, global economic collapse, mass starvation, the end of our current civilization—comes close to the unthinkable nightmare scenario of a major climate change that would render the earth uninhabitable for human life. There's no way of knowing whether we've already missed our window of opportunity to turn things around and passed an irreversible tipping point. It may be too late. If that happens—well, it's some consolation to remember that we sent all that Bach out on the Voyager probe.

After Bush is Out

WE'LL BE OUT OF IRAQ IN A JIFF!

THE CLIMATE WILL GO BACK TO NORMAL!

WE'LL HAVE HEARD THE LAST OF THOSE SILLY CONSERVATIVES!

...AND WE'LL NEVER BE LONELY AGAIN.

"What's Your Plan (When the Shit Hits the Fan)?" April 23rd 2008

I recently received letters from my friends Ken and Jim (depicted in panels 1 and 4 of this cartoon, respectively), who occupy positions at opposite ends of my personal friend spectrum.

Ken, mentioned in last week's artist's statement, is deeply concerned about the phenomenon of Peak Oil and its likely implications for our way of life. He and his wife have uprooted their lives in the suburbs of Washington D.C. and relocated to an energy-independent community in Missouri, where they are hunkering down and laying in provisions for the imminent collapse of our society's petroleum-based infrastructure. A few weeks ago Ken sent a dispatch detailing his progress in implementing his plan:

> ... the plans for an edible food forest here in SW Missouri are developing rapidly. Nutritious perennial vegetables and berries take two or three years to mature, so should be in good production by the time the last-gasp 2009-10 global oil production increase ends. Same with dwarf fruit trees, and revival (via pruning) of some now non-producing old apples and pears. And the annual vegetable gardens will get well under way this year, with poultry to follow. It's not hard to be optimistic here, looking out over the dozens of over-wintering songbirds that spend their days visiting our feeders and sheltering in the bushes and shrubs. Of course I'm typing with gloves on, and Jenny's darning wool socks, but we've kept our winter propane bill under half of what the previous owners spent, and I'm using the warmer days to build up our log pile for next winter by which time we plan to have in an efficient wood-burning stove.

> We spend an average of a day a week at the local thrifts stores, flea markets, and discount outlets building up our tool and garden supplies. Last weekend we went to an Organic Farming conference, and focused on "biological farming" workshops that taught how to rebuild damaged soil, and test plant tissues to check on the results (basically the field science side of the permaculture approach we're taking to edible forestry).

> We're looking forward to spring for the explosion of flowering trees on the property, much more time outside in the barn and gardening sheds, and especially getting back on our bikes.

After describing Ken and his plans in my rather doomy artist's statement last week, I received the following letter from Jim:

Dear Timmy Kreiderkrudd [in-joke, not important],

Not this again. Tim, you know how this kinda talk enrages me. Fuck energy independent Missouri. Didn't more than half of the flatheads in that state vote for Bush in the last election? Mohammedfucker, nothing bad is going to happen. This country has weathered worse shit than this. Christ I am nearly as lazy as people get and I am fine, if I can come out somewhere in the middle then we are going to be OK.

Allah of a bitch, the government is giving poor people money. You think a failing government gives out cash? Ok don't answer that maybe they do. Malthusian catastrophe is something Europeans do, not Americans. I think this temporary collapse of the dollar is Mohammed sent. With the dollar so weak who wants to travel outside the U.S.? It's safer here within the walls of the city. You think the people of the city of Rome suffered as much as the rest of the empire during the collapse? Hells no!

My advice for Pain readers is buy a gun, because when someone kills the dark man that is currently running for king dipshit you are gonna' wanna' defend your Cheez-crunch stash from looters. So readers go buy a gun, it's allowed, you may own a gun it is OK, you won't go to hell for it, it is your right to keep and bear them, only dipshits that think it's wrong and politically incorrect will whine about it.

Also, there is still plenty of oil. If I am wrong and we suffer, so we suffer, we suffer anyway, you suffer, they suffer; we suffer through this tiresome bullshit all day every day. Speaking as a guy who did not eat for more than a month once, I have to say that starving is no worse than heartbreak. You have been nearly murdered, I have had a heart attack, and some poor bastard somewhere in this world was just cheated on by the love of his life. We suffer regardless.

Tell that Missouri-energy-independent-idiot friend of yours to shut the fuck up. Talk about cowardly America-hating liberal. Don't spread his nonsense to your readers. That is just fucking reckless. We are talking about a guy who was going to go and live in New Zealand; this is a

What's Your Plan When the Shit Hits the Fan?

KEN

BOYD

ME

JIM

guy considering an expat lifestyle, not a loyal American. Why does he want to survive this shit so bad anyway? Is he planning on finally getting laid after the crash? Repopulating the world? What is he planning on doing with his gold? Become fucking king of America. All of his bullshit is suspect to me.

Love,
James the Large

I myself am torn between these two ideological poles. Intellectually, I'm closer to Ken on this one. There may be, as Jim suggests, reasons to suspect any apocalyptic certitude; it smacks of what Thomas Pynchon calls the adolescent pose of "somber glee at any idea of mass destruction or decline." Most utopian science fiction, from *Star Trek* to the peak-oil novel *World Made By Hand,* is contingent on the slate being wiped clean by some catastrophe, which always seems to me to be an admission of authorial inadequacy to the challenge of finding some way through the impenetrable mess of the present to a more perfect society.

But peak oil isn't some science-fictional conceit or crackpot conspiracy theory; it's an uncontroversial geological/economic fact that sometime, rather sooner than later, the cost of extracting oil is going to exceed the potential profit, meaning that the price will rise and rise and then finally there just plain won't be any more. What's not as clear is when this will happen and what the repercussions will be. Possible scenarios span the spectrum of optimism from a hasty global adjustment to alternative forms of energy to *Mad Max: Beyond Thunderdome,* the crappy one with Tina Turner.

Ken personally feels that our civilization is still deep in denial about the exhaustibility of fossil fuels and has let too much time elapse without any backup plan. He tends to be cagey about the gruesome details, but I know he fears the worst. Unlike some of his like-minded fellows who are just holing up with canned goods and ammo, Ken has expended a lot of energy entreating his friends to take similar actions before it's too late. Whether Ken's tool purchases have included a firearm to ward off the marauding Boyds of the world I do not know.

My own feeling about Ken's Cassandran crusade echoes Dan Dreiberg's uneasy question about Adrian Veidt in *Watchmen:* "I mean, this is the world's smartest man we're talking about, so who's to say? How can anyone tell if he's gone crazy?" Given this conundrum, it'd probably be wiser to err on the side of caution.

Philosophically, however, my heart inclines toward Jim. Not because I think Jim is right but because it's pleasanter and less work to believe Jim. Of course it's always comforting, in a head-in-the-sand way, to dismiss all this doomsaying, tell ourselves, ahh, everyone's always saying things are going to hell in a handbasket, and assume that eventually we'll figure something out and this shit'll blow over like it always does. But, as my reading of Gibbon's *Decline* has reminded me, sometimes the reason everyone's saying things are going to hell in a handbasket is because in fact they are.

The problem is that, unlike Ken, I am a lazy and disorganized person who does not base my life decisions on abstract ideas, and frankly I find it easier to resign myself to a premature and violent death than to figure out how to invest my money or repair tools or grow plants, at which I have always sucked. My only vague plan in the event of some catastrophic excremental/climate control interaction is to retreat to my undisclosed location on the Chesapeake Bay, where all but those visitors who'll have a lot to offer in the post-apocalyptic environment, if you know what I mean, will be made to feel unwelcome.

Only time will tell which of these two sages sees more truly. In a recent email, Ken offers a wager:

I wonder whether there might also be a small and purely symbolic stake, such as a mutual willingness to have one of us depicted naked and flagellated come Earth Day next year (or a decade from now), whoever has been most vindicated by interim developments?

He also accepts that, as the straight man in this debate, the humor must necessarily be at his expense. "Until," he adds, "it isn't."

TWILIGHT OF THE ASSHOLES

Rising Tensions

THE DEMOCRATIC PRIMARY FIGHT SEEMS LIKELY TO GO TO THE CONVENTION.

NORTH KOREA HELPED SYRIA TO BUILD A NUCLEAR REACTOR.

AFGHANI PRESIDENT KARZAI NARROWLY ESCAPED ASSASSINATION.

THE CHINESE HAVE AGREED TO MEET WITH ENVOYS OF THE DALAI LAMA.

OH AND, UH, SOMETHIN' ABOUT... THOSE GUYS, Y'KNOW, HAMAS...

THERE'S JUST NO POINT TO ANYTHING.

April 30th, 2008

As of this writing it seems inevitable that Hillary Clinton will have to drop out of the race and Barack Obama will be the Democratic nominee for the Presidency. But one hesitates to use words like "inevitable" or "foregone conclusion" in politics—especially when a Clinton is involved. Last week my colleague Sarah Glidden was making noises of relief that at last it was over, Obama had clinched the nomination, Hillary was surely doomed. Tom Hart cautioned her against being lulled into believing that Hillary Clinton was done for. "She's like the Terminator," he said. "Every time you think she's dead, that red eye begins to glow again, or just the mechanical arm comes crawling after you." Which analogy I just plain stole.

Sad that it has finally come to this: Hillary joins my gallery of monsters, along with that unstoppable zombie Joe Lieberman. I have an especially purulent contempt for those Democrats who went cravenly along with the bellicose frenzy back in '03, as opposed to the more cordial, *pro forma* "Morning, Sam/ Morning, Ralph" enmity I feel toward Republicans, who are, by their own cheerful admission, out-and-out villains. My feeling toward Republicans is like my feeling about sharks: of course they're stupid and vicious. It's their nature to be mindless, ravening killing machines. It's nothing personal. They don't know any better. Pretty much the only thing you can do about them is stay out of their waters and, if you're unlucky enough to meet with one, shoot it through its rudimentary brain with a spear gun. But pro-war democrats seem more like cannibals, something unnaturally vile, traitors to the species. In this the radical Muslims and I agree: the most unforgivable sin is apostasy.

I used to feel a reflexive defensiveness on Hillary Clinton's behalf in reaction to all the rabid vituperation that's been spat at her from the wife-beating contingent of the right. But she lost all my sympathy when she voted for the war in Iraq. Always with the Clintons there has been this sense that, well, yes, *this* time they had to tack to the center or defer to the conservatives for reasons of political expediency, but this was only so they could get themselves into position to finally enact their *real* agenda, and show themselves for the progressive reformers they truly are underneath it all. You have to choose your battles. Except we waited eight years for this moment of vindication, and it never quite arrived. Always it was just one more compromise away: "Don't ask, don't tell," NAFTA, wefare reform... But the war vote was one of those moments of truth when the bullshit is supposed to stop, when you cash in all those compromise chips you've spent a career accumulating and stand up for what you really believe. It was, after all, a matter of life and death.

But once again Hillary cast her vote for what clearly seem like the most calculated, cynical, and heartless of reasons. She knew she'd be campaigning for the White House in '08, and feared that a vote against a popular war would be used against her in the election to make her seem weak and sentimental and *womanish*. (The alternative explanation is that she actually believed the Bush administration's rationales for war, in which case she should be denied the Presidency on the basis of her credulity.) There is a harsh justice in the fact that it is this same vote that's hobbled her Presidential run. If, by the time you read this on Wednesday morning, Obama has won a majority of pledged delegates and Hillary has finally conceded defeat, let us bear in mind it was entirely her own fault. It may be true that sexism was a factor in this campaign, but, in the end, I believe the outcome represented a pyrrhic victory for feminism: Hillary Clinton lost on her own merits.

"Can Obama Woo the Shithead Vote?" May 28th 2008

I began drawing this almost immediately after the primary in West Virginia, where Obama lost by a significant margin to Hillary Clinton, who in exit polls was perceived by 100% of voters as "more white." He lost by a wide margin again last week in Kentucky—like West Virginia, another of what are known, among geographers and historians, as "the bumfuck states."

This is an awkward reality for the media to have to package. On the one hand, they have to take every conceivable factor into account in handicapping their electoral horserace, plus any new perceived microtrend or passing interpretation of the poll results is instantly slurped up for rumination on the 24-hour news cycle. Once every four years they have to treat every whim and prejudice and superstition and wackjob theory of the electorate as phenomena to be taken seriously.

The sticky part is, mainstream media also officially likes to pretend that widespread racism no longer exists, and that instances of racial prejudice are some sort of atavistic aberration, like vestigial tails or cannibalism, that can be exposed to the light of public disapproval and purged from the body politic by the ritual of scandal, outrage, and scapegoating. The media raises an outcry, someone apologizes or gets fired, and we can all go on as before. But there it is, this ugly poll result nobody can ignore: 2 in 10 voters in West Virginia and Kentucky are citing race as a "major factor" in their vote.

I don't want to sound like a glass-is-half-empty man; 2 in 10 is better than 10 in 10, which is what it would've been fifty years ago. But those are still some wide margins of loss, and it's hard to politely ignore the fact that there are still a lot of old-school racists out there. The media is torn between the imperative to take them seriously as a voting bloc and their instinctive need to disapprove. For now they're opting to neutrally report the numbers and avoid the delicate "issue" while we all secretly think to ourselves: *crackers, hillbillies, white trash.*

A few weeks ago a friend said she was relieved that Obama had finally given in and worn an American flag lapel pin, because it shut up the sort of people who care about such things and took that issue out of their arsenal. I understood what she meant, but I couldn't bring myself to feel the same way. I was disappointed that he'd given them that silly symbolic victory. I can't believe we still have to take such people seriously and legitimize their idiot bleating about God and country.

Must we keep pretending, at this point, to care what those people think about anything at all? This country is a wreck and a laughingstock today because they got everything they wanted for the last eight years. Does it ever occur to any of these yokels who don't trust Obama because he can't bowl: hey, maybe I don't *want* a guy like me running the country, seeing as how I can't even pay child support or get the fucking cable turned back on? Maybe I want somebody *smarter* than me in charge for a change. We're at a grave and critical moment in this country's history, and we're still being held hostage by the dim suspicions of people who think Obama is a Muslim Manchurian candidate. The situation was well summarized by the *Onion* op-ed: "Yee-Haw! My Vote Cancels Out Y'all's!"

NOW THE CRUCIAL QUESTION IS:

Can Obama Woo The Shithead Vote?

WHAT HE CAN DO:

LEGALLY CHANGE HIS NAME

A BOLD NEW SARTORIAL DIRECTION

RENOUNCE HIS BLACKNESS!

KILL ONE (1) MUSLIM ON LIVE TV

"Now I'll Eat Anything," June 4th 2008

After he lost the Pennsylvania primary to a beer-swilling, whisky-downing Hillary, Obama mordantly announced to his staff, "OK, now I'll eat anything."

—*Newsweek,* 19 May 2008

This makes a good motto for the American political campaign system. A metaphor for every humiliating pose the candidates have to strike, every dumb hat they have to wear, every fanatical or unrealistic position they have to espouse if they want to be president. I unconditionally support Israel no matter what affront to human rights it perpetrates. America has no greater friend than Israel. America has no greater friend than Ireland. America has no greater friend than Poland. There is no greater threat to our national security than Cuba. I will nuke Tehran! Statehood for Puerto Rico! My pappy took me hunting every week when I was a kid. I love the Lord Jesus Christ with all my heart. Bring me a deer—I will kill it! Bring me your squalling baby, its face slick with mucus—I will kiss it. Bring me a pancake that looks like Jesus—I will worship it. I believe marriage is between a man and a woman. I believe Creationism deserves equal footing with Evolution. I will certainly look into your concerns regarding 9-11/ the Disclosure Project/ Stephen King's connection to John Lennon's assassination. I feel more strongly about the issue of nuclear waste at Yucca Mountain than about the threat of al Qaeda, the national health care crisis, and the economy combined. I will make oil prices come back down. Read my lips: No New Taxes. I will deport all the illegal Mexicans. I'll deport the Arabs! I'll line up all the dirty Irish and shoot 'em, just for sweet Jesus' sake please vote for me.

I have made clear my resolute lack of interest in the Israeili/ Palestinian conflict, but even so I cannot help but note a certain let's call it imbalance in American political discourse on this subject. Specifically, that every candidate for the presidency has to convince the electorate that he (or she) is a blindly dogmatic Zionist somewhere to the right of King David. Last week the *Times* interviewed some of the older Jews of Florida who are leery of Obama because they fear he's not pro-Israel enough. There are many among them who believe that Obama is an Arab, that he's Palestinian, that he'll fill the cabinet with the apostles of Farrakhan. Is it some sort of reverse prejudice that this disappoints me? You don't expect any better of the rubes in South Carolina, but the Jews have this reputation for intelligence and education. I guess it goes to show that ignorance and gullibility cut across all boundaries of faith, ethnicity, and class. Or maybe it's just that residency in Florida trumps Judaism, making even the normally keen Semitic mind go bad, like lox left out in the sun.

The panel of Obama eating a Palestinian baby stirred up some trouble. The chairman of an organization called Jews Against Obama wrote an outraged letter-to-the- editor of the *City Paper*, accusing me of "blood libel," which is apparently to regular libel what blood sausage is to regular sausage. A friend of mine who posted the cartoon on a message board got called Goebbels.

There is, as I belatedly recalled, a history of hysterias in which Jews were accused of infanticide and cannibalism. My allusion to this calumny was inadvertent; infantophagy as satiric trope goes back at least to Swift (though in truth I was thinking more of B. Kliban's "Cheesebaby with Our Special Sauce.") The regrettable resonance was admittedly a boneheaded oversight on my part, but I still think it's less a symptom of some sheltered ignorance or insensitivity on my part than a consequence of having grown up in America in the late twentieth century. Such rumors were not exactly rampant among my grade-school classmates in suburban Maryland. They were, at best, a vague story about stuff people used to believe in the Middle Ages, like bodily humours and basilisks. And it seems to me that to refrain from drawing a cartoon like this for the reason that there is a history of such beliefs would be, in a sense, to take those accusations more seriously than they deserve—kind of like refraining from drawing cartoons about the Devil lest people take offense at the implication that their deceased loved ones are even now being poked in the rear with a pitchfork by a horned dude with a tail.

A more egregious error is that it is not kosher to serve meat and dairy products together. I knew this, being a frequent patron of Katz's, where asking for cheese on your pastrami is a serious whatever the Yiddish word for *faux pas* is, and I did consider making the sandwich "w/ mustard," but in the end I went with cheese simply because *cheese* is a funnier word. If I had it all to do over, I would draw the sandwich with mustard, and a pickle on the side. Maybe some black cherry soda. Mmm. Black cherry.

'AFTER HE LOST THE PENNSYLVANIA PRIMARY TO A BEER-SWILLING, WHISKEY-
DOWNING HILLARY, OBAMA MORDANTLY ANNOUNCED TO HIS STAFF, "OKAY...

Now I'll Eat Anything."

—NEWSWEEK,
MAY 19

A PLATE OF SPOTTED OWLS?

PALESTINIAN BABY
(W/ CHEESE)

A RUN FOR THE BORDER!

HIS WORDS

2012

As friend of mine recently wrote me:

> -there's a spaceship on Mars
> -we're all watching a black presidential candidate tromp one of the most detestable democrats around
> -despite all the annoyances, cell phones and the internet are both way better than the communication and research devices available to us in the 20ᵗʰ century

> I conclude that despite the lack of flying cars and pocket lasers I am living in the future, and I like it.

We're living in the future. It's a phrase that's in the air lately. You hear it whenever someone looks up directions on their iPhone or confirms a bet over whether pandas are *ursidæ* or *procyonidæ* via the internet (they're the former) or remembers a black man is a serious candidate for the Presidency.

We're living in the future. I, too, resent the fact that most of the technological innovations these days are in the realm of consumer toys, and that all the truly exciting stuff like personal rocket packs or bubble-domed moon colonies never came to pass. And yet even an irascible old nay-sayer like me has to concede certain undeniable improvements in my own lifetime.

For example, it is now possible, in a lot of places, for gay high school students to be "out" among their peers. In the time and place where I grew up—which wasn't some barbaric shithole like Kansas but a public school in suburban Maryland—this was unimaginable. (To give you youngsters an idea of the general level of sensitivity to such issues in my day, at recess in grade school we played a game called "Smear the Queer"—a.k.a. "Kill the Guy With the Ball" in some regions. Of course we were all preadolescents so the literal meaning of "queer" was abstract at best to us, but still, it's on par with the now-literally-unspeakable "eenie-meenie-miney-moe" variant as an indicator of societal mores, and has one hopes joined it in cultural extinction.) For all conservatives' sneering at the schoolmarmish priggery of political correctness, diversity awareness, and sensitivity training, if fewer kids are being called *faggot* and getting beaten up in this country, it's all been worth it.

Also, stadium seating in movie theaters!

My friend Ken may yet be proven right: maybe this is all a last frantic saturnalia on the lip of the abyss, and the best thing we can do now is hunker down, rig up some solar panels, and start seriously gardening. I am haunted by a remark made by Cormac McCarthy in an interview in the current issue of *Rolling Stone*. McCarthy, who is a fellow at the Santa Fe Institute, a multidisciplinary think tank that addresses long-term human problems, says that if you'd been able to tell a group of intelligent people in the year 1900 what the twentieth century would hold, their response would've been: "You've got to be shitting me."

But I tend to subscribe instead, believe it or not, to the scientific and political optimism of the science-fiction writer Kim Stanley Robinson, who frankly acknowledges the seriousness and complexity of the problems we face but also believes that we can use our intelligence and technology to solve them. As he writes in *Antarctica*, optimism is not some easy, empty-headed, cheerleaderish denial of the facts, but a stubborn and willful act of faith in the face of hopelessness. In an interview he predicts: "It will be a difficult century, and ugly, but I don't think that in the end people are so stupid as to kill themselves off." Robinson envisions futures in which no one is hungry or homeless, in which health care is a right and no one owns land, there's a cap on personal wealth, and women have truly equal status. Which I suppose may sound like some hippy-dippy California liberal *Star Trek* utopia. But we live in a country where slavery is illegal, suffrage is universal, people can practice any religion they want and say anything they like against the government, in a world where Europe is unified and at peace and the Soviet Union evaporated overnight without a fight. Not very long ago this would've seemed like an implausibly optimistic vision of the future.

I'm not sure how to account for this creeping feeling of hope and goodwill. Maybe it's the final defeat of the gutless and hectoring Hillary Clinton, the incredible ascendancy of Barack Obama, and what looks likely to be an embarrassing Dole-like no-contest loss for John McCain. I've also been listening to a lot of Motown, music exuberant with summery optimism. Whatever it is, I have this sense that this country might finally, after seven unendurable years that exhausted my capacity for outrage and gutted my faith in my fellow Americans, be emerging from the Era of Darkness.

We're Living in the Future!

PERSONAL COMMUNICATORS/ ALL-KNOWING COMPUTERS

GAY MARRIAGE!

SPACESHIPS ON MARS!

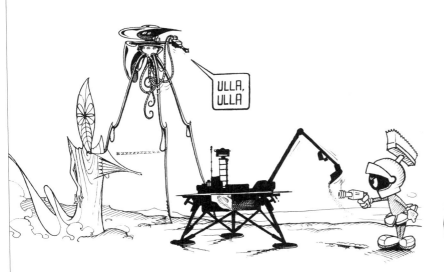

AN HISTORIC CANDIDACY.

In the interest of scientific literacy and the civic peace I should clarify that there is no realistic possibility that the LHC will generate a mini black hole, strangelet, or any other phenomena that might destroy the world. Some doofi did sue the Large Hadron Collider in a Hawaii District Court, demanding that they cease and desist all particle-colliding activities until filing a more detailed Environmental Impact Statement reassuring us that they were not going to accidentally suck us all into Yuggoth.

The U.S. was to have built such a supercollider in Texas, but congress cancelled funding for it back in 1993. Science is one of the stupider things I can think of to get jingoistic about— it's one of the great collaborative intergenerational human undertakings—but it still disappoints me that my own country, which split the atom and landed a man on the moon, decided it didn't have the money to resolve some of the profoundest questions about the nature of reality but did manage to come up with funds for the destruction of Iraq. This seems to me like not being able to afford music lessons for your gifted daughter but somehow always having enough cash on hand to buy cocaine every weekend. It was a symbolic turning of the tide in this country, receding from our high water mark of scientific preeminence. Now the Europeans are hosting the project instead, and we're still debating the monkey trial.

It's funny that evangelicals only stage really organized outcries over evolution, rather than, say, geology or particle physics. How come no picket lines in front of the moon rock repository, where scientists have blasphemously dated basalt back 4.5 billion years, well before the appearance of the Moon on Day Four of Creation five thousand years ago? Why no demand for equal time for Creationism at conferences on string theory, which doesn't acknowledge the hand of a divine creator in supersymmmetry? Am I belaboring my point? It is because they are too stupid to have ever heard of these things. None of their regular sources of information—*Good Morning America*, *USA Today*, *Time* magazine—has alerted them to the threats and temptations posed by bosons, branes or the electroweak force.

Lately I find myself feeling less contemptuous of Creationists than sorry for them. The creation myths of religion were only primitive efforts to understand the origin of the world and the nature of being in the absence of any information. Now, for the first time in history, we're actually able to get at the answers—the actual, correct answers—and most people are too blinded by their emotional attachment to the old bedtime stories to look at the truth now that it's available.

It's especially depressing because the truth, insofar as we're able to apprehend it, is so much more elegant, complex, and beautiful, a far more awful revelation, than the crude fables of religion. Our spiritual lives may be more impoverished, but our picture of this universe is so shockingly immense and rich compared to the dwarfish, arid worldview of five thousand years ago. I recently went to Baltimore's Walters Art Gallery to see an exhibit of ancient maps and an ancillary exhibit of photos from the Hubble telescope. Compare the crude Medieval maps that show the earth as a disc divided cleanly into the continents of Asia, Europe, and Africa (with the Garden of Eden at the center), with the Hubble's Deep Field image—galaxies like handfuls of jewels, each an unreachable island universe teeming with worlds we'll never know. A glimpse of this vision, like seeing Zeus in all his glory, is enough to make you fall to your knees and cover your eyes.

The human imagination is incommensurate to the mystery we inhabit. Biblical, Talmudic, or Koranic literalists remind me of children wrinkling their noses at Belon oysters and asking for more Chef Boy-R-Dee. They want the world to be as simple as they are. This may be one reason that evangelicals, as a group, hired a guy as dumb as they are for the job of running the country; they hoped that intelligence wasn't that important, that guts or faith or "moral clarity" would be enough, which, it turns out, sadly, no.

And yet I share some of Carl Sagan's naive belief that if only science were more widely publicized people might take more of an interest in it, might learn some skepticism, and might even quench some of their thirst for wonder that's otherwise being lucratively slaked with cheap, dehydrating New-Agey booze. Instead we get a steady diet of political gaffes and celebrity gossip, sports and infotainment, Doritos for the mind. Don't mind me, I'm just some snobby Ivory-Tower killjoy who thinks some board of philosopher-kings ought to confiscate all the TiVos and shove string theory and Bach down everyone's throats. Back to Miley and A-Rod.

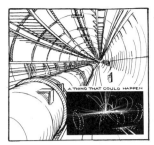

IN AUGUST THE LARGEST PARTICLE ACCELERATOR EVER BUILT WILL BEGIN OPERATIONS, TESTING THE LIMITS OF THE STANDARD MODEL OF PARTICLE PHYSICS. BUT WHO KNOWS WHAT WILL REALLY HAPPEN

Once the Large Hadron Collider Gets Going

IT *COULD* THEORETICALLY CREATE A BLACK HOLE OR *'STRANGELET'* THAT WOULD DEVOUR THE EARTH.

INEVITABLE PROTESTS BY FUNDAMENTALISTS

RETURN OF THE ELDER GODS

OR IT COULD VALIDATE A GRAND *UNIFIED* FIELD THEORY, WHICH WE'LL NEVER EVEN HEAR ABOUT BECAUSE OF SOME *BULLSHIT*.

Professional propagandists in the media are starting to use the word "inevitable" to describe the military confrontation with Iran they're trying to provoke. (I'm reminded of how the same people began referring to Bush's "air of inevitability" in 2000 like an incantation, in order to preordain his nomination.) Iran isn't helping matters by firing off missiles and making with the crazy supervillain rhetoric about wiping Israel off the map. It's as nerve-wracking as watching a drunk wave a knife around and sob incoherent threats while a cop, steadily leveling a gun at him, tells him for the third time to put down the weapon.

Leaving aside the strategic inadvisability and logistical implausibility of opening yet a third front in the War on Terror, it seems like not enough time has passed since the last war to persuade people that another one would be a good idea. As a rule, you usually have to wait for an ignorant new generation to come along that doesn't remember the previous war before you can get them whipped into a jingoistic fervor over the new one. I think what finally overcame our national "Vietnam Syndrome"—the realization that invading countries on the other side of the planet with no clear strategy or objective was a bad idea after all, which passing spasm of sanity was diagnosed by conservatives as a kind of post-traumatic stress disorder or malaise of the national will—was the accumulation of a critical mass of citizens who didn't know shit about Vietnam, so that when the administration cranked up another Gulf of Tonkin hoax and said, *Come on, everybody, we gotta contain Comm—I mean Terrorism or there'll be, like, a domino effect!*, they responded, in unison: *The fuck yeah!*

I'm only forty-one, but I've already seen two war propaganda campaigns, and I can already tell you how they go: Specious proof of the enemy's ill intent will be waved damningly before us and then whipped away and put back in a pocket before anyone can get a good look at it. The spectre of more calamitous attacks on U.S. soil will be invoked. The kinds of dudes who like to chant "U.S.A.!" will chant "U.S.A.!" The rhetorical point will be made that freedom is not free. Second-tier country stars will make some quick money with slavering ass-kicking anthems. Liberals and other such peaceniks will be branded cowards, America-haters, al Qaeda's fifth column. Unrealistic ultimata will be offered, and will, unsurprisingly, pass unmet. The motions will be gone through in congress and at the U.N. Then a lot of people will get killed, nobody will like us, and it'll be a big fiasco, like it always is, every time, and a few years later the dudes who used to chant "U.S.A.!" will be angrily demanding to know what the fuck happened and blaming liberals for their defeat. Wait ten years; repeat.

Liberals may not be quite as easily conditioned as conservatives, but it is possible that our by-now well-justified mistrust of the Bush administration will keep us skeptical and unsupportive of a military action that might for once actually be advisable. Maybe Iran is building nuclear weapons and the first thing they intend to do with them is nuke Jerusalem. Bill Mauldin, no fan of war, said that "[Pacifists] are right ninety percent of the time. It's that other ten percent that worries me."

If there is another terrorist attack in the months leading up to the election, the political posturing will be insufferable. It's impossible to say at this point what the political fallout (ha, ha!) would be in the election. It seems obscene even to consider such a thing, though no doubt there have been late-night conversations at high levels in both campaigns on this subject. Historically, people have fled back into the hairy arms of the abusive daddy party when they're frightened, but since the Bush administration has proven itself incapable of managing an occupation, evacuating U.S. citizens from a disaster area, or even rebuilding a couple of skyscrapers, maybe the myth of the Republican party as at least hardheaded and competent has finally died. But more likely if there's another terrorist attack Barack Obama's middle name will become a terminal liability and we'll elect an old man whose solution to the problem of al Qaeda is to win the Vietman War once and for all.

There Won't Be Any News Until...

WE ATTACK IRAN.

ANOTHER TERRORIST ATTACK

RICH PEOPLE REALIZE THE ECONOMY'S COLLAPSING

... OR THE NEWS I CANNOT EVEN BEAR TO DRAW—

In a recent *New York Times* op-ed on Al Gore' advocacy of 100% conversion to renewable energy sources within ten years, Bob Herbert sounded glumly certain that this ambitious goal would be D.O.A. in the national discourse. Herbert also invoked this country's great defining achievements of the last century: World War II, the Marshall plan, the Civil Rights era, the Apollo program. "When exactly was it that the U.S. became a can't-do society?" he asked.

When *did* we lose faith in our ability to pull off great, audacious things? In Kim Stanley Robinson's trilogy about climate change he envisions unprecedentedly huge, hubristic global engineering projects—the U.S. Army Engineering Corps restarting the stalled thermohaline circulation by dumping trillions of tons of salt into the oceans, for example. What seems so heartbreakingly implausible about this scenario is not the Herculean physical and logistical challenge of it, but the political will that would be necessary to initiate it. I can't envision this country, rigidly ruled as it is by lizard-eyed old oil misers like Dick Cheney, men with mechanical hearts who'd sell out their grandkids' futures before they'd countenance a quarterly drop in profits, converting to renewable sources of energy until they have wrung the very last dime from the last consumer stupid and insecure enough to buy the last Hummer off the last used-car lot in America. I keep thinking of Chris Rock's routine about how, in the old days, we used to cure diseases. "What's the last shit a doctor cured?" he asks. "Polio. You know how long ago polio was? *1952*. That's like the first season of *Lucy*."

The Empire State building took 410 days to construct. It was the tallest building in the word for forty years and remains so in my heart, even as Pluto will always remain our ninth planet. Surrounding the base of the building in my drawing are several monumental structures of the ancient world: the Pharos Lighthouse, the legendary Tower of Babel (drawn after Breughel's depiction), the Great Pyramids, the Hanging Gardens of Babylon, and the Colossus of Rhodes. As an aficionado of very tall buildings and an American citizen I'm increasingly disgusted by the stymied status of the Freedom Tower. It was bad

enough when they replaced Daniel Liebeskind's rather graceful, futuristic design with an ugly hulking bunker that turns a blind concrete face to the street like some titanic cenotaph or Temple of Phobos, a Brutalist monument to the culture of fear fostered by the Bush Administration.

But the fact that it's been seven years since the destruction of the World Trade Center, and that, in that time, we've done nothing at ground zero except sell ghoulish souvenirs to rubbernecking tourists is a shame upon the nation. It seems somehow emblematic of this country's inability to do a single thing right under the reign of its illegitimate idiot frat-boy king. It seems to me that a really inspiring symbolic gesture for President Obama to make soon after his inauguration would be to issue some sort of executive mandate to get something built on that spot pronto. It would provide us all, as a country, some emotional closure on that ghastly open wound, and herald a new era of what America's one true and rightful King called Taking Care of Business.

The embarrassment of Ground Zero is nothing compared to the disgrace of New Orleans. An entire American city was destroyed—and one of our best cities, too, one of the least American, the most untouched by the scourge of Puritanism (I still remember my awe at learning there were *drive-thru daiquiri stands* in New Orleans). And not only did our federal government let it drown, it then, instead of rebuilding it—as we did Berlin, the capital of Hitler's empire—just said, *nah, you know what? On second thought, fuck it*. This is the behavior of junkies and terminal winos, people who no longer care about themselves enough to bother keeping their homes clean or fixing things or carrying out the most basic functions of taking care of themselves. The toilet gets stopped up and they just close the bathroom door and start crapping in a bucket.

Personally I don't think the Bush administration let the people of New Orleans starve on the rooftops because they were black, but because they were poor. This administration doesn't care about anyone who didn't contribute to their campaign. Those people were not only broke, and Democrats—most of

Lost Secrets of the ANCIENT AMERICANS

IT IS SAID THAT THEY ERECTED A
TOWER A THOUSAND FEET HIGH
IN *A SINGLE YEAR.*

...THAT THEY WON A GLOBAL WAR
AGAINST *TWO MAJOR POWERS*
IN *THREE YEARS.*

THAT THEY REBUILT AN ENTIRE
CONTINENT IN *FOUR YEARS.*

...AND SOME LEGENDS TELL THAT
THEY *WALKED ON THE MOON.*

WERE THEY AIDED BY *ANCIENT ASTRONAUTS?*

them probably weren't even voters. And Bush and company still seem to see the whole episode as a P.R. snafu rather than the shameful moral failure that it was. As I've said before, this was the moment when most Americans lost faith in the war in Iraq, because they realized that this government wasn't competent to carry out its most essential functions, much less an ambitious and complicated undertaking like a foreign occupation.

It also laid bare the divide between the elites, by and for whom the government is run, and the citizenry, who are, like the Iraqis, the subjects of an indifferently managed occupation. It became shockingly clear that our government no longer had any intention of keeping up its end of even the most basic Hobbesian social contract. It's a useful lesson to remember in case my friend Ken is right and the next few years see fossil fuel depletion, food shortages, and the general collapse of infrastructure: do not expect the people in charge to do anything to help. By the time most people are considering shooting their fellow churchgoers and PTA members over the last can of creamed corn on the shelf, our leaders will already be on private jets bound for gated compounds in Belize.

The one thing I'm certain we could still do is win a world war, if only someone would fight us in one. But we simply don't fight pitched battles any more. The Russians really let us down when they just collapsed like a stack of towels piled too high instead of duking it out on Battlefield Europe like we were gearing up for for fifty years. Now we've got all these cool toys and no one to play with. We've got radar-invisible planes and our enemies don't have radar. We've got bombs that can vaporize cities and our enemies live in caves. We've got the best-trained army on earth and our enemies have girls blowing themselves up on buses. It's enough to make you take your aircraft carrier and go home.

We used to be as good at rebuilding things as we were at blowing them up. Maybe we didn't completely rebuild Europe in four years, but by the end of the Marshall Plan's implementation the economies of most of the countries in Europe were outperforming their prewar levels. It's hard to believe we managed this when, after seven and six years of occupation, respectively, we can't even get the people of Afghanistan and Iraq to quit blowing each other up already. Gone are the days when you captured the enemy's capital and that was it, game over—as in Capture the Flag, they had to give up.

This 'ancient astronaut' business alluded to in the last panel was huge in my childhood. This assumption that aliens must have helped ancient humans build the Pyramids or Stonehenge speaks of a basic lack of faith in human ingenuity, the same lack of faith evident in the crackpot accusation that the government faked the moon landing, or the 9/11 wackjobs' tired rejoinder that, if you think *their* accusations are incredible, what's *really* hard to believe is that the whole thing was planned by a few guys in a cave! Actually, that's easy to believe; human beings' brilliance is equaled only by their cruelty.

In the same way, I feel like lately Americans have lost some fundamental faith in our own ingenuity and boldness—we no longer believe ourselves capable of great things. Can we really be the blood descendants of the same people who turned the great eastern forest into a megalopolis, the Great Plains into a breadbasket; who built Manhattan and Mount Rushmore and the Hoover Dam; who split the atom, crushed the Third Reich and Imperial Japan, invented the movies and rock and roll, and walked on the moon? This nation of obese, illiterate consumers and litigants, these pampered whining puds who'd sell out the liberties their forefathers died for in exchange for the sake of *safety*? I'm reminded me of how Peter Bogdanovitch sometimes ruefully introduced himself in the 80s: "I used to be Peter Bogdanovitch." We used to be the Americans.

I'm not sentimental about the past, indulging in nostalgia for a time I never knew. I prefer living in a time when polio has been cured, when it's no longer okay to talk about "niggers" or "faggots," when we can see photographs of the moons of Neptune, and a man can view more pornography than existed on the whole planet in 1945 in one afternoon. Even the ancient Greeks romanticized bygone eras; in the time of Homer they believed that they were living in an Iron Age, enervated and decadent compared to the distant Golden Age of larger-than-life heroes like Achilles and Odysseus.

But in the coming years we may have to deal with some of the greatest challenges to civilization and survival that our species has faced since the last ice age, and it seems as if most of us are afraid we're not up to it. There's something wistfully pessimistic about the book *The World Without Us* and the various cable TV specials that have adapted or copied it, with their vividly rendered CGI scenes of our buildings and bridges collapsing, our monuments eroding. There's a morbid yearning behind these visions, disturbingly like an adolescent's fantasies about his own funeral. Adolescents like to daydream about such things because the prospect of facing their actual futures is so unimaginable, and hence terrifying.

Come on, everybody! The game's not over yet! I believe it was Patrick Henry, at a meeting of the delegates of the Colony of Virginia at St. John's Church in Richmond on March 23rd of 1775, who uttered the now-famous speech:

> *Over? Did you say 'over'?* Nothing *is over until we decide it*
> *is! Was it over when the Germans bombed Pearl Harbor? Hell*
> *no! And it ain't over now! 'Cause when the going gets tough...*
> [long pause] *...the tough get goin'! Who's with me? Let's go!*
> *Come on! AAAAAAHHHH—*
> [He runs out alone.]

I was back at my Undisclosed Location all last week, happily deaf to the daily hysterics of the media. I did drive down to my local dive bar to watch Obama's acceptance speech, but all seventeen of their TVs were showing football. I've since returned to The Turret in New York to learn that I didn't miss much news. The Republicans have made history by nominating a woman to the powerless symbolic position of the vice-presidency, only a quarter-century after Democrats did the same thing. Perhaps in 2032 they'll nominate a black man. Who knows?—maybe by the year 3000 they'll support civil unions for homosexuals.

It's been a tempestuous relationship with Obama: flirty interest, infatuation, bitter disillusionment, and reconciliation. I saw my younger colleague Sarah's swoony love for Obama and secretly felt wistful and jealous of her genuine, uncynical, ga-ga enthusiasm for a political candidate. She was experiencing that once-in-a-generation thrill of belonging to a movement instead of a party, being swept up in a wave of mass shared emotion—that sense of inevitable victory over the forces of Old and Evil, as Hunter Thompson described it. My friend Megan and I commiserated: we felt like we'd blown all our hope and enthusiasm on the antiwar protests and the 2004 election, when we actually went door-to-door in Philadelphia getting out the vote. And we got crushed. What's even more mortifying is to think that we'd squandered our youthful passion on *John Kerry*. And now that a genuinely inspiring candidate comes along, we're too old and jaded to get excited about it.

It was his speech on race that won me over. It was the first time I'd heard any politician talk like an adult, daring to acknowledge complexities or express ambivalence, saying in public the sorts of things we all know and live with every day in this country. Sigh. I am easily wooed by a silver tongue.

I was literally just about to send his campaign a check—I had even addressed the envelope—when he cast his FISA vote.[1] Suddenly I hesitated, as though at the altar in Vegas: wait, *who* is this guy again? Matt Taibbi's depressingly well-researched essay on the Obama campaign's donors titrated more cold water onto my initial infatuation. It was like learning that your beautiful new girlfriend is heavily into Ayn Rand or once dated that asshole Marc who works down in marketing.

The sententious dullards who manufacture conventional wisdom on op-ed pages, ever cautious guardians of the *status quo*, like to affect a condescending bemusement that Obama's naïve young supporters are shocked to learn that he turns out to be just another politician—as though maturer, more worldly types are used to being lied to and spied on by the government and no one's ever being held accountable for it. I myself would argue, rather, Fuck that. So I didn't send my check, and for a while Barack and were on the outs. It was sad. I'd see his name and his face on T-shirts on the street and felt like he was going on without me.

Then my friend Boyd, who gravitates toward worst-case scenarios and also likes to let me know important plot points of movies I haven't yet seen, informed me that McCain was now even with Obama in polls, and that some even showed him slightly ahead. It beggared my imagination that anybody other than his immediate family would vote for George Bush in 2004; that anyone would vote Republican *now*, after the last eight years, leaves me boggled. The stupidity of the American voter is without limit; it is like perpetual motion, like faster-than-light drive, freakish, impossible, an affront to the laws of nature. Half the people in this country apparently feel they haven't been fucked over quite enough yet. They are still optimistic that things could be worse.

Obama's nomination speech reminded me why I got on board the Obama bandwagon in the first place. Also persuasive—especially to repentant 2000 Nader voters like myself—was Al Gore's stern "I Told You So" speech, pointing out that the last eight years would've been very different if he had been president. John McCain may not be anywhere near as willfully stupid and mean-spirited as George Bush, but he's still a Republican, and, as Anne LaMott once wrote about the nicest two-year-old she knew, "Of course, that's like saying Albert Speer was the nicest Nazi. He was still a Nazi." So now I'm sending in my check. It's official: I am married to Obama.

---

1 Legislation that effectively protected telecommunications companies that cooperated with the Bush administration's warrantless wiretapping program from legal prosecution.

Obama & Me

A Love Story

I HEARD ABOUT HIM FROM MY FRIEND SARAH, WHO WAS ALL GA-GA FOR HIM.

I WAS LIKE, WHATEVER.

BUT SECRETLY I ENVIED HER. I WONDERED WHETHER I WOULD EVER LOVE AGAIN.

GRADUALLY I GOT INTRIGUED. WHEN I HEARD HIS SPEECH ON RACE, THAT WAS, LIKE, *IT*.

OUR FIRST FIGHT — THE FISA BILL. *THAT* WAS NEARLY A DEALBREAKER.

BUT ONCE YOU'VE SEEN WHAT *ELSE* IS OUT THERE—

YOU REALIZE IT'S TRUE:

"Once You Go Barack, You Never Go Back."

I'm not just making the obvious point that, although all Republicans are not bigots and fag-bashers, all the bigots and fag-bashers seem to be Republicans. It's more that I wish everybody would stop pretending to care about any political ideology at all. Everybody's political philosophy seems to me to be the same: they want to get what they want. Only a handful of weenies who had nothing more fun to do in college have ever bothered to formulate a coherent political ideology, and even they abandon their ideology anytime it becomes inconvenient. Let us look, as an example, to the recent bailout of Fannie Mae and Freddie Mac. All the same rapacious Wall Street types who believe in free markets and deregulation and the ineluctable wisdom of the Invisible Hand are now letting out a vast, shaky sigh of relief that the despised government has come to save their asses now that their various swindles and Ponzi schemes have imploded. Nobody actually believes in, or cares about, limited government; they believe that the government shouldn't be able to keep them from running any scam they can and that they shouldn't have to pay taxes, but they also want the government—meaning taxpayers—to give them eighty billion metric shit-tons of cash after they've blown all theirs on some failed get-rich-quick scheme. They're not so different in their political conviction from some sneering teen anarchist who calls his dad a capitalist asswipe until he needs to borrow a couple hundred dollars to pay for an abortion.[1]

Yeah and speaking of which: another scenario that would

be narratively interesting, which I find I'm kind of rooting for, would be for the father of Bristol Palin's child to panic and bolt. (My friend Myla notes that the whole family clearly uses the same method of birth control.) Right about now, I imagine, that guy's thinking to himself:

Okay, let's just keep cool here, they're probably not going win, we can ride this out, we'll just wait till after this election thing's over and all this crazy bullshit's blown over and then just get in the fuckin' truck and go—Canada, Lower 48, doesn't matter, man, just get a nice little shack somewhere, do some huntin', maybe find a cute little barmaid, yeah, okay, this could all still work out all right for The Kid.

An interesting aside: I turned to Google image search looking for a suitably surly photo of Hilary Clinton to use as a visual reference for my fourth panel, and the one I chose was on what appeared to be a Wikipedia page. But in the course of procrastinating I got to reading the entry, which proved to be so full of errors, distortions, forcibly decontextualized factoids and flat-out lies (example: that Hilary's famous charge about a "vast right-wing conspiracy" referred not to the effort to destroy her husband's political career but to the exponential growth of the internet) that I did a double-take with my nose all wrinkled up and my whole head tilted almost sideways. *Man,* I thought, *this article has clearly been riddled with disinformation by partisan wackos—you'd think even the editors of as notoriously unreliable an information source as Wikipedia would be a little more on the ball.* Then I realized that what I was looking at was a Wikipedia lookalike—the "*Conserva*pedia." I vaguely recalled having heard something about this project a while ago. On the internet, as in real life, conservatives, unwilling to accommodate their political ideology to the facts, have decided to abandon the consensual reality we all formerly cohabited and create their own customized facts to better conform to their ideology. Better that they do it online than in the Middle East.

---

1 An even clearer example was the legal battle over California's Proposition 8, which would have outlawed gay marriage in the state. In the Supreme Court case, gay-rights lawyers argued that the proposition was an illegal revision of the state constitution; lawyers argued that it was only an amendment. Whether Proposition 8 was a constitutional revision or an amendment is a legal distinction so arcane and dull that few people could be expected to care about it at all, much less have an opinion on the matter, but suddenly millions of people were taking passionate sides over the issue, positions which, in 100% of cases, happened to support the outcome they personally wanted to see.

Why Are You Voting Republican in 2008?

BECAUSE I EXPECT VERY SHORTLY TO BE IN THAT TOP 1%.

A LEGITIMATE IDEOLOGICAL BELIEF IN LIMITED GOVERNMENT, STATES' RIGHTS, FREE MARKETS AND A STRONG DEFENSE

BECAUSE IF McCAIN IS ELECTED AND DIES, REAL LIFE WILL BE AS MUCH LIKE *BATTLESTAR GALACTICA* AS POSSIBLE.

HATRED AND FEAR OF CHANGE OF ANY KIND

"IDENTITY POLITICS"

THE SOONER THE AMERICAN EMPIRE FALLS, THE SOONER THE NEW ORDER WILL ARISE FROM THE ASHES

I spent last weekend visiting my friends Jim and Sarah in New Haven, enjoying the respectable pleasures of suburbia: taking Percocets, figure-skating on Wii, watching a TV show called *Destroyed in Seconds* on HDTV. One segment of this last program showcased footage from an air show in which an F-117 Stealth fighter loses a wing, tumbles out of control, and crashes into a residential neighborhood. Even as the fireball erupts over the rooftops the voice of the air show announcer is clearly audible, saying in a relaxed, laconic voice: "Everyone just stay where you are, folks, stay where you are… everything's all right… maybe a good time to get a bite to eat…" Jim and I gaped at each other in astonishment, and thanks to the technology of Tivo were able to listen to this insane monologue again. The announcer reminded me of Kevin Bacon as the ROTC cadet in *Animal House* shrieking, "Remain calm! All is well!" while smoke bombs and ten thousand marbles fill the streets, Bluto in a pirate costume swings down and abducts a sorority girl, and the EAT ME cake splits asunder to reveal The Deathmobile a-snarl, roaring through the chaos.

Everything you hear any government official or financial expert say about the current financial crisis is no different from this announcer's blathering: *Stay where you are, folks. Maybe a good time to get a bite to eat.* John Ralston Saul, in *Voltaire's Bastards*, writes about the reflexive instinct of all governments to avoid panic in all situations, including situations in which panic is the most reasonable response (as when the French government claimed that the prevailing winds were blowing all the radiation from the Chernobyl disaster neatly around France, as if by divine intervention). I've seldom seen it more clearly illustrated than by this scene of an official trying to spin a fiery catastrophe in a housing development as an opportunity to grab a hot dog.

This week I had lunch with my friend Steve, who was once a broker for about two weeks before he quit in horror. "We became a socialist country this week," is how he put it. "Although the beneficiaries are all multibillion-dollar corporations, which is not exactly how I would've planned it." As I pointed out a few weeks ago, the people who own this country champion free markets and small government when they're making money, but scamper for taxpayer bailouts when their crimes are exposed and their con games fall through. In short, they privatize gains and socialize losses, an economic philosophy also known as Heads I Win, Tails You Lose.

Events are conforming disturbingly to the scenario outlined in an email sent to me by my Peak Oil friend Ken back in July: "Over the course of the next few months the US banking and financial system collapses, beginning with another major bank failure (or its equivalent), followed by runs on ordinary savings accounts, then followed in turn very soon by gasoline and diesel shortages, followed shortly thereafter by food shortages." I myself am unconcerned about any of these things because we know that one economic reality will remain constant despite whatever upheavals and calamities may come: *the world will need laughter*. A cartoonist will survive.

Yesterday I spent about an hour on the phone talking to my friend Megan about the collapse of the American Empire. Megan described the opening ceremonies of the Beijing Olympics, a fascist spectacle of perfection reminiscent of Berlin in '36: a perfect little girl singing to the looped-in voice of an angel, one million people drumming in CGI-like unison. Megan reports that their ominous message (it wasn't nearly subtle enough to be called subtext) was: We Can Do Everything Better Than You. Megan, glumly, kinda believes it. We can't do shit in this country any more. We blew it. The Chinese and the Japanese are just waiting for us to default on the mortgage for America now.

Megan's hope is that, once we've been forced to give up our dumb imperial ambitions, we'll maybe remember all those ideals we used to believe in—as she puts it, "You know, America?" I have to say this really doesn't sound much like us to me. It's true that post-imperial nations are usually pleasant places to live: you're left with a decent level of civilization without the headache of maintaining colonies or occupations. But somehow I don't see America going that route. We're too spoiled and pugnacious and stupid. We're not the type to age with dignity; we're more likely to go deep into denial, getting hair plugs and Hummers and trophy wives with silicone tits to stave off our fear of inevitable decline. I see us acting more like Russia, which, twenty years after its own ignominious collapse, is proud of its ruthless thug of a president and invading little nations on its border just to throw its muscle around. I'm picturing President Palin nuking Havanah and all the crewcut Cro-magnons being all like: "Yeah! America is *back*, motherfuckers!"

The Economy Explained

Two of my readers have referred me to an essay published on Edge.org written by Jonathan Haidt, a liberal psychologist, taking a thoughtful look at why people often vote conservative against their own economic interests. I would urge you to read it, but if you're too pressed for time or just too lazy I will try to synopsize: liberalism only addresses moral values of individual freedom and equality, not the equally important ones that Durkheim categorized as ingroup loyalty, respect for authority, and purity. This piece has changed and clarified my thinking on the whole topic; it has the explanatory elegance of a good theory, making more sense of all the data without resorting to reductive judgments like "because they're all idiots"—the equivalent of appealing to supernatural causes in science.

I've always thought it was the Democrats who appealed to the we're-all-in-the-same-boat social contract while the Republican philosophy was more like, *screw you, every man for himself, especially me, jack*. It seems to me that the conservatism the author's talking about is a social/religious conservatism—the Republican base—rather than fiscal conservatism—the Republican leadership. These two factions of conservatism are really at odds at heart, the one hankering after community and ethicality, the other willing to sell out the American dream and the country's future for a rise in profits next quarter. But I suppose the evangelical base knows it's the corporate leadership that gets them access to power, and power is universally seductive. (*"Again, the devil took him to a very high mountain and showed him all the kingdoms of the world and their splendor. 'All this I will give you,"* he said, *'if you will bow down and worship me.'"* –Matthew 4:8, 9.)

It's true that liberalism addresses only secular needs and leaves it to individuals to fend for themselves for community and inclusion and spiritual fulfillment—wisely so, it seems to me. We've had enough of the religion being the state (or, maybe even worse, the state being the religion, as in Stalinism/Maoism/Jong Illism). Historically, it just hasn't worked out all that well. So the utopia of the left is pretty much exclusively concerned with material needs and political rights. The liberal paradise is basically Canada. On the other hand, liberals are also by and large just as lost and starved for spirituality and community as conservatives. And as David Foster Wallace warns in his commencement address to Kenyon College, "in the day-to day trenches of adult life, there is actually no such thing as atheism. There is no such thing as not worshipping. Everybody worships. The only choice we get is what to worship." Among secular liberals there has been a great diaspora into a scattershot variety of newly invented, revived, and updated religions, mystical traditions, and semispiritual practices: pot-smoking Unitarians, wife-swapping Quakers, halfassed Buddhists, Dalai Lamaheads, Hare Krishnas, Wiccans, Druids, Heathens, Asatru (I got a couple of angry letters from devotees of Odin over the cartoon "Science vs. Norse Mythology"), Yoga, Reiki, the Tarot, not to mention the Scientology scam.

And liberals yearn, just as conservatives do, to immerse and lose themselves in some ecstatic, Oceanic mass movement. It's just that our reflexive skepticism prevents us from letting ourselves get carried off on the wave—a skepticism that's usually well justified, since most of the bandwagons we're always being urged to jump on are loaded with mean-drunk bumpkins and headed for the ditch. (I'm thinking of a conservative poster showing a grinning GI, ca. WWII, with the slogan, "How About Rooting for Our Side for a Change, You Liberal Morons.") So we tend to create arbitrary artificial communities–what Kurt Vonnegut called granfalloons—like *Star Trek* conventions or the Burning Man festival, which, although far more harmless and friendly than their conservative counterparts, the Southern Baptist Convention or the Burning Negro festival, are still jerry-rigged and temporary and ultimately unsatisfying.

The problem is that most conservative answers to these deep human needs are simplistic or repressive or obsolete. The conservative paradise, where everyone belongs to one big homogenous group and unanimously reveres and supports the government and maintains strict moral purity, is North Korea. And it gets hard to keep honest, fair, and charitable thoughts about my fellow Americans in my head when the economy's collapsing and what's on CNN is fluff about the dingbat governor of Alaska, whose name the whole country is apparently writing on its notebook covers with little hearts over the *i* in Palin. It seems like, having been ruthlessly screwed by eight years of deregulation, regressive taxation, trickle-down economics, and warmongering, Red America is getting ready to vote for more of

Hey What If the Republicans Win?

NEVER LEAVE NEW YORK CITY AGAIN.

SECEDE, FOUND OWN NATION-STATE

A LITTLE OLD-FASHIONED LEFTIST *REVOLUTIONARY ACTION!*

IF YOU CAN'T BEAT 'EM...

the same, please. A reader of mine described the current election as "the rise of the quatra-annual Great Stupid, ready to wash down the most articulate presidential candidate in decades in a vortex of mind-numbing semi-conscious hatred."

But, see, I'm doing it again. The main challenge in trying to be compassionate and empathetic is always *other fucking people*.

Reading George Saunders's essay in *The Brian-Dead Megaphone* about hanging out with Minutemen, those paramilitary wannabes who patrol the Mexican border, several of whom turn out to be medieval reënactors and have mail-order Russian brides, or Matt Taibbi's account, in *The Great Derangement*, of joining a fundamentalist megachurch in Texas and meeting the deluded divorcees and recovering drug addicts there who don't understand why their kids don't call them, or his description of sitting down to lunch with a group of 9/11 Truthers who'd picketed his office and finding them to be basically nice people who just get all het up on the internet, I'm reminded that the shitheads and dingbats that I vilify in my cartoons are mostly sad, screwed-up, lonely people like myself. A correspondent

once reported to me that Ann Coulter is a genuinely nice person—someone who really listens to you, who laughs out loud at other people's jokes, and a huge Deadhead besides. (Note sure whether, given her literary/public persona, this makes Ann Coulter a better person than I'd imagined or a worse one.) My friend John once told me I was a better person than my beliefs. I think most people are. Religious belief and political ideology always seem to make people act worse than they really are—more simple-minded and sure of themselves, stupider and meaner.[1]

Ask me about all this again in November, though.

---

[1] This turns out, tragically, to have been true even of George W. Bush. Former Special Assistant to the President Matt Latimer, in his own ship-fleeing memoir *Speechless: Tales of a White House Survivor* (let's just leave aside this ultimate debasement of the term *survivor*), tells us that Bush, despite his official policy of supporting the codification of marriage as an institution between a man and a woman, declined to deliver a speech on marriage that contained language denouncing gay marriage, saying: "I'm not going to tell some kid in the audience that he can't get married." I don't know whether this makes me even more furious or breaks my heart. God damn it, George—if you were capable of that kind of basic human decency, why couldn't you have admitted it in public just once, or enacted a little of it into policy?

TWILIGHT OF THE ASSHOLES

Fucked!

★ OR; ★

"Fucked, Fucked, We All Are Fucked"

"THIS SUCKER COULD GO DOWN."
  – GEORGE, 26 SEPTEMBER 2008

THE CHINESE HAVE WALKED IN SPACE.

THE WHOLE UNIVERSE SEEMS TO BE GETTING SUCKED TOWARD ONE SPOT.

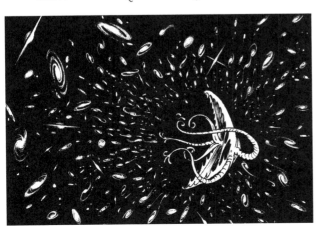

...AND DAVID FOSTER WALLACE IS DEAD.

A friend of mine recently confessed to me that she is secretly looking forward to the new depression. Mostly this is because she was raised on an artistic diet of depression-era kitsch—her grandmother's stories, the Little House books, Loretta Lynn, and Woody Guthrie songs about the dustbowl days. She admits that not actually being poor helped her to maintain her romantic notion of the period.

I'm mostly relieved to see everybody else's supposedly responsible fiscal lives revealed to have been every bit as much a house of cards as was my own. My failure to buy a house or have an IRA or a 401K or ever save any money at all now looks like shrewd, farsighted financial sense. And it's of course pleasant to see Wall Street types being universally reviled as thieving scum. I would've drawn my friends and myself looking on with mild spectatorial interest as brokers hurled themselves from their office ledges, Black Monday-style, but people leaping from skyscrapers has regrettably taken on less cartoonish associations since 9/11.

(Hey by the way: does anyone remember when the Republicans tried to privatize social security and George went on a national tour trying to convince everyone to invest their retirement accounts in the stock market? "The ownership society" was the propaganda term they came up with for this scheme. Can we just publicly take note of the fact that this, like all of the Republicans' other ideas, would've been a disaster? I'm almost sorry they didn't succeed, since if everyone had suddenly lost their retirements on the stock market we might see some Republicans pilloried literally instead of figuratively.)

My friend Ken forwarded me an interesting essay on what its author, Sharon Astyk, calls "ordinary human poverty." Ordinary poverty is the kind described by recollections like "We were poor, but there was always food on the table," or "We were poor, but we didn't know it," as opposed to "pathological poverty"—starvation and squalor. In other words, just getting by. It's the condition humanity has almost always lived in, and most of it still does, and to which we Americans, after a crazed and aberrant interval of living like space-age pharaohs off cheap gas and imaginary money, may soon return.

I have to admit, I also have this probably wrongheaded utopian hope that a post-oil, post-stupendous-wealth America might ultimately be a saner, pleasanter place than the one I've lived in my whole life. I myself have lived a pretty ridiculously privileged life so far, but my needs are also pretty frugal. I never wanted much of the consumer crap that was constantly being foisted on us just to keep the economy churning. I never understood what anybody was doing at work if they weren't physically making something. I've never liked driving and I've always despised the blaring dickhead culture of 4x4s, stretch hummers, and jetskis. I feel like American society used to be more conducive to human happiness and community than it is now: people knew their neighbors instead of living in gated condos; there were main streets instead of shopping malls five miles outside of town. But maybe, as with my friend and her depression kitsch, I've just picked up this idyllic picture from reading Ray Bradbury stories and watching Alfred Hitchcock movies set in small towns.

And even if life was like that once, I worry that it's been so long since we lived in civilized communities, that we've spent so many years screaming at our radios and calling each other faggots and commies on message boards, that we'll have forgotten how to act like human beings in a crisis, and instead of this optimistic vision it'll be Jim holding a shotgun on me as I back slowly down his porch steps, hands raised.

Looking Forward to *The Next Depression*

RIDIN' THE RAILS!

SOME SORTA W.P.A.-DEAL FOR CARTOONISTS

A RESURGENCE OF GUMPTION, ELBOW GREASE, STICK-TO-ITIVENESS

FOLKS PULLIN' TOGETHER!

I finally broke down and drew a Sarah Palin cartoon. What happened was, against my better judgment, I watched the Vice-Presidential debate. I had never seen Sarah Palin on TV before (for reasons of emotional health I did not watch the Republican National Convention). Something about her voice and her face just about rips my skin off. Talking it over with my friend Boyd this morning, we decided that, although Sarah Palin is in fact stupid, she is pretending to be a whole different kind of stupid from the stupid she actually is. She's condescending to affect the provincial, aw-shucks simplemindedness of the voters she appeals to, but in reality she's the kind of dumb cunning bitch who likes to push people around on the PTA or church board. She doesn't know anything at all but she has no doubt that God wants her to be the President. She is the new George. I have had to coin a new acronym to describe her: she's a total M.I.L.K.

Now that Palin has galvanized the critical Braying Ignorant Biddy Vote and brought McCain to a dead heat in some polls, she seems like fair game for humor, as well as an attractive target for our heroic liberal guerilla fuck troops. You know this scheme would work. Every woman I know who has ever personally met Big Bill vouches for the power of his mysterious magnetism. There is always attraction hidden at the heart of all aggression, and vice versa (cf. the disturbing faux confession "I Fucked Ann Coulter," floating around somewhere near the very bottom of the internet, or the brilliant Charles Johnson cartoon from *Player* magazine, ca. 1970, of a Klansman on a street corner watching a hot black chick walk by and envisioning her, in his thought balloon, as a.) naked and b.) lynched). Sarah Palin could not resist the filthy illicit thrill of giving herself up to that big ol' loutish libertine, symbol of the self-indulgent Sixties and touchy-feely liberalism, Slick Willie. Plus you just know she would carry that baby to term, even though it might be the one thing that would make the Republican party rise up in passionate renunciation of its historic pro-choice policy. O Bill, where are you now? This is a situation uniquely suited to your powers, one last chance to be an American hero. Once more, unto the breach!

I had to leave my apartment to draw this cartoon, because at home alone I can mope and laze around and ignore the anxiety and guilt of not doing anything, but being in public usually shames me into productivity. I ended up at one of the few pleasant, quiet little bars in the east village that's not crammed with bellowing sports fags on a Sunday afternoon. As I was sitting there sipping a Leffe and drawing Bill Clinton giving Sarah Palin the old Shock-'n'-Awe treatment, a couple came in with their two little daughters, maybe six and four years old, who, to my horror, climbed up onto the stools on either side of me. The younger one was carrying a hamster in a sort of Habitrail escape pod with a handle. The older one immediately leaned way over into my personal space and watched with unabashed absorption as I drew. The drawing was already well underway, and clearly recognizable as a couple of figures fucking, if you were at all familiar with the configurations of fucking. It made me ill at ease, having this little girl sitting there watching me, but, on the other hand, I figured, it is, after all, a bar, customarily an exclusively adult domain. (I have no objection to kids being in bars but it's sort of like me being on a playground; it is, by definition, their home turf, and I had better have a pretty good reason for being there, like accompanying a legitimate patron of the facilities, and defer to them and not be an asshole and take over the slide.) Also, I was there first. It's not as if I was rushing up to little girls on the street brandishing my dirty cartoons at them. So I kept drawing.

The only thing the girl asked me was, "How come you can draw so good?" (She had an English accent, which only made everything worse.) I answered that I'd had a little bit of natural talent when I was a kid, and I'd kept doing it, a lot, for a long time, and so gradually I got better and better at it. "Practice," said her mother, stressing the moral lesson in persistence and hard work and graciously ignoring the fact that I was drawing people fucking. The girl just kept sitting there intently watching everything I did. She had a bunch of ATM receipts clutched in her hand, which she apparently cherished. Eventually I asked her what was the deal with the receipts, and she explained that she was saving them to give to her friend Elizabeth, because her name was on them (they'd come from the ATM in the bar, which is located on Elizabeth street). I found this kind of charming. At no point did we discuss the fact that I was drawing people fucking. She had a surprising degree of decorum for a six-year-old. Maybe it comes from being English.

This cartoon is completely unfair to John McCain, who, to his credit, has specifically ordered his campaign to refrain from raising the whole Reverend Wright business for fear of appearing to use racial divisions as a wedge. However: John McCain in blackface? How could you think that up and not draw it? I do try to be fair, but when you are cursed with a puerile and inventive mind you sometimes come up with something you have to draw no matter how stupid or wrong it is.

My ex-Marine neighbor down at my Undisclosed Location has been in the know about this Bill Ayers thing for some time now (he's on the other side of the political fence from me, and, like me, tends to access only news sources that confirm his preconceived worldview, so that he and I inhabit wholly separate parallel informational realities) and he's been wondering why the Republicans haven't been making a bigger deal of it. My own answer would be: because it's just not that big a deal. It's desperate. This lame harping on Obama's tenuous connection to a long-ago "domestic terrorist" (which isn't an inaccurate term but is sort of anachronistic—back then I think we called them "militant radicals"), and trying to morph that into a mental image of Obama playing backgammon with Osama, is an indicator of the paucity of dirt there is to be dug up on Obama. This is the one paltry metatarsal they could find way in the back of his closet?

There really are emails going around warning that Obama is the Antichrist. This email's most compelling argument is that the book of Revelation describes the Antichrist as a man in his forties who is Muslim, which would indeed be uncanny if a.) Obama were a Muslim and b.) this were true. The Revelation of St. John was composed either 68 or 95 AD (apparently a hot controversy in biblical-scholarship circles) and Mohammed was born in 570 AD, so you figure it out. Obama also differs from the "Beast" described in Revelation in a number of significant particulars,

such as having only the one head. He is somewhat similar to the Antichrist in the *Left Behind* books, which have perhaps become canonical in certain circles, in that he is charismatic and speaks more than one language, always a suspect sign among Godfearing folk. About the most striking similarity between Obama and the Antichrist is that they are both very popular.

But the "terrorist" business is harder to dismiss as a figment of the dingbat fringe—it's an effort to associate Obama with something subversive, anti-American, foreign, *dark*... After all, he *was* brought up abroad, educated at Muslim schools. All these things seem suspect and sinister to dumb whitebread Wal-Mart Americans who've only ever left the country in Epcot Center—the same people who can't quite put their fingers on the indefinable Something they Just Don't Trust about Obama. These innuendos go about as far toward racism as they can without speaking the forbidden n-word, sort of like horny abstinent teens who've vowed to remain technically virgins 'til marriage but have decided that anal doesn't count. It reminds me of the hilarious climactic scene from Robert Stone's surprisingly prescient first novel, *Hall of Mirrors*: a right-wing radio station sponsors a rally that (intentionally) turns into a race riot, during which a con-artist clergyman delivers a crazed and furious prayer that ends with the frenzied invocation: "Protect and arm us before the black forces of blackness who daily blacken our clear path with their black menace. Amen."

These tactics seem to be roiling up the noisome waters at the very bottom of the Republican base, where fat brainless open-mawed things thrive on a diet of pure shit. Probably most of you have heard about the troubling things being shouted out from among the mobs at McCain/Palin rallies, things like: "Traitor!" "Kill him!" and "Off with his head!" A black cameraman was called "boy." Things are getting ugly.

The Republicans' *Last-Ditch Efforts*

DIRECTLY LINK OBAMA TO 9/11

PLAY UP PARALLELS BETWEEN OBAMA AND THE ANTICHRIST

CROSS-BURNINGS, LYNCHINGS (IN EFFIGY!), APPEARING IN BLACKFACE

GOOD OLD-FASHIONED BALLOT STUFFING

"Republicans' Last-Ditch Efforts," cont.

McCain was himself the victim of a racist smear campaign at the hands of the conscienceless George Bush and subhuman Karl Rove in the '00 primary in South Carolina, where folks will still fall for that sort of thing,[1] and he has now hired some of the same thuggish campaign managers who slandered him then to deploy the same sort of tactics against Obama. So now we're seeing the same old loathsome tricks: repeating lies about Obama's record, twisting his words into sound-bite scandals, pointedly using his villainous middle name, implying that he's secretly some sort of Muslim/terrorist/negro. McCain isn't a racist, but he's apparently not above exploiting racism if it'll get him enough votes to win this thing. A politician with a shot at the Presidency, as Hunter Thompson described it, "is like a bull elk in rut season." He loses all dignity, all integrity, he'll do anything. It's a tragic thing to see a man forfeit honor for glory. The finest thing McCain could do now would be to call off his slavering lipsticked pit bull and run a decent, genial campaign like Bob Dole's in '96, who considered having been nominated by his party to have been the highest honor of his life. I always admired

[1] For you youngsters, the Bush campaign made phone calls implying that McCain had fathered an illegitimate black child. In fact he and his wife had adopted a girl from Bangladesh. This is the so-called "genius" of Republican campaigning as perfected by Karl Rove; find the very finest, most unassailably admirable thing about your opponent and vilify it, twist it into a thing of shame.

Dole for saying, in one of his debates: "If you hate, I don't want your vote."

With less than a month now to go before election Day and the country in a shambles, Obama is ahead in all the polls and even I am cautiously, against my better judgment, starting to hope that maybe, just this once, the shitheads will not win. Of course I've hoped this several times before, only to be sucker-punched and laughed at by the Shithead Nation. Which could well happen again if enough people secretly turn out to be racists behind the electoral booth curtain. Even if Obama does win, it still feels like a depressing confirmation of one's most cynical and misanthropic suspicions that things finally had to get this bad—the country in ruin, mired in two losing wars and on the brink of a global depression—before people would grudgingly consent to vote for someone intelligent for a change. It's hard to believe we might actually have someone smart running the country again; my friend Megan said, "It seems almost bizarre." No doubt as soon as we're at peace and running a surplus again I'm sure the shitheads will vote for another hawkish, tax-cutting demagogue, like an alcoholic with a few months' sobriety under his belt who decides that things are going so well that a coupla beers aren't going to hurt anything.

"A Round for the Losers," November 5th 2008

"A little patience, and we shall see the reign of witches pass over, their spells dissolve, and the people, recovering their true sight, restore their government to its true principles. It is true that in the meantime we are suffering deeply in spirit, & incurring the horrors of a war and long oppressions of enormous public debt...

"And if we feel their power just sufficiently to hoop us together, it will be the happiest situation in which we can exist. If the game runs sometimes against us at home we must have patience till luck turns, and then we shall have an opportunity of winning back the principles we have lost, for this is a game where principles are the stake."

—Thomas Jefferson

November sunshine
The shitheads are on the run
Barack Obama

—reader Samuel Sweelsen

I had to turn this cartoon in on Saturday before heading down to canvass for Obama in Philadelphia for a couple of days, but it wasn't going to run in the paper until Wednesday, the day after election night. Obviously, I decided not to hedge my bets. If I'd been wrong I suppose my cartoon might've been the ironic thing John McCain held gleefully up to the cameras *a la* Harry Truman and the Chicago *Tribune*.

  Pace this cartoon, when Barack Obama won the election I found myself, to my surprise, not much inclined to gloat cruelly over the defeat of the people who have been my ideological enemies for so many years, repellent though many of them are. Instead I felt sorry for them. I don't mean this rhetorically, the way you'll spit, "I feel *sorry* for you!" at someone you loathe. I felt truly sorry for them, the way you'd feel sorry for someone who was tone-deaf at a Bach recital or colorblind at a Bonnard show.

It's the same kind of helpless pity I feel for Creationists when I manage to apprehend some glimpse of the awesome and elegant beauty of evolutionary biology or cosmology. It's sad to imagine how small and paltry and impoverished their world must be. It was a beautiful night, a once in a lifetime moment when, for the first time in a long time, every American could be proud of our nation before the whole world, and those poor surly losers were left out of it, in a self-imposed exile of their own fear.

  For decades, cynical Republican campaign strategists have invoked scary black rapists, trotted out gay-marriage referenda, and railed against the verminous swarm of illegal Mexicans to get their "base" to the polls. As Matt Taibbi pointed out in a recent column, for the last eight years conservatives have controlled all three branches of government and a lot of the media—everything except the culture. And at some point, while they were busy instituting their tax cuts and declaring war on Iraq, minorities became the majority in several U.S. states, and it became uncool for high school kids to call each other "faggot." It happened incrementally, insidiously, under their radar. And this year, when they tried their usual fag-bashing campaign and xenophobic hysteria over immigrants, when they made fun of a candidate's foreign-sounding name and implied that he wasn't a Christian, when they told us all that small-town hicks were the only America that counted, to their helpless dismay, *it didn't work*. That shit only worked back when we had no real problems. But after eight years in power they had made such a stinking wreck of reality that even very stupid people had noticed. (It's regrettable that the only sure way to defeat conservatives is to let them do what they want.) And suddenly they were like some pathetic old warlock whose magic has deserted him, whom you can now walk right up to and punch in the stomach.

  But other than tuning into Fox now and then just to watch Brit Hume sulk, my friends and I didn't waste much mental energy on the losers on election night. It was a moment too pure and joyful to sully with *schadenfreude*. When they called the election for Obama I tried to call my old protest-rally partner Megan Kelso in Seattle and got a "circuits busy" signal for the first time in years—everybody was calling everybody else, like a happy 9/11. When I finally got through to her, she said that these last eight wretched years had occupied so large a chunk of our adulthoods that we'd thought that this was just how the world was: mean-spirited shitheads would always win and we would always lose. We'd forgotten that nothing lasts forever. It was hard to believe it was really over.

The night was full of the sort of transformative moments of grace that usually only happen in movies. John McCain, after debasing himself utterly in his campaign, seemed like the victim of a possession in a horror film after the inhabiting demon has fled, briefly restored to his true self before dying. When Barack Obama stepped onstage into the spotlight of history, it seemed both unreal and yet also as if we were all waking up from some endless, horrid febrile dream. To hear a United States President say the word "gay" in his acceptance speech, to hear him acknowledge the rest of the watching world abroad, to feel like we had a home country we could belong to again—it was all too much for an habitual cynic to take. I raised a toast: "To the Real America."

I now find myself called on to experience emotions that have become alien and suspect from disuse, like pride in my country and faith in my fellow man. My young colleague Sarah Glidden told me she was thrilled to see a spontaneous crowd in the streets of Brooklyn unfurl a giant American flag and chant, "U.S.A.! U.S.A.!"—a spectacle that has only ever repelled her before, since for the last eight years it's invariably meant that someone, somewhere in the world, was getting killed. Last night I was walking through a rain-sheened Union Square and found myself thinking, for the first time since I was about nine: "This really is the greatest country in the world." Watching Obama's speech Tuesday night, hearing him talk about America as a beacon of hope, an example to the world—and knowing that the rest of the world was watching, and that maybe, just this once, it was really true—I realized that some part of me never stopped believing in all that crap. I was reminded, embarrassingly, of the one scene I found moving in the film adaptation of *The Lion, the Witch, and the Wardrobe*, when the Pevensie children meet the earliest and greatest of childhood myths, Father Christmas himself, looking like some splendid medieval lord, and Lucy, the youngest, smiles with quiet vindication and says: "I told you he was real."

Where Are They Now?

JOHN McCAIN

OL' WHATSHERNAME

JOHN EDWARDS AND TIM KREIDER

HILLARY CLINTON

November 19th, 2008

I cannot get enough of the news this week. The Obamas visiting their new home, the White House. Sarah Palin back in Alaska, her office strewn with blue balloons and hung with the kind of banner you'd buy for a kid's birthday party saying: "WELCOME HOME, GOVERNOR." The Republican Party trying to pinpoint just where they went off-message. The South finally relegated to the same irrelevant jerkwater politically that it's always been in reality.

Having allowed myself to wallow unashamedly in the joy of victory, watched digital camera videos of crowds hugging cops on Dekalb Avenue, listened to Obama's books on CD (mellifluously read by the author), and played Bruce Springsteen's "Land of Hope and Dreams" about seventy times, I finally decided to indulge myself in looking in on the reactions of conservatives to the Obama victory.

A mistake, of course. It's not even gratifying to gloat over their defeat, because their perceptions are so out of touch with reality that they're not even abandoning the same field we won. They seem to think that the election of this centrist pro-business Democrat is the end of America, the foundation of some totalitarian Marxist state, the installment of an Islamofascist Quisling in the Oval Office, and that at any moment an elite P.C. corps of jackbooted bull-dyke feminazis is going to kick down their doors and confiscate their cocks I mean guns!, their guns, and shut down forever that last bastion of free speech in the real America, their blogs. One poster noted that all the AK-47s and ammo had disappeared from his local gun shop in the last week.

To quote Penny Robinson: "Dr. Smith, when will you stop acting so silly?" What are these delusional cowards imagining is going to happen? Where are the fascist armies, where the invading Mohammedan horde, the gangs of ravaging negroes, the Yippie fifth column, that they're girding themselves to hold off? I picture them still hunkered down eight years from now, their ammo and canned goods grown dusty and cobwebbed, barricaded against the twin menaces of free health care and renewable energy. In other words, there's this nice hot loaf of banana bread waiting for them— maybe with walnuts or chocolate chips, even—but no, they're too shrewd to be fooled by that old ruse. They're fine with jerky.

What they remind me of is nothing so much as the dwarves in the stable in *The Last Battle*, the final book in Lewis's *Chronicles of Narnia*. (I am aware that this my second Narnia allusion in as many weeks. What can I say? We've stepped through the wardrobe.) The Dwarves, Lewis' allegorical stand-ins for intellectual skeptics, are sitting in a sunlit meadow, and Aslan places a great feast before them, but they still believe they're huddled in a dark stable, and think they've managed to scrounge up an old half-eaten turnip. Aslan explains, "You see, they will not let us help them. They have chosen cunning instead of belief. Their prison is in their minds, yet they are in that prison; and so afraid of being taken in that they cannot be taken out."

When I went to vote back in my Undisclosed Location in rural Maryland, the local Democrats had a little card table set up outside the polling place with some pamphlets and a box of donuts on it. I was asking the ladies at the table about some of the local candidates when a young man walked up and asked, kind of sheepishly, whether the donuts were for anyone who was voting.

"You could have one," they said.

"'Cause I ain't votin' for no black dude, I'll tell you that," he said, relieved and cheerful. (I'll just mention here that this guy did not appear to be 100% Caucasoid himself and refrain from any speculation as to what that might be about.)

"You can't have one," they told him.

I reacted only with my usual repressed shudder of loathing and inward cringe of shame about not opening my mouth in token right-minded protest. For some reason, ignorant bigots are never content to be quietly ignorant and bigoted; they're proud of it, and they want you to know about it, like people who proselytize for Jesus or sell Amway. Meanwhile we liberals tend to keep our own decent and civilized sentiments about equality

BEHOLD, THE HORRORS of The Obama Administration

ISLAMIC BRAINWASHING KICKS IN

PRESIDENT OBAMA REVEALS HIS MIDEAST POLICY

A SOCIALIST WELFARE STATE

THE LONG-AWAITED RACE WAR!

closeted for fear of getting called eggheads or college-boy faggots or (my friend Jim heard this once) "edjumicated idjiots."

My solution to this quandary was to move to New York City, thousands of cultural light-years away from anyplace those Scum Belt dwellers could ever afford or fathom or feel comfortable. It is some consolation that those losers are suddenly feeling confused and frightened and angry, like this isn't their country any more. They're right. *The arc of the moral universe is long, but it bends toward justice.* Eventually—not soon enough, but someday—all those people are going to die off and nobody will even understand why electing a black president was such a big deal, or why gay marriage was ever an issue at all.

I've lately been thinking of a story about a group of black demonstrators who gathered outside Cape Kennedy during the moon landing, indignant that the government was spending so many billions on this useless project when so many people were hungry, homeless, without jobs or medical care. The protesters were not, as would probably happen today, corralled into paddy wagons and detained without charges until the mission was over. Instead, NASA officials went out to meet them, and invited them in to watch the landing with them. This isn't just for white America, they told them. It's for all of us. *We came in peace for all mankind.* Please—come in. We want you to be a part of this historic day. Join us.

This makes for an anticlimactic coda to my donut anecdote, but after I'd voted, I asked the women at the Democratic table whether they'd really withheld the racist guy's donut.

"Nah," they admitted. "We gave him one." (I later learned that it would've been illegal for them not to hand out gifts equitably.)

"Aw," I said. "No donuts for racists!"

And yet, watching Obama's luminous acceptance speech, hearing him say to all those who had bitterly fought his election what I could never have imagined Bush saying to me and my friends—"I hear your voices, I need your help, and I will be your President too"—I was almost glad that that little dirtbag had gotten his donut after all. Yes, I thought, magnanimous in victory: donuts for all. Seeing our first black president, that science-fiction trope for The Future, become a reality, I felt the way people must have felt the night men first walked on the moon.

New Directions for the Republican Party

TRANSFER MALEVOLENT SPIRIT OF REPUBLICANISM TO NEW HOST BODY

START DEMONIZING WHITE PEOPLE

JUST SPLIT THE TOP 1% OF THE WEALTH AND FLEE THE COUNTRY

EXHUME REAGAN

(See overleaf)

Even now the Republicans are regrouping, trying to figure out exactly where they went wrong, looking at new approaches and PR angles to rebrand themselves for 2012. Even the ones who are pretending to do some real soul-searching about the identity and *raison d'etre* of the party seem to be missing the point. I can't help but wonder whether anyone has yet floated the suggestion that they just quit. Maybe it's time to admit that it wasn't a bad candidate or an unfortunate economic crash or a change in demographics but the fact that all their ideas, the core values of conservatism, have turned out to be wrong. That the current confluence of crises, what some have called a "perfect storm"— is not some freak historical accident but the direct consequence of having implemented all their stated policies. Their antipathy toward government and deliberate campaign to enervate it led to the fiascoes of Katrina and the financial crisis. Their insistence on American exceptionalism and the use of force to further our interests abroad led to the disaster of Iraq. And if they'd gotten their way with the "ownership society" and privatized social security Americans would now be calculating how to live the last twenty years of their lives on a monthly budget of nothing.

The fact is, they got to be in complete charge for eight years and do absolutely everything they wanted, and it was a catastrophe. They gutted the constitution, wrecked the military, looted the treasury, and left the country an irreperable mess. The most gracious reaction would be to shake hands all around, say, *Okay, you know what, we fucked that up, sorry, seemed like a good idea at the time but guess not,* and all go their separate ways to pursue careers in fields better suited to their talents than governance—stolid, respectable trades with little capacity for inflicting harm, like shoe store managers, window washers, pastry chefs. Just strike the Big Tent, pull up stakes, split the take, and move on.

It should be admitted, in grudging fairness, that the cabal that's been in for the last eight years bears roughly the same sort of resemblance to Barry-Goldwater conservatism as did the PTL Network to the twelve apostles, or Starship to The Jefferson Airplane. (These are, admittedly, imperfect analogies—not even the Bakkers were as deluded and shameless as the Bush administration, and even Starship rocked harder than Karl Rove.) Their idea of limited government is spying on citizens without warrants and holding them in concentration camps for years without charges. Their fiscal conservatism gave us deficits that hit the gajillion mark for the first time in history and an economy that now resembles Max Ernst's *Europe After the Rains.* Conservatives made a devil's bargain. They really ought to count themselves lucky to get off with mere disgrace. Faust got his eyeballs pinned to the wall.

There were a couple of ideas I didn't get to use for this cartoon, which the Republicans are welcome to use:

1.) A variation on the 9/11 Truther delusion in which the Republicans would conspire to a.) Nuke Manhattan and then b.) frame the Russians, thereby reigniting the Cold War (if you'll permit the oxymoron). The Cold War is the main thing the Republicans still like to point to as their one great triumph (along with finally kicking those freeloading negroes off welfare, but that isn't the sort of thing you can build good monuments to). Though it's not as if Democrats ever advocated capitulation to the Soviets. In fact it was that big closet pinko Nixon who introduced détente and opened relations with the yellow Maoist menace. So I'm not sure what the Republicans have to lay claim to there except that the Soviet empire happened to collapse on a Republican president's watch.

2.) "Return to Their Roots." Idea being that they should resurrect some anachronistic, 19th-century platform, like opposing the gold standard. I researched the origins of the Republican party and learned that they originally formed as an anti-slavery party, specifically opposing the spread of slavery into Kansas. But somehow, picturing a world in which slavery was still a controversial issue, I can't see the modern Republican Party taking the abolitionist position. That's the sort of crackpot extremist stance you'd expect from some hippie fringe group like the A.N.S.W.E.R. coalition. The Federal government depriving small businessmen of their rightful property—their very livelihood—without compensation, crippling the cotton industry and the entire economy of the south? Why, it's class warfare! No—present-day Republicans seem like they'd be more likely to stand up for property owners and states' rights and decry government interference in free enterprise. And if the question of slavery were to come up for a public referendum in Kansas today I don't think it'd even be close.

Already I can feel myself losing interest in politics. I was never a true politics junkie, not in the same way that Hunter Thompson was or Matt Taibbi seems to be. It's just that for the last eight years the reins of power in this nation were in reckless and unreliable hands. We couldn't afford *not* to pay attention. If you're in the back seat of a car and the driver is blacked-out drunk, you sit forward gripping the front seat with your face sticking out between the two front seats shouting very strong suggestions and pleading with them to pull over. But if the driver's sober and trustworthy, you can sit back, relax, stare out the window and let your mind wander, maybe have a little snooze.

America still has all the same problems it had on November 3rd, and they'll take time and work to solve, and I'll do what little I can to help. But I'm not taking a daily interest in who Obama is appointing to cabinet posts, because I trust that, compromised old Washington hacks though they may be, they at least aren't all campaign donors, lobbyists, Jesus freaks and old high school friends of Sarah Palin's. I for one would be content, at this point, to see us return to the bloated, corrupt, and inefficient government we once had.

This week we salute those ordinary people, some of them nameless, who committed absurd and heroic acts of defiance against the forces of humorless authority over the last eight years, who yelled the rude truth over the drone of official lies or committed hilarious blasphemies on the most hallowed grounds of Assholism, cheering our hearts and buoying our spirits in a dark and deeply unfunny time.

The only news story I am currently following with any interest is the fate of this bold shoe-hurling spokesman for the injured and insulted people of Iraq, Muntader al-Zaidi. His trial is set to begin December 31st. According to *The Hindu* (this is an Indian newspaper, not some shadowy informant of mine) Al-Zaidi's brother claims he has been tortured in custody and was forced to write a letter of apology, but that he still insists he would do it again. The Iraqi Minister of Justice denies the accusation. Meanwhile, al-Zaidi has been offered a bride by a wealthy Lebanese family. That's one way to get a girl. As generally happens in these cases, the more you learn about the situation, the more complicated and unappealing it gets: it turns out Al-Zaidi has Baathist party sympathies, which I find a little hard to get behind. But the beauty of his gesture cannot be denied. It was an altogether fitting coda to the ignominious career of George Bush. Blessed be the name of Muntader al-Zaidi, and may St. Hubbins smile upon him.

Dr. Ben Marble, whose house was destroyed by Hurricane Katrina, became briefly famous for repeatedly yelling at Vice-President Dick Cheney, who was conducting a television interview in his neighborhood: "Hey Mister Cheney—go fuck yourself!" (The incident and an interview with Marble are featured in Spike Lee's documentary *When the Levee Breaks*.) When questioned by the Secret Service, he innocently offered the defense that he was only quoting Mr. Cheney's own words, famously snarled at Patrick Leahy on the Senate floor. My friend Ben interviewed Marble shortly after the incident and learned, to his awe and delight, that at the time of his impromptu protest he happened to be wearing a T-shirt that bore the glowering face of Mr. T and the legend: "I PITY THE FOOL."

The website WordNet Daily reported the grave-dancing incident at the Reagan Library on August 9th of 2005: "A California man dubbed a "Satanist" on an online message board has posted photos of himself dancing on President Ronald Reagan's grave, raising the ire of the former chief executive's admirers." In a letter I personally received from the anonymous dancer, he wrote, "Naturally, the Satanism thing is bullshit, as is the "trickle-down effect," as is... you get the idea. Jeezus be with you." We at The Pain are protecting what little information we have regarding his identity as he may still be sought by the Fun Police. As with Dr. Marble, the T-shirt is historically accurate.

I didn't include Stephen Colbert because he's a pretty well-sung hero already, but I do want to commend for honorable mention his speech at the National Press Club dinner. At the time, this speech was greeted with the kind of rigid silence that only an entire ballroom full of asses with sticks jammed way up inside them can produce. The official word was that Colbert's routine had been an embarrassing flop, until it was seen on YouTube by people outside the Washington Press Corps. It was not so much hilarious as jaw-dropping in its face-to-face damnation not only of the incompetence and criminality of the Bush administration but of the obsequious sycophancy and negligence of the press. Hence the somewhat tepid response. All this with George Bush, whose sense of humor is more given to cruelty than self-deprecation, sitting about twelve feet away, trying to imitate an expression of good-natured indulgence. It was like watching Mussolini endure a celebrity roast. It may also have been the only time in his two terms that George Bush was exposed to anything like the truth.

In my last panel I honor those cartoonists who have been my ideological allies and comrades-at-arms over the last eight grueling, dismal years. I'll take this opportunity to salute some of them by name: Steve Bell, Ruben Bolling, Steve Brodner, Tom

Heroes of the Bush Years

BEN MARBLE, M.D.

TOLD DICK CHENEY TO GO FUCK HIMSELF

MUNTADER AL-ZAIDI

THE GUY WHO DANCED
ON REAGAN'S GRAVE

MY COLLEAGUES

"Heroes of the Bush Years," cont.

Hart, Ted Rall, David Rees, and Jen Sorensen all did intelligent, funny, and artful work that cut through conservative bullshit like a charged particle beam through cheap drywall. I wish there'd been a big awards ceremony after it was all over where we'd all get medals.

I don't think that most of us set out to be political cartoonists. What kind of kid is so nerdy and pathetic that he grows up idolizing Herblock or Pat Oliphant? It's dreary work drawing old white men in suits week after week, and the art form has a dispiritingly brief half-life. But the Bush administration wasn't just the opposition party; they were an historical aberration, completely off any ideological spectrum, indifferent to governance and hostile to democracy. They cheated and bullied their way into power and used it to loot the treasury for their campaign donors. They lied without shame and threw away the lives of a lot of poor kids to get more oil for the companies they owned. They were—in one of the rare appropriate uses of the term—anti-American. I, like a lot of artists, felt more or less ethically conscripted into duty for the duration of their regime.

Unfortunately their hold on power long outlasted my passion. Despite the symbolic redemption offered by the Obama victory, I don't think I'll ever forgive my fellow Americans for the 2004 election. I suppose I shouldn't complain about the Bush years—I am, after all, one of the very few people, along with oil companies and military contractors, who derived any benefit from them at all. And I'll admit it was even fun for a while, kind of like being a landscape painter at Krakatoa. But it stopped being funny around the same time people started getting killed, and, like one of those lame sketches buried in the second half of *Saturday Night Live,* it went on much too long. Like Cincinnatus, I will be happy to lay down my weapons and return to a quieter, more dignified civilian life.

It's been axiomatic for me, a sort of defense mechanism during these hopeless years, that I wasn't going to change anyone's minds with cartoons. The best I could hope for, I told myself, was to give some voice and solace to the like-minded, to let sane and reasonable people out there know that they weren't alone—that no, It Wasn't Just Them, they hadn't gone insane, the rest of the country had. But last week I got a donation from a young man at a military academy who wrote that he used to be a Republican and an evangelical Christian, a supporter of President Bush and an opponent of gay marriage, but that he's since come around to being one of us, a dissenting and blasphemous secular liberal—as Falstaff says, "little better than one of the wicked." And one of the influences he cited on his evolution was my own work.

We can't know what effect we have in this world. You just keep beaming your messages into space, and one day, if you're lucky enough to live to see it, maybe the aliens will come.

Good Panels from Bad Cartoons

TAKE THE WEALTH FROM THE **TOP 1%**. AND GIVE IT ALL TO THE **BOTTOM 1%**!

PERMIT KARL ROVE TO LIVE HIS LIFE.

THE EXPANSION OF THE UNIVERSE DUE TO DARK ENERGY WILL ACCELERATE.*

... AND WHAT ABOUT THAT 9/11 GUY, YOU KNOW WHO I MEAN, OBAMA SOMETHING..?

*Rotate word/thought balloons for humorous effect.   [Various dates]

"All Yours," January 21st 2009

I just got back from the Inauguration last night. I was in that crowd you saw on TV, filling the Mall from the Capitol to the Washington Monument. That was me.

Through her unparalleled interpersonal and bartending skills my friend Melissa scored tickets to the Inauguration for our whole group of friends. We left our HQ in Maclean, Virginia at 5:15 A.M. to get the Metro into the District, and it was a good thing we did—we later ran into people who'd *gotten* into D.C. at 5 AM and still didn't get into the inauguration. We spent several hours trapped in a vast, immobile crowd, waiting to get into the designated gate for purple tickets. At one point we saw Jesse Jackson and his entourage up ahead of us, trying to make their way through the crowd on foot, just as fucked as the rest of us. I remembered how he'd been overheard saying he was going to "cut [Obama's] balls off" during the campaign, and I thought, Well, that's what you get for talking shit about Obama—the same color ticket as me. I read later that Jackson never got into the inauguration at all. Neither did Mariah Carey.

When an ambulance forced its way through the crowd, already packed as densely as the subway at rush hour, pressing us even more tightly against the barricades that hemmed us in, we felt there might be the slightest possibility of getting maybe a little bit crushed to death. It was then that Melissa, who was raised to believe that there is always a way to sneak around the rules and avoid getting screwed along with the rubes, struck out away from the crowd and led us all to another approach to the gate, one where the crowd, though just as dense, was indeed shuffling slowly, intermittently forward.

Despite the interminable wait, the frustrating absence of any communication or direction from anyone in charge, the agoraphobic closeness and toe-numbing cold, the people in D.C. that day were, a little halfhearted chanting aside, not ill-tempered or impatient but calm and friendly and humorous, joined together in a spirit of commiseration and fellow-feeling. I heard later that even with a crowd of almost two million people—the largest assembly in the history of Washington, D.C.—there was

not one arrest. Melissa gave our extra ticket to a guy hawking Presidential T-shirts.

We did finally get into the Inaugural area, where every monument was coated and dripping with people, like formations in an Ernst painting. The trees were full of onlookers, too, at whom the cops would periodically yell to get down, and who would sullenly drop down only to be replaced by more climbers five minutes later. I was reminded of Zacchæus, the short tax collector who climbed a sycamore to see Jesus preaching. Never in my lifetime have I seen so many people strain with such intensity and passion to see a single man. And when have you ever seen sportswear emblazoned with the name and face of a U.S. President? You won't find any **GERALD FORD** ballcaps or jackets on Ebay.

It was a racially mixed, polyglot crowd, like a New York City street scene, and strikingly unlike the homogenous mob I saw at Bush's first inaugural—cruel-faced, desiccated coots in cowboy boots and their powdered, mink-enshrouded wives. Older black women were weeping openly, their faces embarrassingly beautiful to see; beaming Asian couples were taking photos of themselves against the background of the crowd. All our trials were worth it to me to know that one of the millions of boos George Bush heard when his name was announced was my own.

I thought of the people I wished had lived a little longer to see this: Hunter Thompson, Kurt Vonnegut, David Foster Wallace. It would've cheered them to see it, at least a little.

The most air-stillingly beautiful moment of the day was Aretha Franklin's "My Country 'Tis of Thee." When she sang the line, "*Land where our fathers died*" a voice behind me shouted, "Yes, they did!" in churchly call-and response. Melissa and Sarah were weeping; I kept laughing for happiness. Obama's speech was the only one we could hear well, so clear and resonant was his voice. I uttered a feeble "h'raay" when he mentioned "non-believers" (despite the politically incorrect nomenclature—we prefer to be called "The Damned"). It was a gesture of inclusion as unexpected and as moving, in its way, as his speaking the word

"gay" in his acceptance speech. In the pauses after any especially welcome or inspiring line, because of the sheer expanse of the crowd and the slow travel time of sound, you could hear the roar of cheers and applause rolling in oceanic waves two miles down the mall, like thunder, or the sea.

After the inauguration I retreated to a mobbed and raucous Irish bar catty-wampus from Union Station, a place where Van Halen was playing real loud and I scarfed down a plate of chicken wings and drank Jack Daniels out of a plastic cup for the first time in years. It was there that I watched George W. Bush leave Washington, D.C. in disgrace. When he ascended the stairway to his plane the whole bar erupted with jeers and hurrahs. I made ecstatic eye contact with a girl I didn't know. Everyone waved *Good riddance, fuckboy,* and raised our beers in ferocious toast. I gave the finger to the screen.

That night my friends and I retired to my Undisclosed Location on the Chesapeake Bay, well north of D.C. I built a fire in the woodstove and we all drank wine and ate baked brie and salad and mushroom risotto. Late that night I put an episode of *The Shadow* on the turntable and we all passed out within minutes. The next morning, after breakfast, we went for a walk on the beach, where we saw a couple of bald eagles flapping over the frozen cove. I played the Star-Spangled Banner on my pump organ before we left the cabin and headed back up 95 to New York City and home.

This morning I overcame my post-election antipathy to politics and forced myself to read the *Times,* figuring that after eight years of relentlessly ghastly and depressing affronts to human decency I owed myself a little good news. I almost couldn't take it. Already President Obama has signed executive orders closing down Guantanamo and the CIA's secret prisons and overturning Bush's efforts to block access to government records. Dennis Blair, Obama's appointee for national director of intelligence, called for oversight and transparency in intelligence and said that counterterrorism must be consistent with American law and the Geneva conventions. He actually used the phrase "speak truth to power."

It is such a pathetic relief just to hear anyone in the government say anything sane or reasonable or obviously true. Can it really be this easy? I know that the Bush administration has left the country gutted, and it's not just a matter of repair but of rebuilding, from the blackened foundations up. But it means so much just to know that the people in charge are smart and responsible and in touch with reality, listening to their soldiers and their spies and their scientists instead of plugging their ears and praying, that they respect the law and believe in democracy. It feels like the Dark Tower toppling, the statue of the Emperor pulled down, the snow melting, and rumors of Aslan returned. (It's embarrassing to have to appeal to so many images from children's literature lately, but apparently it's my only precedent or reference for this experience.)

Most amazing of all, in a way, was the simple photo of President Obama sitting at the desk in the Oval Office. I looked at it for a long time.

L-R: Ellen Twaddell, Melissa Shaw, Sarah Glidden, Jesse Fuchs, Tim Kreider, Boyd White.
(Guest artist: Sarah Glidden)

Apparently Rush Limbaugh slew the crowd at the Conservative Political Action Conference by re-telling jokes I remember my dad telling when I was a kid, except with himself inserted as the punchline (a joke, in this context, ostensibly self-deprecating but in fact self-adulatory), and tossing off feeble two-and-a-half-liners like: "I don't know why people are afraid of liberals. People are always afraid of liberals... but why be afraid of the deranged?" Michael Steele later dismissed Limbaugh by referring to him as an "entertainer," which was not only inaccurate but an affront to hardworking impressionists, puppeteers, jugglers, and mimes. Limbaugh's routine doesn't really qualify as humor—it just alludes to a common set of assumptions. You could substitute any other group-name and it would be funny to anyone who reviles that group—conservatives, the Quebecois, Presbyterians.

Rush really did say that conservatives "love people." It reminded me of an online post I once read by cartoonist Darryl Cagle in which he attempted to articulate the essential difference between liberals and conservatives, explaining, "conservatives trust people." I couldn't imagine whom he thought he was talking about. The same people who want to outlaw abortion, who support illegal wiretapping and torture? The conservatism he admired existed solely in his own head, and bore no resemblance to the one in the real world. Who knows—maybe Rush Limbaugh really is a big loveable fuzzball, as he described himself in a recent interview, despite having constructed a public persona and built a media empire out of hate. (I myself am a nicer person that one might suppose from reading my polemics.) But his, Cagle's, and Newt Gingrich's quotes illuminate a bizarre disconnect between these conservatives' self-image and their actual agenda, one it's hard to attribute to anything but denial.

Offering himself up as an alternative visionary for his moribund party is Clinton-era villain Newt Gingrich, best known and much beloved for re-introducing the concept of public orphanages and poorhouses into the national discourse. A high-contrast black-and-white close-up of Gingrich's bloated face, lit sinisterly from below like Baltar's on the old *Battlestar Galactica,* appeared on the cover of the *New York Times* Magazine two weekends ago. My friends Jim and Sarah and I had to turn it face-down so it would not blight our Sunday morning brunch. Gingrich likes to think of himself as an intellectual, a thinker, although so far his main contributions to the ongoing discourse of Western civilization appear to be 1.) More Money for Us and 2.) The Coloreds Are Wrecking Everything. The traditional twin pillars of conservative ideology: Greed and Bigotry.

I am relieved to see Limbaugh and Gingrich and the rest of these irrepressibly loathsome characters try to belly their way up to the trough of power. The more the Republicans are viewed as the party of fat balding rancorous old Southern white men, the more inevitably they are doomed to marginality and senescence. So bring on Rush and Newt and the rest of the bottom-of-the-barrel crew of hilariously cruel, blustering Dickensian villains. As the last eight years have demonstrated, the best way to ensure conservatives' destruction is to allow them to say clearly and unambiguously what they believe and to enact those ideas.

The Republican Party will be resurgent sooner than anyone would like to think. Like herpes, conservatism lies dormant in the nervous system of the republic, waiting for times of stress, for our resistance to weaken, when it will erupt scabrously anew. And when that day comes I'll feel duty-bound to draw more cartoons about it. But hopefully this one is just a brief dip back into politics, a bemused and contemptuous look back. For the most part I've stopped paying attention. Recently I found myself on a right-wing blog (don't ask why),[1] the kind where it is a foregone conclusion, no longer even under debate, that Obama is a closet Marxist. It made me feel almost physically contaminated, not so much by their specific delusional ideology, distasteful as it was, but by the hysterical, spittle-flecked rhetoric, the uninformed dingbat certitude of it all. Enough already. Enough.

---

1 If you must know, I was conducting an image search for the adult Kim Richards, co-star of *Escape From Witch Mountain,* on whom I had sort of a protosexual crush when I was eight. I find I am way less embarrassed to admit this than I would be to having purposely sought out a right-wing blog. Although I didn't agree with anything said on that website I did appreciate their posting a signed poster of the grownup Kim wearing a white one-piece swimsuit. This is one of those issues on which we can put petty partisan differences aside and truly come together as Americans.

WHO WILL BE
The New Voice of The Republican Party?

RUSH LIMBAUGH?

LET ME TELL YOU WHO WE CONSERVATIVES ARE: WE *LOVE* PEOPLE. *

*ALL QUOTES AUTHENTIC

NEWT GINGRICH?

I THINK ONE OF THE GREAT PROBLEMS WE HAVE IN THE REPUBLICAN PARTY IS THAT WE DON'T ENCOURAGE YOU TO BE NASTY.

MR. POTTER?

I HAPPEN TO KNOW THE BANK TURNED DOWN THIS LOAN, BUT... WE'RE BUILDING HIM A HOUSE WORTH FIVE THOUSAND DOLLARS.

WHAT DOES THAT GET US? A DISCONTENTED, LAZY RABBLE INSTEAD OF A THRIFTY WORKING CLASS! AND ALL BECAUSE A FEW STARRY-EYED DREAMERS STIR THEM UP AND FILL THEIR HEADS WITH A LOT OF IMPOSSIBLE IDEAS.

GRAND MOFF TARKIN?

THE SENATE WILL NO LONGER BE OF ANY CONCERN TO US... THE LAST REMNANTS OF THE OLD REPUBLIC HAVE BEEN SWEPT AWAY.

RE-ANIMATED ABE LINCOLN?

WITH MALICE TOWARD NONE...

SAY TAX CUTS!' 'TAX CUTS!'

...WITH... CHARITY... FOR ALL

GODDAMMIT WHO IS THIS CLOWN?

SOME TOKEN BLACK GUY?

Afterword

The essays collected in this book were originally written as what I facetiously called "artist's statements" to accompany the cartoons when they appeared each week on my website. It's a function of my age, I suppose, that I still regard the Internet as falling somewhere on the scale of respectable publication venues between vanity presses and restroom walls, and my standards for prose that appears in print is much higher. So I wanted to give these pieces at least a quick tie-straightening and hair-smoothing before shooing them out onstage. And yet they also had a certain urgent, sloppy spontaneity that I didn't want to revise out of existence.

I think I had such a horrible time with this job not only because I am a lazy person and a chronic, sometimes terminal, procrastinator, but because I'm a different person than I was when I wrote these pieces. Having to edit them felt like being the executor of my own will. They were written in the heat of a certain historical moment—the grueling, endless second term of the Bush administration, a term I could not believe was even happening. Now that it's over, even I am struck by their tone of shrill, unrelieved rancor. It sometimes makes me wince to read them. No wonder the readers who met me in real life always seemed pleasantly surprised to learn I was so well mannered. Reading over my own political rants now, my main reaction is: Jeez Louise, what a *sore*head.

Of course my current equanimity comes more easily now that the Bush administration is finally gone, not just disgraced but airbrushed from the national consciousness. That whole cast of villains—Rumsfeld, Rice, Gonzalez, Wolfowitz—has dispersed like roaches when you switch on the light and scuttled off to moist, shadowy niches in think tanks or corporate boards. Dick Cheney's been reduced to a harmless, snarling sideshow. And George has gone back to cutting brush in Crawford, only occasionally poking his head back into public to deliver a line like, "When the history of this administration is written at least there's an authoritarian voice saying exactly what happened" to

remind us that no, we're not exaggerating in memory, he really was like that—a malaprop on par with Reverend Spooner or Yogi Berra, with a helpless penchant for Freudian slips that functioned almost like a conscience, blurting out his own worst intentions. He was an inimitable dimwit, an irreplaceable national treasure.

It's easy to forget now how this country felt during the buildup to the Iraq invasion, or after the 2004 election: invincible stupidity triumphant, all intelligent debate suspect and unpatriotic, dissent and compassion discarded as peacetime luxuries, objective reality itself a naive, obsolete standard. Holding my prose up to persnickety literary standards now is a little like holding a man accountable for what he screams while he's being tortured. We were ignored and kept helpless while hateful people did ghastly things in our name. It felt like being held down and spit on by the playground bully for eight years. If my writing sounds paranoid, strident or monotonous now, it's because it was written in reaction to a relentless propaganda campaign and a national media that seemed scarcely separable from it, when it seemed nothing sane or true was being said anywhere in public. The sheer number of times that I had to excise the words "actually," "in fact," or "the truth is" from this manuscript is an indicator of how crushing and noxious was the atmosphere of lies we had to fight through every day. No one would even admit out loud that we were being lied to—I came to hate the craven euphemism "misled" more than any of the Bush regime's more overtly Orwellian slogans.

My colleague Megan Kelso sometimes protested to me, after reading one of my cartoons or artist's statements, that I wasn't being fair in my characterizations of conservatives. I knew she was right, but, as I told her, it wasn't my job to be fair. Being cruelly, childishly unfair is one of the advantages of being a humorist as opposed to a columnist or some other boringly evenhanded commentator. I argued that in an era when conservatives controlled all three branches of government and had their own media empire, dominated the discourse and

The Pen is Mightier Than The Sw

framed every debate before it began, being "fair" was a losing proposition, a sucker's game. Our ideological enemies exploited things like fairness, compassion, ambivalence and intellectual honesty like cheetahs watching for a limp.

I wouldn't exactly recant anything I said or drew in those dismal years. I always rankled at the right-wing epithet "Bush-hater," as if our rightful outrage at Bush's daily affronts to the Constitution, Geneva conventions, common sense and basic human decency were as arbitrary and irrational as misogyny or arachnophobia. My reasons for despising the Bush administration were sane and patriotic and moral. They were liars and torturers and killers, and it would still do my heart good to see them explaining themselves from behind bulletproof glass at the Hague.

But in the end I got burned out and exhausted from being angry and ashamed of my country every day. I once wrote that my function was to be society's liver, refining the toxin of outrage into laughter. Whether I did anybody else any good in this role is not for me to say; what I can tell you is that it's hard on the liver. Perhaps I'm lucky that The Left funds its demagogues so much less lavishly than the Right; if I'd been getting paid as much as Rush Limbaugh does to sound like an aggrieved blowhard for hours every day I might eventually have vanished into my own professional persona. As it was I had to keep it up long after it had stopped feeling like any version of me I wanted to be, and I was relieved to be able to lay it aside. It was the right time and place for polemic, but I'm tired of using art and language as weapons, and look forward to putting them to their peacetime uses. My late friend John, taken aback by the vitriol of some artist's statement, once told me that I was a better person than I pretended to be. I can only hope he's in a position to take some posthumous satisfaction at having been right.

I'm writing this in the summer of 2009. Now all the columnists who wrote persuasively about the urgent moral necessity of invading Iraq are harrumphing that quite a lot of people were misled in that very confusing time, and the same shitheads who used to crank up "Have You Forgotten?" have pretty much forgotten. Obama, like Bush before him, wants to Move Forward, Look to the Future, Not Dwell on the Mistakes of the Past. In other words no one is to be held accountable for any crimes against the Constitution, international law, or humanity that may have been committed. Everyone in America seems to be treating the last eight years like an underage hooker we buried in a sleeping bag outside Nogales.

My colleague Megan recently said that she'd always found those baby boomers who couldn't seem to let go of Vietnam sort of tiresome, but now, after the Bush administration and the war in Iraq, she understands them better. She doesn't think we'll ever quite get over these years; they've left a scar on our psyches, a profound mistrust of our government and a loss of faith in our fellow Americans. Children jeered at us for protesting a stolen election; churchgoing housewives primly approved the deaths of tens of thousands of foreigners; our countrymen eagerly forfeited our collective birthright as American citizens out of fear. If nothing else, we've finally earned the right to tell those aging hippies to shut up about Nixon already. Nixon was like freaking Disraeli or Marcus Aurelius compared to George. They didn't know how good they had it with Nixon.

Barely six months into the Obama administration, it feels like his presidency hasn't really begun yet, any more than Bush's had in August of 2001. It's still just a relief to hear someone smart and sane speak for our country. I've barely been able to bring myself to pay any attention to the news since the election. Sometime soon I'll have to start again; the moral obligation of a citizen to criticize and dissent doesn't diminish when your own preferred party is in power. (It is history's ironic reward for all successful revolutionaries that, after they've finally brought down The Man, they get to be the new Man.) But I have to admit that it's more fun (and less risky) to revile than to hope; it's the difference between watching the guy in the dunking booth and watching the man on the high wire.

I originally wrote an optimistic ending to this afterword in what turned out to be the short-lived idyll of the summer of 2009, but I'm rewriting it just before the book goes to the printer's, in October 2010, a time when the air is turning cold. Having to letter the title of this book, *Twilight of the Assholes*, was a glum exercise in humility, like an act of penance for my hubris in presuming to know the shape of history. My faith in democracy proved to be naïve, and my tentative extension of the benefit of the doubt to my fellow countrymen gravely misplaced. The exhilaration of the 2008 election led me to regard the Bush administration as a grotesque aberration. After eight years of ghastly calamitous fuckups it seemed safe to assume that people would sooner proudly call themselves brownshirts or pederasts than ever identify themselves as Republicans again. I had forgotten that most Americans' knowledge of history only extends as far back as last Thursday. Generations of TV, talk radio, and public school have rendered them so unprecedentedly stupid that they've forfeited the right to an opinion about anything at all—but not, alas, to the vote. The Republican Party has already renamed itself as the Tea Party, found a new generation of candidates among the ranks of the chronically unemployable and clinically insane, and appropriated a spontaneous nationwide surge of grassroots populist antinigger sentiment. The Assholes are ascendant once again.

In a deeper sense, though, my title is more accurate than I'd intended. It seems pretty clear that the United States of America is terminally fucked. We've wrecked our empire with a last frantic scramble for a depleted resource and sunk the economy by investing all our capital in nothing at all. Our only remaining native industries are junk food, casinos, and porn, and the government, corrupted and hobbled by corporate money, has ceased to func-

tion. The body politic is so enfeebled and bloated it's incapable of lifting a finger to develop alternative energies, address global warming, or deflect by even a little any one of the multiple catastrophes racing to see which will be the first to smush us. As in palliative care, the only thing left to do is to keep us as comfortable as possible. We have fulfilled our national destiny according to our own ideal: we lived fast and died young. The corpse, however, may be less than beautiful.

Me, I'm done caring. I believe that these things are important, and that people should continue to care about them; you, for example, should care. It just can't be me any more. Sorry. I put in my time. I cared for years and it nearly killed me. I refuse to return to caring even if the Republicans do win in November, or in 2012. Republican policies only shame and outrage me; financially, they benefit people like me. The people Republicans ruthlessly screw are mostly the ones who vote for them, which I heartily condone. I endorse conservatives' repealing health care reform in their own states, refusing to get flu shots for fear of government nanochips, being allowed to carry concealed guns into bars. This is all just natural selection in action, elegant and just.

I've emigrated to New York City, a civilized island nation off the coast of the decaying behemoth America. Here, people of all races, nations, religions and sexual orientations live together, mostly not killing each other. People read on the subways, at cafés, in the parks. We have Bonnard exhibitions, Mahler symphonies, Kurosawa retrospectives and roller derby. I don't care what happens to the United States anymore. I care about the survival of the human race, and of enlightenment civilization. If it gutters out here it'll flourish elsewhere. It doesn't matter to me who gets to think they're running the world a thousand years from now as long as someone, somewhere, is still watching Akira Kurosawa films.

Tim Kreider
July 2009

October 29th, 2009

Thanks To

Michael Aubert

Chris Beck

Nell Boyce

Jenny Boylan

Rob Content

Phelætia Czochula-Hautpänz

Dave Dudley

Crystal Dunn

Carolyn Ewald

Jim Fisher

Emily Flake

Jesse Fuchs

Lee Gardner

Sarah Glidden

Myla Goldberg

Gary Groth

Tom Hart

Jenny Isaacs

Dave Israel

Isabelle Johnson

Meredith Johnson

Megan Kelso

Mildred Kreider

Jason Little

Aaron Long

Emma McLoughlin

Steve McLoughlin

Alicia Miziolek

John Patton, esq.

Louise Redd

Alex Robinson

Melissa Shaw

Karl Steven

Erik Sunday

Samuel Sweelssen

Ellen Twaddell

Tim Wilson

Boyd White

And to all those readers who offered moral and monetary support through *www.thepaincomics.com*

TIM KREIDER was born and educated in Baltimore, Maryland. His cartoon, "The Pain—When Will It End?," ran in the Baltimore *City Paper* from 1997 to 2009 and also appeared in *The New York Press, The Stranger, Philadelphia Weekly,* and other alternative weeklies. Fantagraphics Books has published two previous collections of his cartoons, *The Pain—When Will It End?* (2004) and *Why Do They Kill Me?* (2005), and he was included in Ted Rall's anthology *Attitude 2: The New Subversive Alternative Cartoonists* (2004). His essays have appeared in *The New York Times, Film Quarterly,* and *The Comics Journal,* and have been frequently anthologized. He appeared on *Nightline* and *ABC World News Online* in defense of Pluto. He divides his time between a turret in New York City and an undisclosed location on the Chesapeake Bay. He is currently working on a collection of essays, titled *We Learn Nothing,* for Free Press at Simon & Schuster.